Becoming a Better Parent:
Ten Things We Need To Know About Parenting

by Robert Lyman Lang, Jr.
LPC, LAC, MAC, SAP

A LANGCO BOOK
Langco Publishing
A subsidiary of FTC LLC

Copyright © 2010 by Robert L Lang

All rights reserved. No part of this publication may be reproduced, distributed, or transmitted in any form or by any means, including photocopying, recording, or other electronic or mechanical methods, without the prior written permission of the publisher, except in the case of properly cited brief quotations that are embodied in critical reviews and certain other noncommercial uses permitted by copyright laws. For permission requests, write to the publisher, addressed "Attention: Permissions Coordinator," at the address or e-mail below.

LANGCO Publishing
228 Meeker St.
Delta, CO 81416
langco.bobl@hotmail.com

Ordering Information:
Special discounts are available on quantity purchases by corporations, associations, and others. For details, contact the publisher at the above address.
For Orders by U.S. trade bookstores and wholesalers, please visit www.Amazon.com.

Cover and format design provided courtesy of Createspace

DEDICATION

This book is dedicated to all past, present, and future parents that struggle to make sense out of what it means being a parent. It is especially offered to all those who are hopelessly caught within the many traps of parenting and needlessly carry the burden of shame on their shoulders like a parental badge of courage. To all those who work with parents are parents, and for all those who will become parents, doing the best they can with what they have. And to my parents, family, wife, and son, whose support has made this journey possible.

TABLE OF CONTENTS

i. Preface: Why Now? A Modern Dilemma (p. 8)
Moving forward
There is hope
Let's get started
Let the journey begin

I. Parental Myths (p. 20)
What it means to be a parent
Myth-busters
Damage control
The importance of parenting
The art and science of parenting

II. Parenting Is Not a Four-Letter Word (p. 36)
The parent license
Becoming a student of parenting
Modern myths about parenting
Great parents are made
Becoming a self-disciplined disciplinarian

III. Fun-n-games and Child's Play (p. 55)
Your work is child's play
Getting down on your child's level
Play is therapy
Develop the power of your imagination
Living life as a game

IV. Where You End and Everything Else Begins (p. 69)
    The wheels on the bus go 'round and 'round
    Becoming the best parent I can be
    Using what works
    Life on the teeter-totter
    You are the best gift you can give

V. Life on Life's Terms (p. 87)
    It's time for an attitude adjustment
    Judge not, lest you be judged
    The power of believing
    True value
    Let's get motivated
    Your perception is everything

VI. It's All About the Relationship (p. 115)
    It's worth the effort
    Being in it for the long haul
    Who said it was going to be easy?
    It takes two to tango
    Hand in hand

VII. Love is Not Enough (p. 128)
    Lessons from a lifeguard
    Responsibility to vs. responsibility for
    What's love got to do with it?
    Listen to your heart
    Take another little piece of my heart

VIII. Do What You Say and Say What You Do (p. 151)
    Can you hear me now?
    Walk the talk
    Lead by example
    Live life as a role model
    Give it another try

IX. Parent, Heal Thyself (p. 169)
    The oxygen mask rule
    Teaching our children to fish
    Bags fly free
    Parenting yourself
    Keep on keepin' on

X. The Big Blue Marble (p. 188)
    Lessons from the playground
    The parent-child system
    The family system
    Societal systems
    The sandbox is for everyone
    Sands of time
    Hope is the best of things

ii. Prologue: Where Do We Go From Here? (p. 211)
    The promise of things to come
    Chaos and butterfly kisses
    Parental harmony and universal strings
    A new direction for parenting

i. Preface: Why Now? A Modern Dilemma

"Where is the wisdom we have lost in knowledge? Where is the knowledge we have lost in information?"

-T. S. Eliot

You might be asking before we even get started, "Why another book on parenting?" A better question might be, "Wouldn't it be great if we had a more complete, comprehensive, and compassionate model about parenting?" After all, this is a central to how we define ourselves as human beings. Hannush (2002) states that it is "through parenting, we learn about who we are and who we can become as human beings."

Let's begin with a gentle urgency as we reorient ourselves to a process of personal enhancement and growth as parents. This is not about right or wrong based perspectives that are often carried forward from our unrealistic expectations, but is based on positive change. *Becoming a better parent* is a continuous self-improvement project dedicated to making a difference in the world.

History has shown that understanding and defining parenting is one of the most fundamental elements of being human. "We, as parents, and those who support us, carry civilization in our arms," (Gurian, 2002). No matter where you stand on the issue, our views about parenting play a significant role in how we identify ourselves, others, and the world around us.

The best hopes for our futures lie within our individual strengths to embrace the process of becoming better parents by not setting ourselves up within the failure of perfection. "The importance of children growing up into responsible adults is critical to the success of the future of our civilization," (Berner, 2007), and how we see the world through our parental lenses shapes all things to come.

This book is intended for professionals and nonprofessionals, alike, who want to develop a better understating of parenting, parents, and our relationships with our children. It is an in-depth look at the driving forces behind what makes us tick as individuals, families, and societies. Designed to support the parent-child relationship, this book attempts to create a more comprehensive view of what it means to be a better parent.

It is intended to support positive change with children, parents, and families. This book can also help professionals from different disciplines find a more inclusive, effective, and relevant model in the study of parenting. Basically, this book is provided for everyone, as parenting affects us all in one way or another.

It is a course of study that delves into the heart of every man, woman, and child so we can better understand the complexities of parenting. By developing a more complete view of parenting, we can more thoroughly understand its implications for the world in which we live. These new passages are the horizons for which we can parent future generations to come.

Through the questioning of our current thoughts about parenting, we can investigate the entire parent-child system so we can "fully examine the implications of our own thoughts and beliefs," (Hilden, 2007). Hilden states that it is by our willingness to carry the burden of change and to "withstand personal jeopardy" that we are able to create a "society where wonder is welcomed and critical thinking is recognized as indispensable."

First and foremost, we must realize that *becoming a better parent* is not about making better children. This is often a suggestive notion that has been readily adopted and has become the downfall of most of our modern parenting perspectives. The idea that we can mix together all the right ingredients for a parental soup that we can then force-feed to our children, is only a recipe for disaster. By realizing that parents and children are uniquely separate, but interrelated, parts of a complex interconnected social system, we can find new pathways for understanding.

This book provides a new parental perspective that values the individual, reinforces our relationships, and stresses the importance of the distinctive aspects of both the parts and whole of the parent-child system. Our exclusive views about parenting, based on the parent, child, or their varied relationships as separate components, only minimizes our ability to study the individual, family, child, or the processes that connect them.

Individuality, what Stern (1938) called the "problem of the 20th century," consists of all those unaccounted for, independent variables that make the soup of life so intriguing. He was one of the first to propose that "an entire system of thought" was needed to understand these "personalistic aspects" that made us the most human. In other words, the free will and choice of our individuality is why 'you can lead a horse to water, but you can't make him drink.'

It seems that the problem of dealing with individual differences and our connections has followed us into the 21st century. We can find a way out of this impasse by taking into account both the parts and the whole of the parent-child system. This inclusive approach to parenting can provide us a way to study the real world aspects and effects of what *becoming a better parent* can mean in creating a better future for our children. Our future is tied to our past and it is through knowledge, reason, and wisdom that we can make a difference in the world today.

Current parenting approaches have made it difficult to address these aspects of free will and choice that are often the driving forces behind the parent-child system. Self-determinism can be considered a highly complex set of interactive dynamics that work independently and together within the parent-child system. These, in turn, interact with an internal personal processing system that determines how we perceive ourselves, others, and the world around us.

The interplay of these dynamics within the parent-child system are wondrous, if not perplexing, and cannot be fully explained or appreciated with our current models. Simply put, no matter how many 'king's horses or king's men' we have acquired in regard to parenting, our current models are often unable to determine how to put the parental Humpty Dumpty back together again.' Baer (2008) and his colleagues indicate that psychologists tend to avoid this topic "like it's a 6-ton elephant sitting in the room" and is an important consideration for adopting an expanded multidiscipline approach to parenting.

Moving forward

"Life is like riding a bicycle. To keep your balance you must keep moving."

-Albert Einstein

The challenge has been to find a way for us to make sense of the entire parent-child system. It is only by constructing a model that considers the interactive dynamics of both the parts and whole of the parent-child system that we can fully comprehend the complexities of parenting. Sperry's (1993) "synergy paradigms" proposed that "it is by the very nature of what and how we think, based on either the whole or part that may limit our ability to understand complex systems." In short, the interactions of the parts and whole of the entire parent-child system need to be explored if we truly want to have a better understanding of parenting.

"Multitheoretical psychotherapy" (Brooks-Harris, 2008) shows some promise as an integrative model for parenting, while other "humanistic systems models," as proposed by Bailey (1994) and Boulding (1985), also have potential. There seems to be a reoccurring theme emerging, indicating that something else is needed. Holden (2010) suggests that parenting "reflects a dynamic and ongoing process" that is "characterized, in part, by change." He goes on to state that there are many dynamic variables of the parent-child system that are "multidimensional and can be highly differentiated" based on "a two-person, bidirectional process."

To complicate things further, our current parenting models have seemingly lost their way on the modern technological information superhighways. Our current parenting perspectives have not been able to keep pace with the ever-changing landscapes of our technological world. Parenting fads come and go and do not have enough flexibility or sustainability to respond to the ever-changing needs of our growing world.

Popular parenting techniques often only offer specific advice and lack a pervasive methodology to effect real change across both time and space in the parenting continuum. Research paradigms, on the other hand, miss the importance that dynamic change agents have within the parent-child system. Still other case studies, theories, and anecdotal responses to the problem also fall short in developing more responsive models of parenting.

It is only by blending these approaches that we have a chance of developing a parenting model that has the adaptability to guide us into a better understanding of what it means to become a better parent. What we need is a more comprehensive bio-psycho-sociological systems approach to parenting. Cummings and his colleagues (2000) have suggested that we need to look at "parenting practices as dependent on the biopsychosocial context within which they are embedded."

My examination, experience, and practice in the study of parenting since 1983, has made it evidently clear that we need a major reframe of our current parenting models. I have read and used hundreds of reference books and articles in successfully working with thousands of parents, children, and families. However, at times, I have found myself at a loss and often have to combine and add to a number of different resources to address the specific issues in finding the right fit for success.

The problem remains that although there exists a great deal of helpful information, much of which is referenced extensively in this book, it is often focused on only a relative few aspects of the entire parenting process. Cowan (2009) suggests that we need a systems approach to parenting and proposes "five domain models" so we can see these dynamic influences from a multidimensional perspective including; "family-focused, parent-focused, child-focused, marital-focused and parent-child focused."

Current research has revealed that the "data does not support a narrow view of the parenting process," (Darling and Steinberg, 1993). Approaches that have taken this minimalistic opinion of parenting have often reduced our overall views of the entire parenting continuum by focusing on only a few isolated variables. Other, more subjective approaches, on the other hand, dole out advice to parents in dealing with specific elements of a child's development.

Still other approaches often over-emphasize the separate elements of the parent-child interactions that include communication, education, tools, techniques, strategies, styles, and methods. As important as all of these approaches have been to furthering our understanding of parenting, they have somehow missed the overall target and indirectly contribute to an underlying fault that runs through the heart of parenting.

There is hope

"I hope our wisdom will grow with our power, and teach us, that the less we use our power the greater it will be."
-Thomas Jefferson

The true complexity of parenting has created gaps in understanding, as we continue to experience the accelerated rates of change that bombard us from every direction. Most of our current models are unable to embrace an evolving vision for parenting that allows us to deal with instantaneous information. A new perspective is needed that will allow us to see beyond the current stereotypes and allow us to be better equipped to support rapid change that can assist us on our search.

Parents are faced with many challenges that keep changing, as suggested by Douglas (2004), who states that parental expectations are rising, "parents are working more, spend less time with their children and feel as if they cannot do an adequate job of parenting while working full-time." "Being a parent today is a lot tougher than it was a generation ago" and parents "are concerned about the negative effects of popular culture on their children."

Flexible structures are needed to account for all the systems aspects that work for all parents in all situations. Steinberg (2004) states we need an approach "that cuts across different issues and different age periods" and is grounded in what has been shown to work. Though this seems to be an impossible task, the hope is that this book will allow people to break free from the commonly held beliefs and misconceptions about parenting.

Becoming a Better Parent is intended to bridge these gaps, fill in the cracks, and create an overpass for the crevasses within our current models of parenting so we can make way for a new parental philosophy. By using the information in this book, we can create a multifaceted approach to parenting that is based on the entire parent-child system.

This book is designed as course of study that will help parents everywhere become parent-students and create a model based on their own strengths and talents. It will span the current barriers and obstacles and blend historical, empirical, and practical knowledge that will help us better understand the wisdom of what it means to be a good parent.

Parenting encompasses so much more than what our traditional perspectives can account for or provide. Our once-conventional roles of parenting are continuously being altered as our views about the current culture of parents may now include single parents, adoptive parents, foster parents, grandparents, care takers, guardians, and communities, to mention only a few.

Questioning our modern views about parenting is forcing us to break free from our ingrained beliefs and redefine the very nature of who we are. We need to shift our focus to the processes that can foster personal growth, create an atmosphere of interdependence, and build our relationships so that we can make this world a better place for our children.

Becoming A Better Parent

This book is written as a guide through the parental maze, and is intended to help you find your way through the confusion that has evolved out of these modern myths of parenting, so you may develop your own path to parental self-discovery.

Let's get started

"Let your mind start a journey thru a strange new world. Leave all thoughts of the world you knew before. Let your soul take you where you long to be...Close your eyes let your spirit start to soar, and you'll live as you've never lived before."
-Erich Fromm

The parental journey begins by first developing a framework for understanding the nature of who we are, then expanding this concept to include the connections of our relationships, and eventually develops into the ways in which we include the world around us. In developing a circular understanding of our relationships with all things, we can start to envision the complexities of who we are as parents and find more effective ways to connect with our children.

We can then move forward and take the steps needed to map out a new path of parental self-discovery. It is only by defining who we are within a system that we can overcome our parental traps and debunk the long-standing myths about parenting. By outlining an effective strategy for change, we can shed the toxic shame that exists in the unrealistic expectations found in our parental control. Albert Ellis said, "Where is it written that others must act the way we want them to? It may be preferable, but not necessary."

Building on this foundation, we can begin to build our own strengths and abilities, foster relationships with others, and find useful tactics methods that will lead to *becoming a better parent*. This parenting pyramid, as outlined by Webster-Stratton (1992), suggests a hierarchical approach that starts with understanding ourselves and builds on our relationships with others so we can continue the search for practical solutions and overcome the obstacles we can encounter as parents.

We can create an understanding of what it means to be a good parent by expanding our potential for growth and enhancing our relationships. In addition, we will also start the process of adapting a more responsive, rather than reactive, stance to our rapidly changing world, and thus create a more effective vision for parenting in the future.

Every journey begins with the first step. Our first ventures into the world as parents are often taken on the unsteady legs of the unknown. These first attempts at dealing with the uncertainty of parenting must be taken in small steps so we can develop the strength, security, and habits necessary to succeed in developing our own pace and stride. This internal rhythm can be found within and is the harmony that gives us our best hope for a better future.

The children of tomorrow are our future and, until we are able to develop a better understanding of parenting, we will continue to struggle to make sense out of the dynamics that foster these relationships. The relationship that exists between parent and child is a mystery that needs to be explored so we can develop a more comprehensive view of parenting. Our success as parents, and for that of our futures, lies in what we are able to discover about ourselves, our children, and others along the way. It is our passageway to our own parental truth.

This journey can only be experienced through a shared connection with our children and others. These are the shared personal and professional stories of hope and tragedy that have been disclosed by family, friends, colleagues, mentors, and clients. It has been a path that has been dedicated to uncovering the mysteries, debunking the myths, freeing the traps, and creating a personal power that is echoed through the soft whispers of truth.

These parental truths can only be revealed, not seen; they can only be known, not proven; they can only be valued, not kept. These cherished insights often remain elusive aspects of our parental reality as we are often trying to find the quick fix for our children. It is our ability to let go and accept the uncertainty of the journey that makes it so exciting.

We must begin to recognize that the paths we share with our children on this journey are parallel processes that may not always look alike. What's important is that we start to realize that we can share these trips in life and expand on our experiences together through our relationships. The roads we travel may have many different hills, peaks, and valleys, and may take many divergent twists, turns, and curves.

It is this diversity that adds to the extensive, rich, and fascinating aspects that make our lives uniquely ours. In preparing for this journey, we need to take advantage of all the possibilities that might be, prepare the best we can, and put one foot in front of the other. This is a race that can only be run and winning is found in the heart to continue when the road ahead gets tough.

Let the journey begin

"To finish the moment, to find the journey's end in every step of the road, to live the greatest number of good hours, is wisdom."

-Ralph Waldo Emerson

There are no parent guarantees and "there is no such thing as a perfect parent," as suggested by Steinberg (2004). *Becoming a better parent* is a process, not an event, and its rewards come from making the most of what we have to give. It represents an ongoing life's work; rich with the treasures found not only in the search, learning, practice, and training, but also in the personal experiences and stories of your life.

Hopefully, this book will inspire you to open doors and provide the necessary means to embark on a parental journey of your own. In other words, we should seek to understand parenting on a deeper level so we can see that "human beings do not grow up and adults do not parent in isolation, but in multiple contexts," (Bornstein & Cheah, 2006).

I remember my grandmother saying that "children don't come with instructions," and the same holds true for parents. We instinctively know that there are no all-inclusive parental handbooks for parents and we need to strongly question anyone who would claim differently. If there were such a thing, it would most likely resemble an incompressible, 'some assembly required,' encyclopedia-sized index manual that came with a box full of missing spare parts.

By creating a parental compass that points within, we can start to find our own internal directions to *becoming a better parent*. Historically, parenting was something that was handed down from generation to generation and what we learned about parenting came from our parents and family. This training method for future generations also creates a systemic cultural problem in our ability to transform our fundamental mindsets about parenting. We have become dependent on these oral traditions from our past that are fast becoming outdated and insufficient in preparing parents for the future.

Finding our way through the parental maze can be difficult and many of us have often found ourselves lost on this journey. Brown (2000) says, "I read years ago that it was not the responsibility of parents to pave the road for their children but to provide a road map." Elias, Tobias, & Friedlander stated, "As parents travel down the *Emotionally Intelligent Parenting* highway, there are going to be signs along the way."

This book, then, allows us to use our internal parental compass on the road map of life and is provided as a hitchhiker's guide to parenting. By developing a more compressive understanding of parenting, we can read these signs more clearly. To navigate the sometimes treacherous roads of parenting, we need a good internal compass, strong map-reading skills, and the ability to understand the road signs along the way.

Our continued efforts to develop a more comprehensive and inclusive understanding of parenting are essential so we can work together on making this a better place for all our children's tomorrows. It is only by focusing on the process within the parental journey that we can hope to make a difference in our children's lives. This parental undertaking can be distressing as we have trouble making sense out of all the variables that make up the complexity of parenting.

The problem is that "there is no one psychological pathway to parenthood," (Barnes, & Balber, 2007). In their exploration of the parental journey, they discuss the "facts, fiction, and fantasy held within the myths of parenting," and state that our "journey into parenthood begins long before the baby arrives."

Parenting encompasses more than the parents, more than our children, more than the tools, techniques, and advice that we have picked up along the way; and is more than the dependent variables studied by empirical research. The hope is that this book will help you find your true path to parenting that lies within.

Robert Lang

I. Parental Myths

"If there is anything that we wish to change in the child, we should first examine it and see whether it is not something that could better be changed in ourselves."

-C.G. Jung

What it means to be a good parent is a question that has plagued mankind since the beginning of time. Our views about parenting have fueled endless controversy and generate the perceptual lens from which we see the world. Igniting mythology, fueling history, and sparking modern scientific thought, our views about parenting have formed the story of us all.

We, now more than ever, need to create a new human narrative for the parental phenomena. We can challenge ourselves to see beyond the current beliefs and accept a more open definition of the parent-child system. We can seek new questions that provide insight, inspire hope, mold values, build on the past, predict the future, and outline the basic structures for our parental existence. By shaping our destiny, we can define the success for parenting future generations.

Our search needs to seek the parenting unknown, as Goodnow (2006) suggests, so we can ask the questions that "consider making comparisons within a culture (across subgroups, across historical times, or across generations)." These questions have become a consuming passion that have driven the very pages of this book and exemplify a life's treasure that keeps giving. Our questions continue to reveal truths about the nature of being a parent, the processes of parenting, the state of parenthood, and our parental philosophies.

Asking more of these questions continues to peel the layers of the parent onion back so we can begin to recognize and use more effective models of parenting based on the system dynamics of the parent, child, their relationship, and surroundings. This *"socio-ecological* framework" provides us a way to look at the entire parent system as interdependent spheres of influence, (Deater-Deckard, 2004).

Struggling to understand these questions provides us an appreciation of just how difficult it can be to grasp the complexities of parenting. Our efforts to create a more universal understanding of this complicated field of study require a more holistic perspective—a new "parentology," (Johnson, 1982). Johnson suggests that the study of parenting "is a serious (and universal) condition that has gone unnoticed and paid little attention to."

Becoming students of parenting will allow us to focus on the entire human experience and create a systems model that supports the significance of the interrelated connections with our children and the world around us. We can seek "an integrated systematic exposition of the nature, variety, and function of the social ties that bind human beings together" (Bronfenbrenner, 1990).

It is a treacherous obstacle course that is not for the faint of heart; an introspective journey of self-discovery that you must be willing to take on your own. The passage can be perilous and misleading, making it easy for you to lose your bearings. Just keep in mind that the quest for answers exists within. We must resist the minimalist temptation to accept an over-generalized approach to parenting and seek a more complete view of the parent, child, and their relationship.

Our current one–size-fits-all ideas about parenting have become narrow, shallow, and inconsequential. Agich (2003) suggests that we need to shed the "narrow notion of parenting and family that prevail in today's society" and move to a wider range of *paternalism*.

Robert Lang

What it means to be a parent

"Parents wonder why the streams are bitter, when they themselves have poisoned the fountain."

-John Locke

Bill Cosby once said that "child raising is still a dark continent and no one really knows anything. You just need a lot of love and luck—and, of course, courage." Having a road map for exploring this "dark continent" would be nice. How to become a better parent is a growth process that is experienced from within. From the time we first conceptualize our role as a parent by playing house when we are children, to the time we conceive our first child, this evolving process begins to mold our views about the world.

Parenting represents the time in our life when all things seem to come to a screeching halt and we allow ourselves to evaluate our ideas about parenting. These questions about parenting go through a number of transformations in our lives and can become less about parenting and more about "what are we going to do with our children." Chaos is often the driving force behind these internal processes, and, although the individual details may vary, the intent, meaning, and purpose of these cries for help are unmistakably clear.

Anyone can give you a general idea about what it means to be a good parent. However, the answers given are often as varied and vague as our current models of parenting. These differences contribute to one of the fundamental flaws about how we see ourselves or others as parents. These views about parenting, no matter how skewed, are often based on false belief systems that have become ingrained parental patterns. The perceptual distortions differ not only from person to person, but also within the cultural dimensions of time and space. What might be true in one moment can be radically different in another.

Ask a college freshman, "What does it mean to be a good parent?" and you will get a detailed, if not candid, answer. Repeat that question to the same person again 10 years later, when they are faced with the real panic of having their first child, and the answers can reveal a significant difference. I'm sure the answers to this great parenting question have also been different at different times and within different cultures but contain the same elements of uncertainty.

The real terror of parenting replaces our initial panic when we settle into the day-in, day-out struggles of being a parent. Although shrouded in good intentions, our views about *parental control*, create the central theme behind the majority of our modern myths about parenting. This unhealthy force breaks down the parent-child boundaries and shifts the focus on parenting to the child and away from the parent.

Our questions become the impossible '**HOW DO I'** questions, as listed in the table below. These questions tend to define who we are as parents in terms of our children, a process called *childing,* and narrows the focus our parental outcomes on our children. To find our true path to *becoming a better parent*, we must be able to overcome our fear, see past these shame-based questions, and let go of trying to control anyone's life other than our own.

"HOW DO I"
"Prevent my child from getting hurt?"
"Tell my child to behave?"
"Force my child to do their chores?"
"Get my child to do their homework?"
"Make my child listen me and mind?"
"Keep my child from being disrespectful?"
"Convince my child to not hurt others?"
"End my child's acting out?"
"Stop my child from getting into trouble?"

Table 1

These shame-based questions probably have a ring of familiarity about them, especially if you are dealing with the 24 hours a day, 7 days a week, and 365 days a year task of being a parent. The problem inherent in these questions is that we are asking all the right questions for all the wrong reasons. Our love for our children is our greatest asset, but our loving intentions can sometimes create the strongest traps we face as parents.

It cannot be emphasized enough that the problem with these questions is that they have little to do with being a parent and everything to do with trying to control our children. Aldort (2005) states that "control is ineffective whether it is gentle coercion or covert manipulation, the very control we use causes the problems we are trying to solve." These misconceptions of parental control perpetuate an irrational belief system that drives the nature of the modern parenting dilemma and negatively infects our relationships with our children.

Shame-based parenting is a concept that is often an unintended consequence of our current parenting models. This concept becomes very evident when parents define themselves in terms of their children. Unhealthy or toxic shame is a process whereby the concrete black and white principles of self are dictated in a one-dimensional, "absolutizing or internalization process where a person believes himself to be flawed or defective," (Bradshaw, 1988).

Parents that find themselves stuck in this trap often end up feeling inadequate, ineffective and insecure. When this process becomes entangled it sets the stage for a spiraling emotional cycle of shame. This leads to feelings of hopelessness, helplessness and worthlessness. Shame, like any of our emotions, can be used in a healthy manner when it supports and empowers personal change from within.

Healthy shame is an emotion that communicates internally by letting us know that something we have done, thought, or felt goes against our own set of core values. It acts as our emotional consciousness and works most effectively when it is based on what we do and not on who we are. By changing these shame-based questions to the '**HOW CAN I**' questions listed in the following table, we can start to shed this toxic shame of parenting and focus on the relationships with our children that can make a difference.

"HOW CAN I"
"Help my child from getting hurt?"
"Support my child in making good decisions?"
"Assist my child's learning?"
"Build the relationship with my child?"
"Communicate better with my child?"
"Model respect for my child?"
"Promote positive behaviors with my child?"
"Facilitate positive change with my child?"
"Encourage my child to grow?"

Table 2

It's not only the questions we ask, it's the reasons why we are asking that often set up some of the most common traps we face as parents. Most parents want the best for their children and the purpose of the questions we are asking, although well-meaning, become misdirected when we see our children start to go astray.

Parents often bring their children into counseling wanting the all the right answers to all the wrong questions. They are trapped within the controlling aspects of the '**HOW DO I'** questions listed above, and become overwhelmed by the process of parenting by saying that, "nothing we are doing is working."

These parents are often dealing with children that have serious behavioral problems and tend to project their ideas about control or perfection by saying "you need to fix my child." By helping parents understand the difference between dealing with and fixing behaviors, they can turn away from the shame that binds them to this way of thinking and they can start to focus on what truly works for them as parents.

"What works for us as parents?" is a question that needs to be explored in more detail as we develop an evolving philosophy toward parenting, based on "choice psychology," (Primason, 2004), and "choice theory," (Glasser, 1998). These approaches also support the idea that "we choose everything we do" and "everyone chooses their behavior."

When we ask the question, "Is it working?" we need to look more closely at the question and define what 'working' means. By asking who's working?, what's working?, when does it need to work?, why does it work?, and how do we know it's working?, we can study the choices we make more carefully.

These are some of the ways in which we can analyze the working relationships within the parent-child system. This organizational management approach to parenting, directed at the principles of work, provides us a way to understand that if we want "to attain a change in someone else's behavior, start with yours," (Magee, 1998).

In setting up behavioral interventions with families, parents will often say, "We have already tried that and it doesn't work." When I ask parents to "tell me what they mean by 'it doesn't work,' they will generally say something like, "Because they're still doing it." Parents stuck within this trap, often exhibit the characteristics of what can be called 'magical thinking' and assume that their children are the developmental extensions from their past.

These are a set of "erroneous beliefs that one's thoughts, words, or actions will cause or prevent a specific outcome in some way that defies commonly understood laws of cause and effect," (DSM-IV-TR, 2000). Once we can break free from the trap created by our own 'magical thinking,' we can stop believing that we can change our children or prevent them from getting hurt. We can then start to deal with the reality that is parenting and begin to focus on making a difference in the lives of our children.

To truly make a difference in our children's lives, we must be able to distinguish between the aspects of parental influence from control, fixing, or changing our children. By focusing on the influence we have with our children and not the control we have over them, we can start to understand that "parenting is central to childhood, to child development, and to society's long-term investment in children," (Bornstein, 2003). He states that "we can influence not just some, but all, positive characteristics and values we want to see children develop."

Becoming A Better Parent

It is only through the realization that building our relationships creates influence that we are able to make a difference. We, as parents, have a tremendous responsibility in utilizing our influence within the relationships with our children and must have our children's best interests at heart, remembering that there is a difference between selflessness and selfishness.

Changing our views about parenting away from this toxic shame that binds us to the trap of parental control can open the doors for a new direction. This is not an easy task and changing the questions we ask as parents is only the first step. These new questions provide us the internal directional links that can change not only the questions we ask, but our thoughts, feelings, and behaviors that can reshape the dynamics of parenting in the future.

Redirecting our questions can challenge our current views about parenting and transform the ways in which we see the nature of the entire parent-child system. It is the nature of how we perceive parenting that has set up these parental traps that ensnare us into believing in the illusions of control. To avoid these traps on the road of parenting, we need to start asking the questions that will set us free and keep us from falling back in.

Myth-Busters

"The great enemy of the truth is very often not the lie—deliberate, contrived and dishonest—but the myth—persistent, persuasive, and unrealistic."
-John F. Kennedy

We, as individuals and as a society, can have unrealistic, unattainable, and unreasonable expectations for parents, based upon their children. This is the basis for a concept of *childing*; a core belief system that generates inaccurate myths about parenting, defined in terms of the child. This *parent trap* immobilizes our efforts and has more to do with being a good child than it does with *becoming a better parent.*

These maladaptive models are often supported by evidenced-based partial truths that inadvertently support and maintain our positions of parental control. Consisting of twisted and distorted slants on parenting, these models have gone to great lengths to show how parenting is associated with the successes or failures of our children. Although our understanding of what contributes to a child's accomplishments or misfortunes is an important aspect of parenting, it can often be misused to perpetuate the myth of parental control.

Understanding our children can be enlightening in developing insight into ourselves. The problem comes not from trying to understand our children, but from how we use this information. Parents often misuse this information as a tactic to gain leverage over their children in the hopes that this will get their child to do the right thing. Parents can also create these unrealistic expectations for their children, based upon their own childhood needs that were not met.

Whatever the causes, our false expectations are placed directly at the feet of parental influence, indirectly implying that parents have the ability to control the outcomes for their children. If we could only use this knowledge to enhance our own self-understanding and build our relationships with our children, we would be moving closer to our path of parental self-discovery.

Our parental truth comes from within and sees the futility in trying to control our children. It recognizes the challenges we all face in trying to control our lives and redirects our efforts at managing our own thoughts, feelings, and behaviors so we can deal more effectively with our children.

Parental control builds a spiraling trap that can capture our children in an identity net of confusion, as they lose more of who they are and become empty reflections of their parents. We falsely believe that if we do all the right things as parents, then our children will do all the right things.

The truth is that the more we try to control our children the more out of control things can become. These shame-based ideas lie at the core of what diminishes our roles as parents to have a positive influence in our children's lives. These damaging beliefs become failed attempts that inadvertently focus our attention as parents on regaining even more control.

This process is often seen within parent-child power struggles. Gordon (2000) describes these processes as the misuse of a "parental power" and states that "it is paradoxical, but true, that parents lose influence by using power." It seems that what matters most in our children's lives is the influence we have through our relationships and not the control we think we have in our role as parents.

Damage control

"Children are not our property, and they are not ours to control any more than we were our parents' property or theirs to control."

-Richard Bach

Parents share a common delusion that imposes our wills onto our children. These expectations are often projected and generate a false parental reality that states, "if we can only find a way to get our children to do what we want, then our children will succeed, and we will be seen as good parents." The dilemma we all face with this set of parenting beliefs is that we become only distorted reflections of our own children. It minimizes our role as parents, de-emphasizes our relationships, and disempowers our children.

When we base our parental success on our children, it creates a cultural atmosphere of non-accountability and blame. Segal (2005) suggests that learning to "manage our children's behaviors," through understanding, not control, can set us free from these "parent traps" and we can then experience the true rewards of being a parent.

Finding the answers to the questions posed in *"Becoming a Better Parent,"* like many of the mysteries we experience in life, can be extremely complicated, deeply involved, and profoundly difficult to grasp. There are volumes of materials on parenting presented in various mediums that have attempted to address this problem.

These references have been an invaluable resource in my own search and the behavioral strategies and techniques that are outlined within them can be very effective parental tools. *"Becoming a Better Parent"* does not attempt to eliminate any of these legitimate parenting approaches, but is provided as a means to break free from the cycle of control and shame that is often overlooked in these other approaches which reinforce the parent trap.

If we can shed ourselves from these inferences of parental control, we can then use these strategies to build our relationships, foster personal growth, and facilitate healthy boundaries within the parent-child system, reminding us that it is the process, not what we do as parents, that matters most.

Parents can often misuse these powerful tactics as an additional means of controlling their children, thus making them only oversimplified behavioral manipulations. These often fail to address the real dynamics of parenting and tend to amplify the myth of parental control. Segal (2005) has readers sign a contract to assure the information provided is used to "become a better parent and not control your child."

Modern views about parenting subtly imply that we have the ability to control our children and have to sign a contract to prevent it. Control is an illusion that does not exist in a world of free will, and choices rule the day, whether through indirect or more direct means.

We have mistakenly bought into our beliefs that by finding the right carrot (or theory), our children will do the right thing, because, after all, 'it's for their own good.' Parental control is a false belief system that is often reinforced culturally. When our views about being a good parent become dependent on our children our expectations are set up to fail.

Becoming A Better Parent

The importance of parenting

"There is no job more important than parenting. This I believe."

-Dr. Benjamin Carson

Parenting plays an immeasurable role in our lives and forms the relationships that construct the societies in which we live. It has far-reaching implications that define the world around us, whether we are willing participants or not. It impacts public policy, societal expectations, cultural boundaries, and our expectations of the world. These norms, rules, and laws are used to govern and reflect our ingrained attitudes and beliefs about parenting.

In fact, our very existence in this world is dependent on what it means to be a good parent. According to Goode (2001), "it is not only possible for us to improve our relationships with our children for future generations, it is imperative." It is our abilities as parents to let go of the shame that binds us and the control that traps us so we can build significance in the relationships with our children that make a difference in the future.

The interesting phenomenon about our current views about parenting is that we have over-emphasized *childing*, continued to reinforce the *parental trap*, minimized individuality, and overlooked the parent-child system. This focus has created an ever-escalating social dilemma that continues to affect our concepts of personal responsibility and societal accountability, a process that has cultivated a social no-fault attitude, and has generated an alarming increase in social problems that overwhelm our legal system, inundate our social services agencies, and give rise to public unrest.

The problem is that by blaming parents, we enable individuals to look for fault in everyone and everything else. Barber (2000) suggest there is a strong link between our current social problems and parenting, stating that "low parental investment" can lead to "poverty, teen pregnancy, drug abuse, increased divorce rates, conflictual relationships, and crime."

We must realize that being involved in our children's lives is an important aspect of parenting but does not guarantee the outcomes for our children. It is only one of the many variables of the parent-child system.

The reason why we have placed so much emphasis on parenting is because it represents the cornerstone upon which everything else is based. Without a well-developed understanding of what it means to be a good parent, our efforts to grow as a civilization will fail. Karl Menninger said that "what's done to children, they will do to society," and this realization has plagued mankind throughout history.

Becoming enlightened parents will allow us to explore all the other possibilities that exist and come to the recognition that there might be a correlation between our current social problems and our modern day myths about parenting. Embarking on this journey of parental discovery will emphasize the respect, responsibility, and reverence needed to make a perceptual shift in what it means to be a good parent for parenting's sake.

Society has been relentlessly haunted by the idea of control that often results in reduced personal responsibly, human atrocities, and historical tragedy. Based on commonly shared societal delusions about parenting, we continue to reinforce our current social problems and push the idea of social justice to the extreme.

These beliefs serve as a false set of convictions that weaken personal responsibility and parental accountability. When we judge ourselves harshly on these unrealistic expectations of control, we diminish everyone's personal power. Our views about how well-mannered, well-behaved, well-disciplined, well-adjusted, and perfect our children are, damage the very nature of what it means to be an effective parent.

Controlling expectations can often be seen in the looks of disapproval that we, as parents, get when our child is "acting out" in a grocery store. Even more damaging, is the positive reinforcing process of praise given to parents when their children act like little angels. These parental images become empty holographic reflections of our children and add to the ever-growing social dilemmas we face; because, after all, it is "all the parent's fault," according to many "pop psychology therapists," (Harris, 1998).

This is the fault line that runs through the heart of parenting and is what creates the damaging effects of the earthquakes centered in blame. We have been so preoccupied with the causes and effects of parenting that we have missed out on the processes that shape, influence, and empower us all. It's not about fault or blame but responsibility and change.

The art and science of parenting

"Parenting in today's world is both science (facts and principles gained by systematic study) and art (skill in conducting a human activity)."

-Ramey (2009)

Parenting represents a unique tapestry that is intertwined with our understanding of the complex variables required to be a good parent. It is only through joining the elements within the entire parent-child system that we can create a realistic approach to parenting.

We need a new model of parenting that is based on the unique individual strengths, talents, and abilities of both the parent and child, as well as the interconnectedness they have with one another and the world around them.

Through this new orientation, we can escape from the hold of the *parent trap,* become empowered, and trust in the relationships with our children. A systemic paradigm that Bardill (1997) describes as a "holistic view that allows us to get beyond emotional right/wrong thinking about human relationships."

"Becoming a Better Parent" represents a delicate balance between theory and approach, conception and practice, as well as ideology and practicality. Its roots are strongly embedded in both the art and science of human understanding. A good parent must be prepared to do more than just use the tools and techniques of the trade.

We must be willing to develop an artistic touch and vision in making our own renditions and interpretations in its application in the real world. Combining the art and science of parenting will allow us to create a more inclusive systems model of understanding.

Through our own personal development as students of parentology, we can become the artist, using our internal vision that brings together the science of the brush, color, and canvas to create our own parental masterpiece, without covering our children in paint through the process.

Parenting is an allusive concept that is perplexing enough without having to attach the extra shame that is associated with the absolute logic of our current linear parental models. By focusing on parenting as a system, we can start to envision the complexities of parenthood, empower the lives of parents, and enrich the relationships with their children.

This systemic view of parenting, as suggested by Solomon & George (1996), and expanded on by Stienberg & Pianta (2006), provides some directions for future studies but still remains locked within the cause and effect dynamics of *childing* that are held tightly within the grasp of the "parent trap."

The key lies in knowing that that there is no shame in parenting. From the simplest of tasks to the more elaborate dynamics, it is the noblest of our human endeavors. Parenting is all about process; it's not an event. It's the ebb and flow of the parenting and the interconnected nature of our relationships that creates the desired outcomes we so desperately seek for our children.

Unless we are able to reinforce the distinct boundaries that exist within the entire parent-child system as separate and whole interactions together, we are destined to perpetuate the ongoing myths of parenting and will become lost on our journey. To become better students of parenting, we must "study parents from their own perspective, not just as socializing agents of their children" (Mayseless, 2006).

To transform our current beliefs, we must incorporate the art of science, create meaning though purpose, and provide a new internal direction from within. This new guide for parents can be found within the wisdom of the well-known words of the Serenity Prayer: *"God grant me the serenity to accept the things I cannot change, the courage to change the things I can, and the wisdom to know the difference,"* (Reinhold Niebuhr).

II. Parenting is Not a Four-letter Word

"What lingers from the parent's individual past, unresolved or incomplete, often becomes part of her or his irrational parenting."

-Virginia Satir

Basically we get one of two choices about parenting. One, do what our parents did when we were growing up, or two, do something different. It is the very nature of our search for something else that defines our paths as parents.

It's not that our parents did anything wrong or that they were to blame, because, after all, they were faced with the same limitations. It's just that we need a more proactive approach to learning to be good students of parenting. Learning to be a good parent means we need to start asking better questions.

This is not an easy task and pushes us to seek new creative solutions outside of the box and away from our old parenting paradigms. We need more cohesive structures to effectively facilitate our response to rapid change.

Asking the right questions, provides us a way to look for the opportunities that exist within that drives us as parents. These questions can include, "what do I need to change?, how do I change things or shut them down?, and what new things can I try and when?" (Taffinder, 2006).

Our parental evolution has created an historical dilemma that established a gap in our generational learning curve. This historical learning curve generated new insights about parenting every generation, or roughly "22 years,"(Carlson, 2009). Carlson who also states that "generational timeframes vary based on shared cultural experiences" and "generally represents the amount of time it takes for one generation to grow up and have children of their own" (Howe & Strauss, 2000).

These timeframes never presented a pressing problem for us in the past because we, as parents, had the time to adjust to change. This is no longer the case as the rates of change continue to accelerate. The information that once took generations to accumulate is now accessible in an instant. Our past parental trial and error methods of change are outdated and need an overhaul.

Our history has been unavoidably altered by our technological advances, which continue to grow at alarming rates. Prior to the industrial revolution, social change occurred roughly once in every 100 years, or four generations. After the industrial revolution, the same change occurred in half the time.

These changes now take less than five years and according to Kurzweil (2005), this "technological change is so rapid and profound it represents a rupture in the fabric of human history." We are now at an unprecedented time in history where we can access information instantly and expand our awareness of parenting beyond imagination.

This vast cultural spectrum of human existence "requires a continuing, ongoing stepping out of old reality constructs to engage in the social construction of reality" (Anderson 1990). This information gives us the ability to ask questions about parenting that works so we can share the wisdom from all ages, cultures, and walks of life.

The effects from this rapid rate of change are creating a ripple effect felt across the globe and are challenging the status quo. Thomas Jefferson said that "a little rebellion, now and then, is a good thing, and is as necessary in the political world as storms in the physical," and a little rebellion within our views about parenting is needed to accommodate room for growth and define our search for answers.

It is precisely our ability as parents to handle rapid change that drives us in making a difference in our children's lives. However as important as these issues remain, there are no educational courses of study, no licensure requirements, no parenting degrees, no parenting science, and foremost, no universal understanding of what it means to be a good parent.

The parent license

"From where can your authority and license as a parent come from, when you who are old, do worse things?"
-Juvenal

In the movie "Parenthood," Keanu Reeves' character, Tod Higgins, reflects on parenting and states, "You know, Ms. Buckman, you need a license to buy a dog or drive a car—hell, you need a license to catch a fish, but they'll let any butt-reamin' asshole be a father."

Although there is some debate on the issue, the answer to our current parenting dilemma does not exist within governmental control, regulation or licensure. However, there seems to be an underlying consensus that added attention needs to be made in training our future generations on the importance of parenting.

Socrates once said, "Fellow citizens, why do you burn and scrape every stone to gather wealth, and take so little care of your children to who you must one day relinquish all." Socrates proposes an effective way for us to reframe our parenting questions. "Socratic questioning" is an effective tool for our parental growth that challenges current logic and enables us to "develop empathic critical thinking in building communities of learning," (Weil, 2004).

When we can apply these questions to parenting we can start to imagine a relationship with our children that will encourage growth, enhance learning, and foster a healthy sense of interdependency. The structure and discipline inherent in these types of questions forces us to look within. This insight will provide us a way to make the changes we need as to build more effective relationships with our children.

Becoming A Better Parent

Psycho-educational models like "The Incredible Years" (Webster-Stratton, 1992) and "Parent Effectiveness Training" (Gordan, 2000), have had proven success and provide a good starting point. I have used these models extensively in my practice and found them very useful with the clients I have worked with over the years. Where these directions might take us in the future is a question worth probing and might lead us to developing a more enlightened path of parental discovery.

Looking beyond our current shame and blame based models of parenting, we can start to create a vision of parenting for the future that is not based on unrealistic expectations and which encourages the genuine and real opportunities that exist within the parent-child system. By breaking through the myths of parenting, we can honor the challenges we all face in *becoming a better parent* so we can learn from our mistakes.

A new enlightened learning approach that fosters our ability to question the status quo and can make the lasting changes that truly make a difference in our children's world—a world where leadership replaces regulation, actions speak louder than words, and personal responsibility flourishes.

Creating an open-minded, free-thinking world where individual free will and choice are the driving forces behind positive change. "Parental involvement with their children" is a vital key to support this era in the parenting process so we can overcome the modern dilemmas we now face in keeping pace with the "explosion in mobile and online media, " (Foehr, Rideout & Roberts, 2010).

Becoming a student of parenting

"Life is a succession of lessons which must be lived to be understood."
-Helen Keller

My work with parents and children has revealed an interesting multigenerational phenomenon related to reoccurring parental patterns. Adapting our views about parenting is much more complex than it seems and represents a paradox that often only perpetuates "just more of the same,' (Waltchwick, Weakland & Fisch, 1974).

This type of "first order change" is "what might appear like a change at first glance is really just more of the same." This pattern creates the reoccurring parental traps that we are trying to avoid and represents the repetitive parenting cycles that have a tendency to spiral in on themselves.

The following is an example of a fist order multigenerational repeating pattern and represents a common parental paradox called a "polarized interactional pattern" or PIP (Watzlawick, Beavin & Jackson, 1967).

> *Jill grows up in an authoritarian family where her parents feel it's their role to be in control. Jill feels stifled by her parents' control and makes a vow that she will "never be that way with her children when she grows up." These interactions intensify over time and become entrenched as Jill develops her own ideas of parenting. She becomes more rebellious in reaction to her parents control, and starts to have problems with school. This only reinforces Jill's resistance to her parents' control and her anti-establishment commitment to do things differently than her parents did.*
>
> *Jill graduates, grows up, moves on with her life, and marries Mike, who also grew up in an authoritarian home. They both take a more laissez-faire approach with their daughter, Mikkela. Their permissive, let it be, style is not accepted by either of their families and they are always making unwanted suggestions about what the two of them need to do differently as parents. This interaction also intensifies as Mikkela grows up and she starts to resent what she calls her parents' 'alternative life style and approach to parenting.' She develops social problems in school, feeling like she doesn't fit in, and vows "that she will never allow this to happen to her children."*

Mikkela, too, grows up, moves on with her life, and gets married to John, against her parents' wishes. John grew up in an authoritarian family and states that "what was good enough for me is good enough for my kids." The two of them adopt a more conservative parenting style, based on what they call a return to "traditional family values." This interactional pattern continues to be a source of conflict for Mikkela's family as the authoritarian parenting style re-emerges, in spite of Jill's attempt to change this pattern in her family.

Interactional patterns can repeat or skip generations as seen above. What Jill found out was that doing something different than her parents did, only created a repetitive cycle that was passed on to her daughter.

Patterns can also be observed within reoccurring dysfunctional family patterns associated with abuse, neglect, substance use disorders, mental illness, and domestic violence. These can be seen as the biblical references to the "sins of the father" that continue to punish "the children for the sin of the fathers to the third and fourth generation." (Exodus 20:5)

Often passed down from one generation to the next, these ingrained patterns make it challenging to truly change our parental perspectives. It seems as though we need a more deliberate approach to change within the parent system.

Our efforts to break free from these destructive cycles go beyond doing something different than our parents did. It requires that we become true students of parenting and start to ask the questions that will lead us away from these mental prisons into the freedom of a new direction.

Robert Lang

Modern myths about parenting

"We cannot become better than we are; we cannot become stronger than we are; we cannot love more than we do; we cannot change our will or character, but we can change our vision of a child."

-Soloveychik

Parenting myths come in many forms and are made up of ingrained beliefs that generate iconic superheroes. These are often idolized versions of our own parental needs and wishes. The modern media mass produce these images that range from cartoons to sitcoms and from commercials to movies.

These iconic idols are like demigods, borrowed from ancient Greek mythology, who have superhuman abilities and can leap tall children with a single bound. These unrealistic parenting expectations create stress and feelings of hopelessness that reduce our self-esteem and self-confidence.

The idea of a *natural-born parent* is based on the genetic theory that some people are born to be good parents. They possess an innate natural ability to parent that takes place automatically. Although there is some research that suggests the possibility of a parent gene, "the provision of parenting is influenced by attitudes derived from the parent's family of origin as well as by genetically influenced parental temperamental characteristics," (Kendler, 1996).

It seems that these biological attributes must be developed, honed, and fine-tuned to make a difference in the parent-child relationship. Like any other God-given genetic ability, we can only recognize our full potential by building on our strengths. A 'natural' must use and build on what they have been given so they can learn and grow along the parenting continuum.

Athletic ability is a common set of skills that is often strongly linked to genetics and is described as being 'kissed by the gods.' The nature vs. nurture debate has been going on for a long time and is often strongly linked to the concept of athletic ability. Although our genetic makeup contributes to our physical limitations and abilities, most great athletes view their success as being more directly related to their work ethics.

Performance-based psychology has been extensively studied by Bouchard, Malina & Pérusse (1997), and emphasizes the roles that both genetic and environmental factors play in the development of athletic ability. They point out that "both are intrinsically linked in the sense that it is impossible to understand the genetic basis of a trait without making assumptions about nurture and vice-versa."

If, for example, a top athlete were to rely solely on his innate abilities and talents—neglecting motivation, practice, dedication, and hard work— he would be incapable of achieving the success he desires. It is only by building on these intrinsic attributes that true athletes can become top performers.

Parenting ability can be seen as the hidden potential that lies within all of us and is often referred to as the "field." It represents an internal mental process that creates our 'visionary dreams' of the future—a rich history that outlines our human fascination with predicting the future that includes both "Judeo-Christian and Native American traditions," (Bulkeley, 2001).

This field is also fictionally described in the novel "The Legend of Bagger Vance," as "a place of true reality that vividly flows with everything in the universe and is intimately linked and contributes to the authenticity of all possibilities."

It is what Einstein called a "unified field theory" that generally tried to describe the unseen forces that existed within the space-time continuum and connected all things. This parental "Field of Dreams" is where the real possibilities exist for the parent-child system that state, 'if we build it he will come.' Playing on the fields within our hearts and minds can allow us to seek this universal connection where we can focus on the steps of progress rather than the pillars of perfection.

Becoming a better parent means we must do more than rely on our innate parenting abilities. We must prepare the field within for the enormous responsibility that is parenting. In other words, there is no such thing as a natural-born parent, just like there is no such thing as a perfect parent. Natural parents, who seem to have taken to parenting like ducks to water, are only able to accomplish such feats with self-dedication, self-discipline, and personal responsibility.

We can only realize the gift of our true authentic parenting potential through hard work, practice, dedication, and devotion. Building this place of possibilities is where we can dream of a future for our children, internalize the field for our relationships, and transcend our own personal stories to soar where eagles dare.

"Supermom," or the "too good mother," (Voirst, 1998), is a modern day figment of our parental imagination that has developed out of the additional roles that women have taken outside of the home. These professional, hardworking, and active mothers have felt the pressures of assuming more responsibilities in addition to those they still retain within the home.

This supermom's supernatural ability to be all, do all, for all, is best reflected in the made-for-television ad by Electrolux. This commercial, with the theme from *"Bewitched"* playing in the background, suggests that these supermoms can be 'even more amazing' by 'juggling even more things in the day.'

The tragedy of these stereotypes is the unrealistic expectations that have been thrust upon the women of today. These images have created a damaging standard that set women up for perceived failure and can cause feelings of inadequacy. These distortions of the modern feminine psyche include images such as Barbie, Twiggy, June Cleaver, Elyse Keaton and Clair Huxtable. Although Barbie and Twiggy are not iconic images of the supermom, they symbolize the idealistic views that women have had to live with.

These images have inspired some but have done irreversible damage to others in diverting the real truth of what constitutes a woman and mother. Women and mothers deserve more credit and respect than these plastic images have allotted. This form of typecasting is only another way to oppress the unique individual characteristics so we can all become a one-dimensional, cardboard-cutout action figure that someone else created.

Becoming A Better Parent

Understanding what it means to be a good parent is supermom enough, or what Voirst (1998) discusses as the "good enough mother." This idea is not the opposite of the *supermom* as suggested by the images of Rosanne Conner ("*Roseanne,*" 1988), Peg Bundy ("*Married with Children,*" 1987), or Marge Simpson ("*The Simpsons,*" 1989), but instead is based on balance, wholeness, and acceptance of our true gifts as a person. To commit ourselves to the idea of *becoming a better parent* requires that we look beyond the myth of the supermom.

By dedicating ourselves to becoming the best parents we can be, we can let go of the perfectionist ideas of having to be more, do more, and contribute more to our families and children. Women can learn to grow beyond these false images and accept the realities of motherhood, which are far more rewarding than any myth can hope to be. This foundation is the true grit of parenting in which miracles are performed every day and eliminate the need for some made-up fantasy supermom—a place where moms can wake up, look in the mirror, and feel empowered as a parent.

The *ideal dad* is another romantic legend, created out of myth to define our roles as fathers. The real challenges faced in being a father have exposed this fatherly ideal as a fraud. Our views about fathers have been shaped by cultural narratives, patriarchal religions, and mythological stories. These ideas provide limited ways for men to defined their masculinity and dictate our roles as fathers and husbands.

Recently, the men's movement and the advocacy for father's rights in the parenting process has gained some momentum in redefining who we are as men and provides us with an expanded view of fatherhood. Taken from a variety of orientations, these new directions for defining who we are as men has given rise to a broader spectrum of what it means to be a husband, father, and man.

Classical psychoanalytical ideas of the *ideal dad* probe the deep-seated areas of our conscious and unconscious minds and rely heavily on past mythological representations. These conceptions of an imaginary figurehead are based on the absent father, as described by Freud (1905), and the symbolic father, as described by Jung (1969).

These are both empty representations of what a father can be. These psychosexual representations are based on classical oedipal mythology where the hero archetypes must rescue their mother and wage battle against their father to symbolically become a man. By transcending these theoretical fantasies, we can break free from the myth of the *ideal dad* and reconstruct our understanding of what it truly means to be a good parent, father, and man.

Epic sagas told throughout human history, as in *"Bible"* (2008), *"Buddhavacana"* (1991), *"Star Wars"* (1977), and *"Iron John"* (1992), have fueled a never-ending stream of conceptualized father figures. Great philosophers, such as Plato and Descartes, have also created these icons of fatherhood and have also contributed to our illusions of the *ideal dad*. A father's role as a parent remains somewhat elusive and has gone through many changes in a short period of time.

Our identity as a complete parent within the role of a father will allow us to pass on this endearing legacy to the next generation so we can become more than the legend. By surpassing these myths of the *ideal dad*, we can see ourselves as compassionate, caring, and devout fathers so that we can provide our children with the "heart, intelligence, and spirit of free men," (Soloveychik, 2008).

These fatherly myths have created, perpetuated, and supported the historical and cultural phenomenon of the "absentee father," (Santoro & Santoro, 2004). The U.S Census Bureau reports that only "about 15 percent of fathers were custodial parents, 55 percent, had visitation privileges, 7 percent had joint custody, but 38 percent had neither." According to the National Center for Fathering, 72.2 percent of the U.S. population see fatherlessness as "the most significant family or social problem facing America."

The studies on the role of fathers done by the National Fatherhood Initiative, showed a number of "negative effects of father absence and a number of positive effects of father involvement." These expanded views on the role of parents are paving the way for us to redefine what it means to be an actively involved, caring, and nurturing father, and break away from the myths of the *idea dad*.

The *perfect family* is another myth contained within our views about parenting. Our status efforts in trying to 'keep up with the Joneses' can create havoc in our lives as well as the lives of our children. This three bedroom, two bathroom, two-car garage, white picket fence, with two children (preferably one boy and one girl), and a dog, is the Norman Rockwell image of the perfect modern suburban American family.

Stereotypical families like these have been a mirage created on some distant highway of our minds that is preoccupied with "chasing the American dream" (Adams, 1931). The great American melting pot with its diversity, rapid social change, nontraditional gender roles, blended families, and differing parent roles has never lent itself to a one-size-fits-all view of the family. These fantasies are often based on pop culture portrayals such as "*The Cosby Show*" (1984), "*The Brady Bunch*" (1969), and "*Family Ties*" (1982).

Media perpetuates and profits from these covert messages to reinforce commonly held illusions that project them into stardom. Contained within these perfect families, or their sarcastic counterparts, are the unrealistic values and attitudes that lie within our own hidden fantasies and desires.

Media portrayals of these perfect family images go back to the early days of television with programs like "*Father Knows Best*" (1954) and "*Leave It to Beaver*" (1957). Literary representations have also contributed to the myth of the perfect family with examples that include "*Little House in the Big Woods*" (1953) and "*The Swiss Family Robinson*" (1812).

We have bought into what is being sold because it's something we want. These often less than benign and overly simplistic portrayals of the perfect family demonstrate the curiously optimistic, warm, humorous, and well-functioning side of family life. Despite some difficult situations that these families face, the wise and all-knowing parents end up resolving the issues through the power of righteous moral thinking and good old wholesome values.

Our insatiable appetite for these unrealistic views of family life is a need that feeds the incredible popularity of these feel-good representations. "*The Incredibles*" (2004), is another illustration, showing a family of superheroes that can save the world not only with their superhuman abilities, but also with their perfect family skills in working together.

I have known and worked with many people who have been negatively impacted by this myth of the perfect family and have expressed distress about how their past or present family experiences did not measure up to their own naive perfectionistic expectations. These myths about what family life should, ought, and need to be, have created unrealistic internalized standards that are often adopted as second families when ours don't measure up.

These expectations for our families often lead to unattainable goals and disappointments no matter how caring, well-intentioned, and loving our parents might have been. This contrast between the realistic view the fantasy view of the perfect family was a major theme in the movie "*Pleasantville*" (1998), where, through some magical transformation, the imperfect family becomes whole. This sets the stage for our harsh judgment of real parents and the real life we live every day and is often passed on as a negative byproduct of the perfect family that is based on some of the following rules:

1. *The perfect family's parents always get along and never fight.*
2. *The perfect family's children are always cooperative and willing to help out.*
3. *Perfect families get along without conflict.*
4. *Perfect families have a supportive, loving, and involved extended family*
5. *The perfect family never has any serious problems.*
6. *The perfect family never has any unresolved problems.*
7. *The perfect family has parents that have total control over their children.*
8. *Perfect families have perfect mothers and fathers.*
9. *The perfect family is made up of one father, one mother, and 2.5 children.*

10. Perfect families make upstanding citizens for their communities.
11. The perfect family is always pleasant.

Our human need to see the happy ending in every perfect family story is deeply rooted within our own emotional system. This emotional dynamic, although momentarily uplifting, is based on avoiding pain and seeking pleasure. It drives our desires to experience the pleasantness of the perfect family and avoid the pain sometimes created by our everyday family realities. The difficulty with this type of family perfectionism is— what is often most perfect about our families is our imperfections.

The poet Robert Hillyer once said that "perfectionism is a dangerous state of mind in an imperfect world." This idea of perfectionism is often linked to both *internal* and *external negative schemas* that "lead you to make mistakes in your interpretation of events," (Bosco, 1999). Bosco states that these irrational schemas lead to automatic "emotional reactions, behavioral responses, and sometimes, physiological events, such as having your heart race or your stomach ache."

Letting go of this perfectionism can develop a more proactive and realistic approach in asking more of the questions that will lead to learning something beyond what these false images could ever imagine.

Great parents are made

"Here is my chance. This is the only chance for a weak, incapable, and imperfect parent."
-Soloveychik

Changing our perspectives, attitude, values, perceptions, and beliefs can move us away from trying to be a perfect parent and help us focus on becoming the best parent we can be. These questions can change what 'could have been' to everything that 'can be.' Through this course of study, we can start to direct our parenting attempts to break free from these intergenerational patterns and false expectations.

Parenting is not defined within any particular time, space, or age, and represents a lifelong process of change and growth. The effective stewardship of our lives, our societies, and our world contains a parent principle that defines who we are as humans. Comprehending the importance of this parenting process is pivotal in explaining our true identity, which is more than the sum of its parts.

It is impossible for us to separate our views about parenting from the whole as this represents our connection to all things. Whether we were raised by our parents, grandparents, foster parents, relatives, in a group home, boarding school, orphanage, or a kibbutz, our views about who we are can be determined by our views about parenting.

Whatever messages we received, adopted, and used from our past can make a huge impact in how we see ourselves. Descartes said, "I think, therefore I am," and a great deal of research has supported this idea in that what we believe about ourselves is most often true. Preskill and Torres (1999) describe that the "values, beliefs, assumptions, and knowledge that have been developed over time, are thought of as 'truths,' and are what guide people in their everyday lives."

Generally speaking, then, if we believe we can't be a good parent, then we won't. If, on the other hand, we believe we can be a good parent, then we can. Aside from its linear reference, we must go beyond changing our patterned thoughts and include our emotional and behavioral systems to do whatever it takes to succeed in *becoming a better parent*. This 'do whatever it takes' attitude is often one of the keys that holds the promise of a brighter future for tomorrow's generations, whether we decide to have children of our own or not.

Becoming a better parent means that we can began to see the potential and opportunity in ourselves so we can overcome the built-in illusions of these false idols of parenting. We can start to appreciate the time, energy, and effort it truly takes to develop a positive and meaningful relationship with our children. Letting go of the idea that we can make some parental

'Jeannie' or 'Supernanny' appear out of a bottle is about realizing that these myths and expectations are unrealistic, static, and unnecessary components of our parental identity.

Our parental identities can be so much more than these idealistic fantasies could have ever imagined. Generational expectations are often reinforced by individual efforts to have another chance at overcoming our own mistakes from the past.

Developing our new parental identity out of these ashes, like a Phoenix rising out of our past, we can now turn our attention to making progress rather than being perfect, learning rather than knowing, and becoming rather than being. This brings everything we ever have been and everything we will ever be into the present so we can transform the moment into all its possibilities.

Becoming a self-disciplined disciplinarian

"With self-discipline, most anything is possible."
-Theodore Roosevelt

Discipline refers to the systematic instruction of our children but often carries a negative association with it being attributed to punishment. In its Latin root form, discipline is directly related to the process of teaching and learning, and involves a more pervasive view of the intimate connection that exists between teacher and student.

This view expands on the aspects of behavioral modification and includes the emotional, cognitive, and social aspects of the entire learning process. It is a method of "modeling character, teaching self-control, and reinforcing acceptable behavior in our children," (Papalia et al, 2006). However, to accomplish this task with our children, we first need to become disciplined ourselves.

We can then create a positive learning experience, consistently set behavioral limits, and structure effective guidelines that will allow our children to reach their own full potential. Tragically, it is often hypocrisy that rules this parental process, as reflected by an old cliché, "Do as I say, not as I do." In the worst cases, it can lead to our tragic fears of abuse as the control associated with "discipline gone wrong," (Schwartz & Isser, 2007).

Discipline is a complex process of the parent-child system that is in a constant state of "dynamic equilibrium, " (Headey & Wearing, 1989). The processes "within complex living systems usually oscillates between constancy and change," (Thommen & Wettstein, 2009). They report that these "transformational and change processes do not always proceed on a continuous and linear courrse; rather, there is often evidence of qualitative ruptures and transitions linked to chaotic developments."

Dynamic equilibrium is an oxymoron, of sorts, in that it combines the contradictory terms of 'dynamic,' meaning a continuous and productive activity or change, and 'equilibrium,' meaning a state of rest or balance. However, combining these two ideas gives us an accurate mental picture of the turbulent internal process of discipline as a parent.

Parents are continuously searching for answers to find what kind of discipline will work. We are often perplexed by this illusive dilemma within the parenting system, and once again are fooled by the parent traps of control and magical thinking. Not fully understanding the complicated dynamics of 'what works for one person in one place and time might not work for another,' we end up making statements such as, "It worked when he was younger, "It worked for his brother, "It's not working anymore," or "It stopped working altogether."

These statements are made within the illusions of discipline when it is directed at our children and we find ourselves faced with the same old trap of parental control. Discipline can be a very effective teaching tool for our children as long as we remember to start from within. "Parents must become disciplined parents before their children will most likely become self-disciplined, " (Wyckoff & Unell, 2002).

Discipline, like many of the elements of being a parent, is a complicated practice that does not have a single answer that can be applied to all situations. Vasiloff (2003) identifies self-discipline in terms of "learning" as a kind of discipleship that "builds character." Self-discipline, as defined by Tracy (2009), is "the ability to do what you should do, when you should do it, whether you feel like it or not." Tracy also suggests that our success is based on our mastery of our goals, courage, and persistence through self-discipline.

Our willingness to embrace taking on the role of students learning to become self-disciplined disciplinarians gives us the ability to connect with our children and lead the way by example, making it easier to 'practice what we preach.'

When faced with these challenges, we often resort to common flaws in the discipline process by using those good old 'parent standbys' such as, "because I said so" or "because I'm the parent, that's why." We must be willing, as role models for our children, to adopt a new mindset that children are meant to be seen and heard— which sets the stage for learning to occur.

We, as parents, often minimize our role in the learning process and must realize that "children learn by what they see and hear you do. All the lectures in the world will not compensate for the example parents set for their children," Christopherson (2002). The impact of our parenting styles, approaches, techniques, and strategies, on our ability to discipline or teach our children, has everything to do with our relationships and little to do with the implementation of these tactics.

To become disciplined parents, we must become students by learning the science and applying the art of parenting. It is only through our ability to become self-disciplined parental disciplinarians that we can develop and train ourselves in the self-will needed to transform our role as a parent with our children. Vasiloff (2003) suggests the following ways to model self-discipline so we can 'practice what we preach' with our children by:

- Using active listening
- Following the rules
- Asking questions and practice sharing
- Using and developing your social skills

- Working cooperatively
- Understanding and explaining rules
- Accomplishing tasks on your own
- Demonstrating positive leadership
- Using effective communication strategies
- Staying organized
- Working on resolving problems
- Initiating multiple solutions
- Distinguishing between fact and feeling
- Getting involved and doing service work

Within the parenting literature, a great deal of time, energy, and effort has been devoted to parental discipline, with significant contributions having been made. But, again, like many of our parenting approaches, the complex nature of the dynamic process of discipline in the parent-child system is still being missed. Without first appreciating the multifaceted nature of the entire parenting system, discipline can be used for all the wrong reasons.

When it comes to discipline, it is often not the 'how,' but the 'why' that creates a problem. The problem generally lies in the 'why' we discipline and not 'how' we discipline—except for the more controlling forms of discipline that are all maladaptive, no matter what, why, when, where, or how. We must remember that our role in the discipline process is to *teach* our children, not to *make* them learn.

If our efforts are directed at controlling the learning process for our children, then we are setting up a power struggle and we decrease our effectiveness. We need the discipline to practice patience, tolerance, and forgiveness that consistently structures, encourages, and reinforces the natural curiosity of our children to learn.

III. Fun-n-games and Child's Play

"You can discover more about a person in an hour of play than in a year of conversation."

-Plato

In using play as a medium, I am often fascinated by how this process helps facilitate the connection between parents and children. These imaginative gifts are glimpses into the world from a child's perspective. Tasks that we, as parents, often take for granted and view as labor, are the worlds of wonderment in our child's play.

These imaginative gifts make up the fertile playgrounds of their inquisitive minds; a place where we can join with their imaginations and take an active role as the drama unfolds. Play is a powerful source of creativity offered as an open invitation to breathe the reified air that holds the promise for all things great and small. However, this is only restating what Jesus once said, "Let the little children come to me, and do not hinder them, for the kingdom of heaven belongs to such as these." (Matthew 19:14)

The power of play has provided tremendous therapeutic outcomes for both adults and children within my practice. The research done by Eisenstadt and his colleagues (1993) supports these findings and indicates that "play can be very useful in creating positive therapeutic outcomes." Shifts in our perceptions created through play can have a significant impact on our views about the world.

Humor is one of the greatest benefits from our reframing experiences in life through play. By approaching life from a child's perspective, we can see our everyday struggles as more playful opportunities, giving us the unique ability to see the humor in all things. Research by Klein (1989) has shown that this humor can also have an added health benefits as it raises our natural "endorphin levels, decreases depression, fights off stress, and boosts our immune system."

Our need to play and have fun is deeply embedded within the human emotional system and is reflected in the proverb "all work and no play makes Jack a dull boy." Play is one of our most essential needs and can enhance our emotional health and well-being. Our ability to tap into these playful resources allows for a powerful interchange so we can connect with our children and foster the significance in our relationships.

Play can be an enjoyable experience and is a process where children will feel understood and supported. "Play offers parents a wonderful opportunity to engage fully with their children" (Ginsburg, 2007). He states that "parents who have the opportunity to glimpse into their children's world learn to communicate more effectively with their children and are given another setting to offer gentle, nurturing guidance" as well as "gain a fuller understanding of their perspective."

In order for us to make an emotional connection within the parent-child relationship, we need to consider our perceptions, attitudes, and beliefs of fun. Whether a behavior is fun or not is related to our interpretation of its meaning. Our thinking, feeling, and behaving systems are what determine our social interactions and define what we see as having fun.

It is our ideas, not the activity or materials that matter in having fun. I have seen children having fun and playing for hours with the fallen limbs of trees, pretending that they are knights on a quest to slay a dragon, or using empty boxes to create their own secret hiding places. These are the building blocks of our own imaginations and create the fun within play.

Becoming A Better Parent

Your work is child's play

"Play is often talked about as if it were a relief from serious learning. But, for children, play is serious learning. Play is really the work of childhood."
-Mister Rogers

There is an interesting transformation that takes place with our opinions about playing and having fun as we get older, that is best illustrated by the often misused and misinterpreted letter of John to the Corinthians when he says, "When I was a child, I spoke as a child, I understood as a child, I thought as a child; but when I became a man, I put away childish things."
(1 Corinthians 13:11) Our misconceptions about the role play has in parenting often perpetuates misinterpretations of this passage, as there is a vast difference between being child*like* and being child*ish*.

Keeping this in mind, we are again reminded that our attitudes, beliefs, values, motivations, and judgments are highly influenced by our ideas of reference, no matter what their origins might be. Whether these are biblically-based or emanate from the "*Origin of the Species*," (1998), our mindsets are dictated by these philosophical orientations. By re-evaluating the usefulness of these rigidly held dogmatic themes that often fly in the face of reason, we can facilitate change and let go of our old preconceived notions of parenting.

We must possess the sensitivity, receptiveness, openness, innocence, and imaginative characteristics of a child to set the stage for overcoming our childish, simplistic, stubborn persistence with ineffective parenting patterns. These take all the fun out of life and limit our ability to connect with our children.

Playing must be a priority so we can put the fun and humor back into our lives as parents. It is through our childlike playfulness that we can see the true wonders and mysteries of the world. Our childlike eyes give us new insight into parenting or, as expressed in a song by Reamonn, that says, in part, "Why do we make it so hard? This world is so complicated, until we see it through the eyes of a child."

Our work needs to be seen as child's play. Imagine our life and a workplace filled with joy, creativity, amazement, and compassion, and that also fosters individual growth, values learning, encourages productivity and cultivates cooperative collaboration. Organizational philosophies such as these have been a reality for some of the most successful modern entrepreneurial endeavors and include companies like Intellectual Ventures, Apple, Disney, and Yahoo, to mention only a few.

This wisdom comes from a sacred place that cannot be found in the white pillars of academia, the columns of justice, or in the boardrooms of the Fortune 500. These are the simply joys that are found on the playgrounds of the world. In his book "All I Really Need to Know I Learned in Kindergarten," (Ballantine Publishing, 1986), Fulghum states that this wisdom comes from understanding a simple balance. A simplicity that includes, to paraphrase, 'everything, playing fair, putting things back where you found them, saying you're sorry when you hurt somebody, warm cookies and cold milk are good for you, and living a balanced life - learn some and think some and draw and paint and sing and dance and play and work every day some.'

Looking at the world with the fresh eyes and amazement of our own youth allows all things to become possible and the limitations that are driven by our own internalized mindsets can be put to rest. Having fun is a relatively simple task that requires small shifts in our perception about play and we can regain that silly sense of humor that is childlike.

If we can transform the opportunity that exists in our everyday lives into humorous gifts, then we can expand our fun factor to unlimited potentials. Imagine if we were able to transform our everyday common experiences of waiting in line or driving in traffic into comedy, or to greet people that you meet with the creative power of a smile—then our duties can become filled with the enthusiasm of youth. Tuck (2003) states that this "is an invitation to go on a journey within to try to see through the eyes of a child once again."

At this point you're probably hearing those same old messages in your head saying, "Yeah, but life isn't meant to be all fun and games," "Get real and act your age," or "Grow up, already." Of course you would be right to say that life is not all fun and games—but it isn't all fear and suffering either. Life represents a balance between obstacles and opportunities. It is only when we can accept the pointlessness of controlling other people, places, or things, that we can began to honor ourselves, others, and the world around us.

Our journey as a parent has divergent paths, rich with opportunities and challenges, and it is our triumphant return to the joy, play, fun, and humor of our youth, that allows true healing to take place. "So, let the children play, inside your heart always. And death you will defy, 'cause your youth will never die." Creed. "Never Die." *Human Clay*.)

Getting down on your child's level

"When you are dealing with a child, keep all your wits about you and sit in the floor."
-Austin O'Malley

To join our children at play, we need to get down on their level. This strategy, of getting down on our child's level, is described very effectively in the parenting program "The Incredible Years," as developed by Webster-Stratton (1992). Webster-Stratton suggests that this represents an open invitation into a world that gives us each the ability to connect and build a deeper, more meaningful, relationship with our children.

Brazelton's work, "What Every Baby Knows," (1983 and 1998), was instrumental in developing an understanding of the importance of this parent-child interaction. This set the stage for developments within pediatrics to build parent-child relationships that facilitate positive change. This has continued to evolve into what has become "Parent-Child Interaction Therapy," or PCIT, as described by Zisser & Eyberg (2010).

These cooperative play interactions between the parent and child take two primary forms that are either child or parent directed. However, whatever form they take, it is imperative that we, as parents, engage in our children's world of play and not force our grownup illusions on our children. The following is a list of strategies that have been taken from a number of approaches I have used over the years, to help you get the most out of the play with your children:

- *Play like a child and let them educate you on how.*
- *Slow down and make time; it's a process you don't need to finish.*
- *Clear your mind of all expectations and just let the play happen.*
- *Pay close attention and be an active participant.*
- *Avoid power struggles and be open to bending the rules.*
- *Follow your children's lead and build up the process.*
- *Use all the aspects of communication to connect with your child.*
- *Be genuine, sincere, appreciative, and use lots of praise.*
- *Fake it 'til you make it, and try copying what your child's doing.*
- *Ask for your child's help; this is their area of expertise.*
- *Be flexible, open, and responsive to changes in direction during play.*
- *Use structure, provide limits, and be consistent without being demanding or rigid.*

Entering into this wondrous world of our children's play can sometimes be a terrifying proposition for parents who have long ago given up such 'childish things and have no time in their busy lives for such nonsense.' Parents often resist and sometimes refuse to get down and play with their children when there is no adult stuff, including 'big chairs or big tables' allowed in the play room.

Becoming A Better Parent

These cases often require coaching, modeling, and teaching so parents can relearn the art of play. Rigidity replaced by a youthful suppleness—allowing parents to peer into their children's eyes and see the universe of wonder held within. "Loosening up – literally and figuratively – also helps, as most of us adults are rather stiff when we try to get down on the floor and play" (Cohen, 2002).

I have had the privilege of seeing these parents become as comfortable on the floor as they were sitting around a conference table or sprawled out on a couch glued to the television. Being able to witness the longing of a child's heart being filled with the joy of playing a game of "Chutes and Ladders" with their parents for the first time, is an honor I'm proud to share.

Little things matter the most in our children's lives, and to be a part of these small miracles is a life affirming process. Cherishing the obvious emotional expressions that take place between parent and child during these times reveals the powerful nature of these bonds. Our relationships during play morph and recreate a connection that touches the deepest places in our hearts, minds, and souls.

Observing these parents get down, let go, and roll around on the floor with their children seems to tap a part of something long-forgotten but well-remembered. Memories that flood the playroom with a new joy rediscovered in this internal fountain of youth as portrayed in *The Twilight Zone's* "Kick the Can," (1962).

Play is the key that opens doors to the child that survives within all of us and desperately wants to reach out. Studies have shown that play is essential for child development and also offers the "ideal opportunity for parents to engage fully with their children," (Ginsberg, 2007).

Play is not only important in building a healthy relationship with your children it is the most effective way to connect with them. Bonds formed by joining our children in their world will provide the means by which you can support them in growing into yours.

Robert Lang

Play is therapy

"A person's maturity consists in having found again the seriousness one had as a child, at play."
-Friedrich Nietzsche

"Play as Therapy" is defined by Stagnitti, Cooper & Whiteford (2009), who discuss how mental healthcare professionals view play as an effective treatment tool. They also suggest that "practitioners often have a difficult time agreeing on the theories and practices that make up play-based therapeutic approaches."

Even this type of therapy is being called to grow up as Stagnitti, Cooper & Whiteford (2009), point out that "the interventions and approaches based on play are increasingly being called into question as the mental health field attempts to provide more uniform evidence-based practices."

Stagnitti, Cooper & Whiteford (2009), seem to suggest three relevant points. One, that play is essential for human growth. Two, that play is imperative in building the parent-child relationship; and three, that parents need to be involved.

Play therapy provides a more comprehensive approach when parents take an active role in this powerful process. If we, as parents, want to engage our children, we must be willing to embrace a mindset that play is the most important work we do.

Our views on play are changing and creating a "widening belief that play is not a trivial or childish pursuit, but rather a prime pillar of mental health, along with love and work," (Schaefer, 2002). It seems as if play presents a number of benefits for adults by helping them explore creative problem solving through the utilization of other, more 'right brain,' interactive activities.

Becoming childlike reconnects the neural pathways of our youth and rekindles the embers that once burned bright. By moving from our adult versions of "adulterated play," as defined by Donaldson (1993), to more spontaneous, improvisational, and free forms of childlike play, we can start to experience the full joy of this youthful elixir. Anderson (2002) taps these humorous ways in which laughter can inspire us so we "never have to act our age." He points out that we need to find the "ways to get the fun back into life."

Play can be a source of calmness and relaxation while simultaneously stimulating our minds and bodies. Being playful can assist us as parents in being more inventive, smart, happy, flexible, and resilient. It can help develop our imaginations, foser creativity, and improve our ability to deal with and manage all of life's challenges. As stated before, play promotes our physical and mental health, reduces stress levels, and improves our immune system's ability to fight off disease.

More importantly, it allows us to shape the nature of our relationships with our children. Laughter brings people together and builds strong, healthy relationships. By making a conscious effort to incorporate more humor and play into our daily interactions, we can improve the connections with our children, loved ones, co-workers, family members, and friends.

Brown & Vaughan (2009) have made a number of significant contributions in realizing the benefits of play, concluding through their studies that play is "a powerful force in nature that determines our very survival as a species." Their research has shown how play facilitates "brain development, supports fairness, reinforces equality, encourages empathy, and promotes psychological and physical health." They argue that work and play are mutually supportive, noting that "play increases efficiency and productivity in the work place."

Play is a state of mind that can often be described as a time when we feel most alive. It is through our play that we can activate our sense of humor and create healing laughter, which "can reduce stress and revitalize our bodies," (Miller et al., 2005). Their research supports the old saying that 'laughter is the best medicine,' and they suggest that this "definitely appears to be true when it comes to protecting your heart."

Laurence (2009) further suggested that we should adopt an "attitude of playfulness" in which our minds are "open to uncensored, iconoclastic, silly, or outrageous thoughts." He states that "we need to think funny by seeing the flip side of every situation." He thinks that we should "laugh at the incongruities in everyday situations, whether they involve you or someone else."

Laurence (2009) also points out that our laughter should be directed at behaviors in "what people do and not for who they are." Most importantly, he suggests that we need to be able to "laugh at ourselves with acceptance and delight." He states that we should "make others laugh and use our sense of humor to have fun and not to be funny," a spirit that comes from a place of humility.

By embracing these tools, we can connect with our own playful inner child, span the generation gap, and foster a sense of humor so we can transform our relationships with our children. This transformation makes the burdens of life more bearable. Abraham Lincoln once said, "With the fearful strain that is on us night and day, if I did not laugh I should die."

Develop the power of your imagination

"The imagination is a place all by itself—a separate country. You've heard of the French or the British nation. Well, this is the imagi-nation. It's a wonderful place."
-Kris Kringle ("*Miracle on 34th Street,*" 1947)

This incredible place of imagination, as described by Kris Kringle, is a glorious and endless universe of pretend that stretches our ability to form a mental image of something that is not perceived through our other senses. Different than illusions or delusions, it is the ability of the mind to build mental constructs, objects, or events that do not exist, are not present or are not part of the past.

Everyone possesses an imaginative ability, but, as with any skill, we must use this as parents if we want to continue to develop. Imagination makes it possible to experience a whole world inside the mind and gives us the ability to look outside of ourselves, empathize with others, and see the world from different points of view.

Becoming A Better Parent

Manifesting itself in many forms, our imagination enables us to mentally restructure choices from our past and explore the possibilities of the future. These mental constructs are important in creating our daydreams, mental images, hopes, aspirations, and our visions of tomorrow that provide a sense of happiness, calmness, contentment, well-being, and serenity.

Our imagination is an important tool that can be used to help relieve stress, reduce tension, assist in problem solving, and develop our intuition and insight. It can assist in the expansion of wisdom that encompasses more than our accumulated knowledge and is a pathway for realizing all that we are, have been, and ever will be. Imagination is an energetic resonating conduit that defines our thoughts, feelings, and behaviors, and structures our efforts to build all our futures of tomorrow.

I often work with parents and children to expand their imaginations together and thus build a closer relationship. Parents and children working together in a number of different creative mediums such as play, storytelling, art, music, and writing, are able to access their experiences in different ways that utilize untapped personal potential. Once a barrier, these obstructions can now flow freely within the innovative gift of our own imaginations.

Our imaginative capabilities as parents can also supply us with the ability to generate new pathways for change. Research by Russ (2009), suggests that parents that use their own imaginations promote imaginative children "that can generate different ideas about a topic. The ability to generate alternatives allows children to become better problem solvers."

Tapping into these imaginative internal resources we can start to use these creative mediums in ways that we never thought possible. No longer trapped by the fears, inadequacies, and learned behaviors, we can welcome these childlike things from our past and move forward with a renewed hope. We can begin to use these mechanisms in initiating the places in which we can build the relationships with our children.

Overcoming the mental constructs about these things as being childish, we can use a mindful approach, as outlined by Germer (2005), in the application of our imaginations. He suggests that by using mindfulness in "relating to the experience," we can "lessen the sting of life's difficulties" and overcome our "past conditioning, present circumstances, genetic predispositions, or any number of interacting factors." Simply stated, we can become more mindful in relating to the experiences we have with our children on a daily basis in new, imaginative, and creative ways.

Living life as a game

"Life's a game. All you have to do—is know how to play it."
-Unknown

The game of life presents us with an ongoing collection of constant and compelling choices in which we are endlessly searching for purpose and meaning. This game of life can be infinitely complex and is why we are compelled to play. The challenge of playing this game as a parent is learning to enjoy the experience with our children so we can grow, learn, and have fun. Getting the most out of this game means that we need to develop our playing skills, give it our all, and embrace life in its totality.

There are many games in life and many ways in which to play them that can dictate the opportunities for everyone to win. Rules for the game of life are discovered along the way and everyone's game is determined by how it's played. Playing the game of life as parent means we can hit the 'restart button' as many times as we need to, so we can find more effective ways in which to connect with our children.

Philosophical traditions have been investigating how to play the game of life for centuries, and have come up with a simple common axiom that says, "It's not whether you win or lose, but how you play the game." There are an endless number of games that we play in life, including those we play with parenting, work, school, finances, emotions, safety, stability, security, family, health, wellness, and spirituality.

These sub-games, and the reasons we play them, can divert our attention away from the far more expansive game of life itself. We can find ourselves locked into the purpose and meaning that drive these sub-games and "lose sight of the goal and probably lose the game," (Kofman, 2006). He states that learning how to play the game of life well, means we need to heed the echoes from the past and "not focus on egocentric cravings, and express our highest virtue in every action."

Transforming our parental views about how play and how we perceive the game of life, can make our experiences with our children that much more rewarding. "Life is not a battle; it is a game," (Shinn, 2011). She states that the game of life is about "giving and receiving" and suggests that our minds are the most powerful tools we have in playing this game. She also says that if used properly, we can attain "happiness, peace, prosperity, healing, forgiveness, and faith that are all part of the "Divine Design."

Life played by this design frees us from the rigidity of our legalistic expectations in a world of scarcity and forms the internal pathways of game lived in abundance. Winning and competition can be redefined in terms of sportsmanship where the spirit of collaboration and team work become our free passes to success. These can be the most wonderful, incredible, and astonishing aspects of our lives, if we decide to play, and commit ourselves to studying our own game of life.

Understanding the rules of the game provides the structure in our lives. These rules can either enhance or confine the experience of playing the game. We are given no instructions or rules for this game, we are only given a box and it is up to us to figure it out. How we define the rules determines the outcomes for the game and provides us the way to create our own success in winning. I'm reminded of the movie *Big Daddy* when Julian creates his own rules for a card game he calls "I win." No matter what hand Julian is dealt, he always wins.

So it is with the game of life—we are dealt the hands we are given and what matters most is how we play them. These rules are the "universal truths that everyone inherently knows but has forgotten somewhere along the way. They form the foundation of how we can live a fulfilling, meaningful life," (Carter-Scott, 1998).

Deciding to play the game is only the first step. By becoming students of the game, we can start to find our best fit, learn the rules, and take the time to understand what it means to become the masters of our own lives. To become a master of this game can take a lifetime and requires that we become apprentices in recognizing that 'the more I know, the more I realize I don't know.' Mike Sexton was given credit for saying that *Texas Hold'em* is a game that "takes a minute to learn and a lifetime to master."

The same can be said for parenting, where we can spend our entire lives trying to find our "sweet-spot, where our giftedness resides," (Lucado, 2005). This is a place where the game and real life are in balance and produce the purpose, meaning, and joy of what living life to its fullest can bring.
It is a place where we become fully engaged in the process of life, where we start to value the experiences for what they are, and develop a state of oneness that flows from all things. This is about living life by "being in the zone," (Csikszentmihalyi, 1997). The game of life is supposed to be fun, so find your sweet spot, learn to live in the zone, and go out there and play to have fun!

IV. Where You End and Everything Else Begins

"Boundaries bring order to our lives, strengthen our relationships with others and ourselves, and are essential to our mental and physical health."
                                                                    -Anne Katherine

Boundaries define where we end and everything else begins. They determine our roles as parents and "define our interactions with others," (Petronio, 2002). They "affect communication patterns," (Agazarian, 2004), and "structure hierarchies," (Minuchin, 1974).

Built from our internal dynamics, they act like magnets and either hold systems together or push them apart. Good boundaries bring a sense of balance to our lives and a sense of chaos when they become unhealthy. Our boundaries can give us a clearer sense of ourselves and our place in the world. Simply put, boundaries separate who I am from everything else. It is an interdependent systems phenomenon that determines how we interact with the outside world and how we allow the outside world to interact with us.

With healthy boundaries, we can have the assurance that comes from knowing we can and will protect ourselves from situations and circumstances that occur in our lives. Boundaries are important in the relationships with our children because they determine where we end and our children begin. If we do not develop a healthy sense of boundaries with and for our children, then it becomes difficult for us to form healthy relationships with them.

These boundaries provide the structures that are needed to establish a foundation for the interactions taking place between us and our children. Our boundary connections form the bonds of the parent-child relationship and can make an important difference within our role as a parent. If we make the effort to define our boundaries with our children, our relationships will improve, becoming more complete and balanced.

Boundaries are formed throughout our lives and are characterized by Minuchin (1974) as a "continuum from enmeshment through semi-diffuse permeability to rigidity." He also indicates that our boundaries are characterized by a "hierarchy of power, typically with the parents having more power than a child." Minuchin suggests that in healthy families, "parent-children boundaries are both clear and semi-permeable," allowing both systems to interact together with a degree of autonomy and interdependence.

These family system structures are not too rigid nor too aloof, and provide for our children's needs for support, nurturance, and guidance that encourage healthy development. He points out that "dysfunctional families" exhibit mixed subsystems or coalitions that manifest improper power hierarchies where boundaries become "enmeshed."

Parents can take a leadership role in educating their children in asserting healthy boundaries. Boundaries foster self-respect, establish limits, and define your own personal space. They act as filters, messengers, and an internal guidance system for developing personal responsibility. Our thoughts, feelings, and behaviors determine our boundaries that then regulate our interactions, responses, and reactions to the world around us.

Expressing our boundaries is how we present ourselves to the world. It is a social learning process that is built on the mutual balance of respect, consideration, and compassion. "Healthy boundaries protect without isolating, contain without imprisoning, and preserve identity while permitting external conditions," (Katherine, 1994). Leading the way for our children will allow us to set the 'Goldilocks' standard for our boundaries, to ensure that they aren't too weak or too strong, too distant or too close, too soft or too firm—but just right.

The wheels on the bus go 'round and 'round

"Change does not roll in on the wheels of inevitability, but comes through continuous struggle."
-Martin Luther King, Jr.

Boundaries are where the rubber of our 'parent wheels' meet the road; vessels that separate, define, interact, and hold all the elements of a system together. They are visible and unseen, flexible and rigid, and are the pushy, pully, stretchy, barriers within and around the parent-child system.

From the simplest form of our skin, to more the complex nature of our social structures, they can be as concrete as the shape of our bodies and as obscure as a thought. They exist as a "quantitative and qualitative," (Bowen, 1994), "continuum," (Minuchin, 1994), that is represented on "different levels," (Linden, 2008). Each of these approaches allows us to build a model that can provide us the insights we need into how these boundaries impact and define the parent-child system.

These boundaries form the structural outlines for our physical, emotional, psychological, social, and spiritual constructs of the world. They are the elements of the *personal boundary wheel*, as listed in Diagram 1, as follows, that provide the structure for our lives. These take into account a three-dimensional view of the width, depth, and breadth of our boundaries, as a defining mechanism for each of the components of the human system.

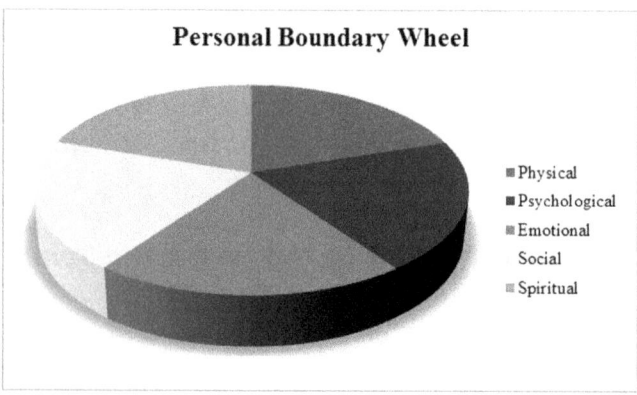

Diagram 1

Recognizing the importance that balanced healthy boundaries play, we can create a visual representation of how to keep things rolling smoothly. If, for example, our emotional system gets out of whack, we know this can make for a bumpy ride—until we are able to restore some sense of balance.

If we don't find a way to resolve this emotional imbalance, this can start to affect other boundaries as well. These disruptions can continue to grow and create even more imbalance to the overall system. If these continue to go unresolved, we compound the problem and things will continue to become more unstable.

The more out of balance and pervasive these imbalances become, the bumpier the ride gets. For example, if a car hits a rut in the road, one wheel can become unbalanced and begin to vibrate and shake.

If it is not fixed, the unbalanced wheel can affect the systems of the car and it will compound the problem. The more ruts we hit, the more problems we create, and the more difficult the car will be to drive. If the problems continue without being fixed, the car may present a serious risk to the driver, passengers, or others.

Boundaries, therefore, play an important role in how we, as parents, interact with our children and affect our ability to share information and connect with others. They are created in an effort to manage our environments and deal with other individuals and systems that are a part of our world. They can create problems when they break down, and play an important role in the development of more serious psychological, psychiatric, and emotional behaviors or addictive disorders.

These boundaries are a major factor in developing healthy relationships with our children and can affect their own abilities to develop healthy boundaries of their own. Mate's (2003) research shows a connection between "confused emotional boundaries and a confused immune system, which fails to defend, or may even turn on itself." He states that when our boundaries are weakened, they make "us more susceptible to invasion—emotional and physical."

Becoming the best parent I can be

"Self-image sets the boundaries of individual accomplishment."
-Maxwell Maltz

Healthy parental identities are enhanced by the structures contained within our own internalized self-concept. We are separate and unique individuals, but also part of those around us. This separate but belonging boundary "creates an atmosphere of trust," as outlined by Kerig (2006). We learn a great deal about ourselves by our interactions with others and our experiences in the world.

Our boundaries are determined by the way we interact with others and how they respond to us. We are responsible for the creation of the mental constructs that define who we are and orient our *self* to the world. We must look within, and start asking the questions that can modify unhealthy boundaries and change the internalized messages we grew up with. We can become trapped by these mindsets when we are unable to challenge our own way of thinking and buy into a form of self-elitism that fools us into believing 'it's my way or the highway.'

Parenting is a lifelong process that provides us many opportunities to learn what it takes to *become a better parent.*

From our experiences as children, to our awareness as adults and parents, our lives are forever touched by our views about parenting. Becoming childlike provides the intuitive medium through which we can learn how to heal and deepen our connections with ourselves and with others.

We must come to recognize that our future is not determined by our past and we can overcome our own misperceptions and preconceived notions about parenting. We can create and change our own life's narrative that continues to shape that way in which we parent. "When we become free from the baggage of the past, we can live more fully with a flexible sense of fresh anticipation and spontaneity," (Hartzell & Siegel, 2003). They state that we all "want to be the best parent we can be" and that by re-parenting ourselves, we can make sense out of our own past experiences and integrate them into our own "coherent ongoing life story."

In light of these sometimes "self-fulfilling prophecies," (Merton, 1948). I am always fascinated by the resiliency individuals show in overcoming their own personal tragedies (created by poorly defined historical boundaries) and ending up becoming more than what they ever imagined. These self-contained constructs of our own minds become the putty in which true "multigenerational healing," (Bowen, 1994) can take place.

Outshining the hidden recesses and traps in order to realize the significance of our lives, is more about who we are than what we do. Taking these steps will allow us to establish a healthy, balanced sense of boundaries so we can overcome these obstacles of our past and avoid the trap of becoming "human doings as opposed to a human beings," (Bradshaw, 1988).

Boundaries are powerful protective mechanisms that form strong internal points of reference for the *self* and are difficult to change. Boundary transformations require an internal awakening so we can get beyond ourselves to see other options.

Recognizing that our own best thinking made us either too defensive or too vulnerable, we can start to ask the questions and use our connected insights to facilitate positive change. By tapping into this internal source of strength, we can start to "heal the child within—as we realize our true self, we begin to live from, and as, who we really are," Whitefield (1994).

Using what works

"Feelings of worth can flourish only in an atmosphere where individual differences are appreciated, mistakes are tolerated, communication is open, and rules are flexible—the kind of atmosphere that is found in a nurturing family."
-Virginia Satir

Parenting styles and practices represent two of the many intertwined variables on the parenting continuum. Parenting practices include more goal-directed activities, such as the type of discipline used, parenting techniques, and coping strategies. Parenting styles are related more to the relationship dynamics that affect the overall emotional climate of the parent-child interactions.

These two areas have been major areas of focus (Darling & Steinberg, 1993) in developing our scientific understanding of parenting. Focusing on only these two specific elements of the entire parent-child system is like eating a peanut butter and jelly sandwich without the bread or jelly—it's just peanut butter. Although peanut butter is an important ingredient, we also need to include the bread and jelly, in all their variations, for it to truly be a peanut butter and jelly sandwich.

It is only by bringing all the parts of a peanut butter and jelly sandwich together within the structures of the whole that we can enjoy the entire sandwich without making a sloppy mess. It is the parts, the whole, their structures, and how they are combined, that make for a good peanut butter and jelly sandwich—and it is the parts and how they are structured together within the whole of parenting that can make a difference in the lives of our children.

When the multivariable aspects of parenting are combined within the 'whole ball of wax, the whole enchilada, the whole nine yards, and the whole 'shebang.' we can begin to understand what determines our abilities to parent effectively. If we use effective behavioral interventions, techniques, and strategies, but fail to reinforce the social learning dynamics or emotional integration of these experiences within the relationships with our children, we minimize our role as a parent.

For example, if we see our child banging their head against the wall in frustration because they want a cookie, we could use a number of approaches, styles, and techniques that foster our nurturing interactions to support learning and redirect behaviors. We can take this opportunity to build our relationship and encourage our children to develop more effective ways to regulate their emotional experiences and increase their frustration tolerance. Or, we could just eliminate the behavior altogether by giving them the cookie, or use an intervention that will stop the crying.

These approaches miss the bigger picture and minimize our overall understanding of what really works. Parenting is a difficult and complex process, and if we take the softer way out, we can be assured we will not make things easier in the long run. We must be willing to take "The Road Less Traveled" (Peck, 1978), and know that the choices we face make for a difficult and challenging road ahead.

Although some (Darling & Steinberg, 1993) have suggested an integration of these parenting factors, we must also extend our understanding to include the dynamic interplay and social context of all of the factors, as well. It is only then that we can avoid the cookie-cutter theories of parenting and get down to the real work required in studying what it really means to be a good parent. It is only by addressing all of these factors simultaneously within the parent-child system that gives us greater predicative abilities.

This orientation can also allow us to construct more effective models for parenting. We must focus within to comprehend our own internal structures and boundaries so we can improve our connections and build stronger and more influential relationships with our children. This provides us a genuine sense of validation and reinforces our children's emotional intelligence, personal development, and social interdependence, so they can grow up to develop their own interdependent identity.

Parents can find their own sense of balance between the internal boundaries of their emotions, thoughts, and behaviors. These internal processes will be able to support, facilitate, model, and encourage the same healthy internal boundaries for their children. Parents who are able to effectively resolve their own internalized conflicts, negative moods, and problems in life, are able to assist their children with healthy problem-solving.

In contrast, parents who have ineffective patterns of emotional regulation, coping strategies, and problem-solving skills, struggle to model the necessary skills for their children's success. These patterns seem to suggest that our parental influence has greater significance when we are able to 'practice what we preach.' We experience the world as perceived through the structures of our boundaries that are received from our five primary senses which include hearing, sight, touch, smell, and taste. We also have a number of somatosensory systems that can include "emotions, balance, movement, kinetic, temperature, directional, spatial, temporal, and personal," (Anderson, & Emmons, 1996).

These form the inner schematics of awareness that are connected to our conscious and unconscious *self*. They are what Carl Jung (1969) called the "inner space of the psyche," and is what defines the *self*. It is a sense of self-awareness that is contained within our sixth sense of mindfulness. Contrary to the psychic aspects of mysticism, this inner sensory processing system is behind the self-affirming statement, "I think therefore I am," (Descartes).

These sensory processes link our experiences to our thoughts, feelings, and behaviors, and form our orientations of *self* in the world. By using these sensory systems, we can become more mindful of our self-core that drives our destiny from within. The key for understanding ourselves as parents lies within the internal processes of these experiences.

They make up our perceptions of our past, the possibilities of our future, and the reality of our present. These interconnected networks make up the structural components of how we think, feel, and act. These dynamics form the inner workings of the *self-core*, as outlined in Diagram 2, as follows, and are defined by the structural boundaries of *self*.

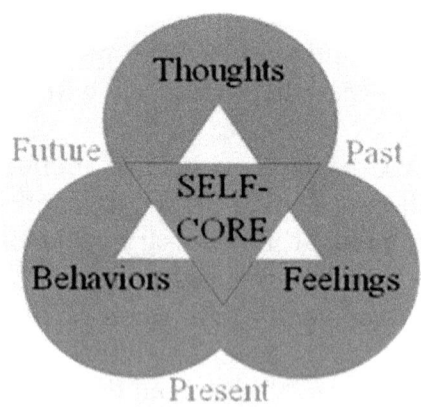

Diagram 2

Looking inward, to our own internal system dynamics, gives us the personal power we need to make sense of the world. Our thoughts, feelings, and behaviors are interdependent systems unto themselves, and their inner workings, within and between each other, make it possible for us to deal with the changes that take place continuously.

Sanna & Chang (2006) imply that it is "our thoughts, feelings, and behaviors over time, which are inexorably intertwined and intermingled." They go on to suggest that these elements of the parent system are state-dependent within time and space, and that "we are all affected by our pasts, assessments of our presents, and our futures."

...nding more time focused on the entire parent-child ... ...n provide us the opportunity for growth and learning so we can stop trying to control. The fact remains that we cannot control anyone or anything other than ourselves and, even then, it's more about managing, regulating, and directing our lives than it is about control—yet we must be able to recognize that, no matter how effective we become as parents, some children will continue to have problems that lie beyond our reach.

More interesting, is the phenomenon of how some children, in spite of the negative influences of their parents, situations, or circumstances, overcome these barriers and defy the scientific odds by going on to accomplish great things. We should keep in mind that *becoming a better parent* is a "continuous quality improvement process," (Deming, 1986), for us, as parents, and is not an event based on the choices our children make.

You are the best gift you can give

"The value of a man resides in what he gives and not in what he is capable of receiving."
-Albert Einstein

Heading out into the great parental unknown with a newly-developed sense of who we are, can give us the confidence to say what we mean and mean what we say. With healthy personal boundaries intact, we can feel a sense of ease and become more of the parent we want to be. Knowing that we are protected and comfortable in our abilities to handle anything that life throws our way, we can now focus on ourselves and on building our relationships with our children.

In being responsible for our own thoughts, feelings, and behaviors, we can now shift our attention to *becoming a better parent*. No longer do we have to waste time, energy, and effort on changing our children, other people, places, situations, o circumstances, to fit our belief systems. We can now share that gift which is most precious—who *we* really are.

Flexibility and letting go are values that make forgiveness possible and allow us to accept ourselves and others for who we really are. We no longer need to defend or justify our pretentions and we can design a path for living that establishes healthy boundaries with our children that are "kind, gentle, respectful, and firm," (Lundberg & Lundberg, 2000). We can now build relationships with our children with a renewed emphasis on the importance of personal choice and responsibility; a new emphasis on teaching from which we can learn from our children and grow as students of parenting.

By openly and honestly dealing with the here and now, we can look beyond our control to see the gift that letting go brings, and make way for a brighter future. We can now share our lives with our children and develop a much more profound understanding of who we are as parents.

It is through our new-found ability that we can openly express our hopes, fears, successes, and failures, so we can create significance in our relationships with our children. In this continued effort of building our relationships, we are reminded that the most important legacy for our children comes "straight from the heart," (Brian Adams, *Cuts Like a Knife*, 1983).

Forging our way into the world with this new parenting philosophy, we can shift our focus to doing all the right things for all the right reasons; we can nurture our children, recognize their needs, and help them reach their full potential, without becoming "enmeshed," (Minuchin, 1974).

The mysterious illusions of the parent trap are washed away, revealing the seeds of success that will truly allow our children the opportunity to blossom and thrive. Parenting within a "whole parent/whole child," (Berends, 1997), can support our "child's gifts and dreams, to build their self-esteem, and empower them for personal success," (Goode, 2001).

Becoming A Better Parent

We can now draw on an awareness that will foster emotional openness, increase self-esteem, and support the development of all the different levels of intelligence for our children. We can move forward in *becoming a better parent* and come to appreciate the dream by fully understanding, accepting, and celebrating the individuality, uniqueness, and interdependence within the entire parent-child system.

This parent-child system is a metaphor that can be used to create a new direction in understanding the social and emotional dynamics across multiple levels, which regulate not only a child's development, but also our own parental and personal growth. This can open our hearts and minds to a more powerful and thoughtful way of parenting that gives us the capability to envision a more hopeful future for our children's tomorrows.

Being whole is the gift of parenting that continues to give. We often take a perspective of "scarcity" (Castle, 2007) in our views about parenting, and end up feeling that we never have enough time and that what we do is never good enough. Caught in a vicious cycle driven by scarcity, over-stimulation, and emptiness, we feel incomplete and deny ourselves and our children the greatest gift of all—the gift of love.

This theme unfolds in a number of ways, from sayings like 'you can't always get what you want' and 'money doesn't grow on trees,' to fairy tales like "*Cinderella*" (animated film by Walt Disney,1950) and "*Jack and the Beanstalk*" (Joseph Jacobs, *English Fairy Tales*, 1890). The underlying message is that there's never enough to go around. The irony of these tales is that if we let go of trying to be more of what we are not, we free ourselves to find the resources within to make a difference with what we already have.

Love is the gift of wholeness that creates a bridge, connecting our hearts with those of our children so we can feed "the hunger for love and appreciation in this world," (Mother Teresa).

Robert Lang

Life on the teeter-totter

"Early to bed, early to rise, makes a man healthy, wealthy, and wise."
-Benjamin Franklin

People have different philosophies and often disagree about what makes a person successful in life. Some say it is wealth, while others state it is wisdom, still others proclaim it is serenity, and then there are those who will argue, "If you don't have your health, you don't have anything." This debate has been argued throughout human history in a number of different arenas, including medicine, philosophy, psychology, and theology.

It is doubtful that we will arrive at an answer that will satisfy everyone. Still, the issue remains an important aspect of our lives and often determines our views about being a successful parent. However, there is one common perspective that continues to emerge from these different disciplines and it centers on the idea of balance.

Tracy (2005) suggests that "just as your car runs more smoothly and requires less energy to go faster and farther when the wheels are in perfect alignment, you perform better when your thoughts, feelings, goals, and values are in balance." Greenfeld (2009) also states that "if you stay motivated, focused, relaxed, and set small attainable goals, you have a much better chance at achieving your optimal balanced success."

Success in life is a shared experience that seems to be identifiable and occurs more deeply when all the aspects of our life are in balance. Robbins (2003) gives examples of how successful people have developed an "ultimate formula for success" and states that "great success is inseparable from the physical, intellectual, and spiritual energy that allows us to make the most of what we have."

Committing to a balanced way of life means we need to create a holistic approach that promotes health, wisdom, wealth, and happiness. When we are able to achieve a sense of balance in life, we can "create our own reality" and experience "total success," (Anthony, 2004).

Finding this balance as a parent can be an elusive task in today's world, as we are required to manage a variety of roles and wear many hats. Developing healthy internal boundaries to manage the separate and different interactive systems of our life such as work, family, play, community, school, church, and friends, can provide us the necessary framework for balanced success.

To maintain a sense of balance in these highly complex internalized social systems of *self*, means that we need to empathize the concepts related to "dynamic equilibrium," (Baily, 1990). Dynamic equilibrium states that complex social systems are in a constant state of change and managing this "nonequilibrium phenomenon" represents a state of balance for a system. Like living our lives on a teeter-totter, we are continuously challenged to weigh and juggle all the differing aspects of our life to achieve success.

By maintaining healthy boundaries in becoming psychologically sound, physically fit, emotionally stable, socially connected, and spiritually in tune, we can achieve a lively, evolving sense of balance. Hall & Richter (1989) have stated that what people need is "to have clear boundaries and some degree of separation" within all aspects of their lives in order to create a sense of balance.

Our boundaries play an important role in balancing the entire parent-child system and define our internal and external realities. These physical, psychological, emotional, spiritual, and social influences are connecting points of the self into the world (see Diagram 3, as follows). They are represented as five spheres of personal influence that are self-regulated and create our mental schemas of life.

They can be seen as reflections of ourselves in the world that are internally generated by the interactions of our thoughts, feelings, and behaviors within the context of our relationships. This holistic perspective includes the projection of self as mind, body, and spirit. Who we are and how we are seen is then defined by the *self* in terms of our mental constructs that are created within and are shaped by both the internal and external influences in our lives.

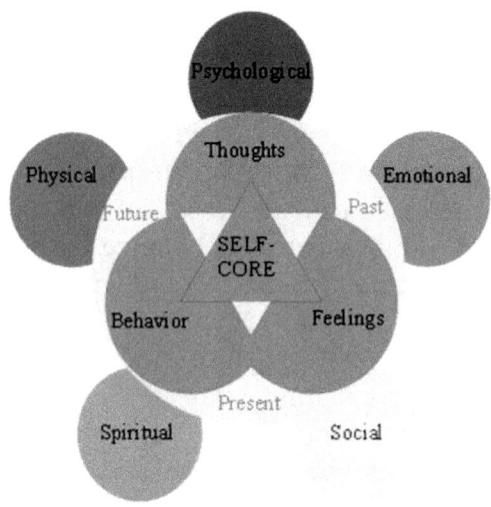

Diagram 3

This multidimensional system framework provides the personal dimensions we need to achieve an ongoing balancing act for our future success. Using this model provides us a tool that truly reflects the value of complete balance in all areas of our life. Nash & Stevenson (2004) suggest that "success is not about one thing nor an infinite number of things; it is about just enough."

Like Goldilocks, it seems as if our search for balanced success is based on proportions in life that are "just right." Their research suggests that these proportions are made up of just the right amounts of "happiness, achievement, significance, and legacy." If we apply this approach to each of our spheres of influence within our systems of understanding, we can expect a balanced success in each of the following areas of our life:

- *Physical:* To find physical balance in our lives doesn't mean we all have to prepare for ultra-marathons or become couch potatoes. It means that we are seeking balanced proportions in what

and how we eat, exercise, sleep, relax, play, and take care of ourselves physically. This is why most exercise or diet programs that are based on excess or scarcity fail. As we seek to balance ourselves physically, we have more energy and vitality to achieve balanced success.
- *Emotional:* Being emotionally balanced does not mean that we carry our hearts on our sleeves or become stoic figures of emotional control. Seeking emotional balance means that we are always developing, redefining, and refining our "emotional intelligence" (Wharam, 2009) to effectively regulate our emotional states. We can learn to accept all feelings without judgment, including those of others. We can become open to finding positive outlets for balanced emotional health and can start to feel the true depth of our souls.
- *Spiritual:* Our focus here needs to be on spiritual balance and not religious fervor. Often the concepts of religion and spirituality are confused and can create imbalance across systems. This is not about going to church, but about implementing the deep spiritual aspects of our faith. These reflect the concepts of balance in our most noble pursuits of success that include harmony, peace, serenity, and love. By being in tune and connected from within, we can find spiritual balance in our lives.
- *Psychological:* The field of "positive psychology" (Seligman, 2002) has comprised a model for psychological balance. They propose that our happiness and well-being is focused on balancing success in three areas: pleasure, engagement, and meaning. These areas are outlined again by Peterson, Park & Seligman (2005), and are called "the pleasant life, the good life, and the meaningful life." Balance within these three areas of our life

can foster our psychological health and promote our happiness.
- *Social:* The "social balance theory" (Heider, 1958) is an effective framework for understanding balance in social systems. This is where our beliefs and desires play a central role in guiding our interactions with others. Based on how an individual perceives and analyzes their likes and dislikes, social conditions, other people, and their interconnectedness, is instrumental in achieving balance in this area (Goldman, 1993). However, we must also take into consideration both intra- and inter- relational system dynamics to fully understand our ability to achieve social balance.

The interplay of these five spheres of influence with our own thoughts, feelings, and behaviors, as well as the social connections we have with others and the world around us, is critical in achieving a sense of balanced success in our lives. There are those who argue, however, that balance stifles creativity, motivation, and drive, and that we would never have the Mozarts, Jordans, Twains, or Michelangelos of this world if they all strived for balance. I would counter that perspective by questioning how many other countless Picassos, Beethovens, Fischers, Verns, or Einsteins we have lost forever, due to unbalanced parental obsessions based on excess.

Striving for balanced success is not about compromise, sacrifice, barter, or exchange, as is often misperceived. It is more about living all areas of life "with passion!" as Robbins (2003) exclaims. A world of parental abundance does not exist in the excess or scarcities of the parent trap. We must seek to understand that the more balance we have, the more abundance we create; and the more abundance we create the more we have to give to our children.

V. Life on Life's Terms

"The more you complain about the problems you have, the more problems you'll have to complain about; and the more you express gratitude for what you have, the more things you'll have to express gratitude for."

-Zig Ziglar

Life is not easy, especially when you're a parent. How we deal with difficulties in life is based on willingness, acceptance, and openness to change. Our creative abilities in using our personal processing systems are what allow us to recognize these opportunities in our life. These internalized mindsets are created by the interactive dynamics of the entire human system. These highly complex "social systems," (Parsons, 1964), make up who we are and are the internal "cognitive, cathartic, and evaluative orientation" that define the *self*.

These constructs are created by our mental schemas and filtered through our spheres of influence. They are the intangible aspects of our conscious and unconscious *self*. They form the intuitive and deliberate sets of processes within our sensory systems that determine the ongoing frames of reference for everything in our lives. We can now expand on our constructs of *self, the parent system core*, and *systems of self*, to include the mental schemas that make up our attitudes, judgments, beliefs, values, and motivations, as illustrated in Diagram 4, as follows, in the *self*-system.

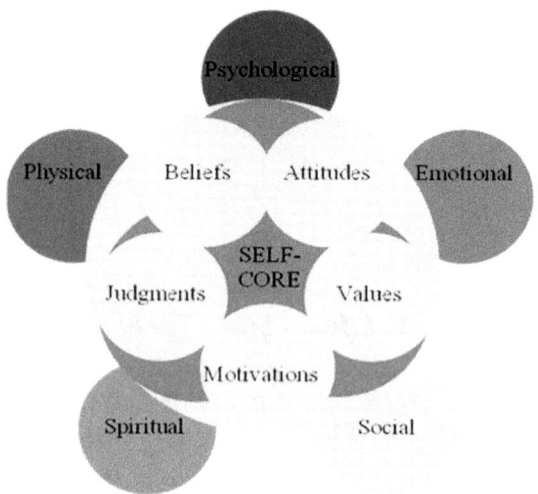

Diagram 4

"Who are we?" This question continues to push the envelope of human understanding. Who we are as parents is continued within this search and is defined by the entire parent-child system. As we continue to develop this parental construct, we can bring the layers of the onion together and begin to truly appreciate the complexity that is parenting. Now that we have broad foundation for understating the parent-child system, let's take a closer look at the processes that make us a parent.

The personal characteristics that make us the most human can be described by "descriptive psychology," (Ossorio, 2005). He states that using a "developmental schema" within the context of a "conceptual system," we can develop a better understanding of human nature. He proposes four questions that can drive our search for meaning as parents that include:
1) "Why do people do what they do?"
2) "What are the differences and similarities among people?"
3) "How come people are the way they are?" and
4) "What kind of world do we live in?"

Within these questions about our 'humanness,' is contained the evocative search that has fueled all modern schools of thought. It is a unique blend of poetry, philosophy, history, and science that can reveal the infinite combination of variables, interactions, and relationships that define who we are as parents.

These individual humanistic features are outlined by Bandura (1999), and include the concepts of "subjectivity, deliberative self-guidance, and reflective self-reactiveness." They are elusive concepts of *self* that require us to expand our understanding of human nature beyond cognitive, behavioral, and affective representations. Bandura states that, "we cannot reduce human nature to a by-product of mental processes and the exchange of input and output."

In other words, our thoughts, feelings, and behaviors are more than just the bystanders of internal processes and are integral agents of the experiences themselves. These manifestations are contained within our attitudes, judgments, beliefs, values, and motivations.

It's time for an attitude adjustment

"There is little difference in people, but that little difference makes a big difference. The little difference is attitude. The big difference is whether it is positive or negative."
-W. Clement Stone

Attitudes usually refer to our tendency to respond either positively or negatively towards people, places, and things. They are our opinions and views that are based upon our interpretations and perceptions of our experiences as seen through the filters within our spheres of influence. They represent "the evaluative integration and abstractions of affect, behavior, and cognitions," (Crano & Prislin, 2006).

These are often referred to as the "ABCs of Attitude" (affect, behavior and cognition), and are reflected in the way we think, feel, and act. Attitudes also have a top down and bottom up function that operate within an intensity scale and are strongly linked to our other mental schemas. Our parental attitudes can color every aspect of our world and act like a kaleidoscope for our senses. Depending on the internal structure of the mirrors, contents, and intensity of light, it can create a vibrant array of multifaceted colors, or it can make everything dark and dreary.

As parents, we have all probably used the phrase, "I'm having a bad day," and we don't have to look very far to see that our attitudes have a major part to play in this drama. These bad days can originate from many sources, but our evaluations of whether it's bad or not are generated from within.

I continue to be fascinated by the phenomenon that the very things in life that can create the most stress are often the same things that can create the greatest joy. So, if it is not the people, places, or things outside of us that cause our positive or negative attitudes in life, then we must be willing to look deeper within for answers.

By looking within, we can reveal the culprits of these attitudes that are often attributed to our views about those things we see as good and bad as a function of experience. Perceptions may change and circumstances vary, but how we determine if they are good or bad is a matter of our attitude. The following are two examples of ways in which our attitude affects our day.

- *Bad day attitude:*

> *I had a hard time getting up today and hit the snooze button three times before getting out of bed. I feel tired and groggy because I didn't get a good night's sleep. I tossed and turned all night long, worrying about a stupid deadline I have at work. I struggled getting my child up and ready for school. I began to feel rushed, pressured, and hurried as I raced to get my child out the door and in the car as we race off down the road. I know I'm*

going to be late to work so I called in, made up some lame excuse, an stressed out the rest of the way. At work, I had to spend the entire morning trying to mend fences with a customer because of a coworker's mistake. I felt frustrated because it's not my problem and I was unable to work on my own project that was due at the end of the day. I went to lunch with a close friend, but was preoccupied with work and spent the entire time complaining, feeling pressured, and could only think about how I could be back at the office and working on this project. When I got back to the office, I had a message from my child's teacher who informed me that my child has been having difficulty with math. I finished the project in time and handed it in on time. My boss informed me that the deadline changed and the project did not have to be done until the end of the week. I walked away, shaking my head, saying to myself, "He could have told me that earlier." I called the school and defensively asked the teacher what she was going to do about the problem. I left work frazzled and picked up my child from daycare, feeling overwhelmed, headed home, and, upon arriving at home, told my spouse that I had a "bad day."

- *Good day attitude:*

I decided to get a little more sleep and set the alarm for a half hour later than normal. I woke up feeling re-energized and ready for the day. I felt rested because I was able to let go of my worries from the day before and got a good night's sleep. My child had difficulty getting up, so I took some additional time to make sure my child was ready to begin the day off on the right foot. I made an effort to stay relaxed and took the extra time to get my child ready and off to school.

I knew I would be late for work and called in to apologize, saying, "I'll be a few minutes late." While at work, I helped a coworker with a customer service problem and took the time to look for solutions to overcome the issue. I felt useful, helpful, and confident, and looked forward to finishing the project that was due this afternoon. I went to lunch with a close friend who supports my efforts, and I felt a sense of gratitude for their friendship. After lunch I got a message from my child's teacher who informed me that my child has been having difficulty with math. I finished my project, handed it to my boss, who informed me that the deadline had changed and the project was not due until the end of the week. I felt a sense of relief and accomplishment that it was already completed and out of the way. I had some extra time and called my child's teacher and we discussed a plan to help out with math. I left my work at work and couldn't wait to pick up my child from daycare. I headed home and, upon my arrival at home, told my spouse that I had a "good day."

Attitudes affect the entire parent-child relationship and act like a contagious virus spreading throughout the system. The question we need to ask ourselves is, "What kind of attitude do we want to spread?" There are at least "thirty-four distinguishable models of attitude change," (Suedfeld, 2009). In fact, he goes on to say that the "very definition of 'attitude' has been embroiled in controversy."

This does not seem to have diminished our interest in how our attitudes are formed or changed. These can generally be described by four general theories of attitude that include "consistency theories, learning theories, social judgment theories, and functional theories," (Eagly & Chaiken, 1993). Basically, these theories of attitude state that attitudes are formed and maintained through our emotional, behavioral, cognitive, and social processes that, in turn, help us learn, establish consistency, determine influence, and outline the purpose they serve.

Attitudes are self-regulating systems unto themselves and are shaped by the internal and external forces in our lives. These forces work together with our experiences to create perceptual windows that become our attitudes. These processes are highly influenced by these dynamics and change the direction of our attitudes. Our likes and dislikes are the preferences that are governed by our attitudes.

This is why this area of study has been so heavily applied to the fields of marketing and advertising. Like a personal kaleidoscope, these small shifts, tiny turns, and slight movements, along with some additional light, can give us the ability to create an entire new spectrum for our attitude. If we don't like the images we see through our own perceptual window, we can make the needed adjustments and rearrange the colored bits of glass to give our lives a little attitude.

Judge not, lest you be judged

"Everything that irritates us about others can lead us to an understanding of ourselves."

-Carl Jung

Judgments represent the personal processing system containing an internal critic that operates our evaluation and decision making processes. There seems to be a great deal of evidence indicating that our judgments contain a "dual processing function" that, in general, are either "automatic and reflexive or conscious and reflective," (Betsch et al., 2008). We all have our own positions, notions, interpretation, and opinions regarding the world in which we live.

These opinions form, operate, and maintain the mental schemas that define our judgments and are another integral part of our personal processing system. Although judgments can have different meanings, including those with legal and religious connotations, for our purposes, we will be focusing on the psychological aspects that deal with the "evaluation process related to decision making," (*Oxford Dictionary*). The psychology of judgment includes the underlying aspects of how we use "automatic and deliberate thought processes that influence how decisions and problems are conceptualized and how future possibilities in life are evaluated," (Hastie & Dawes, 2010).

First impressions are reflexive judgments that take place within the first three seconds of any situation that we are faced with, where evaluations are made and then acted upon. These snap judgments are made in the "blink of an eye," (Gladwell, 2005), whether we are conscious of them or not. We often have a tendency to first 'judge a book by its cover,' and then evaluate whether or not our intuitions and gut reactions were correct. Carlson, Vazire, & Furr (2010) state that these "calibrations act like an internal gauge" and bridge the gap between the dual processes of our judgment system.

This allows us to either quickly trust in our instincts or be more deliberate and gather additional information if needed. Weinstein (1980) has shown that optimistic people are more likely to have good events happen to them, while pessimists are more likely to have bad events happen to them—suggesting that if we get into the habit of second guessing ourselves, we seem to make poorer decisions.

By fine tuning both aspects of our judgment processing systems, we can make better decisions and avoid the biases, errors, and traps of parenting, as outlined by Plous (1993). These dynamics can feed the 'parent trap,' as we discussed earlier, and are common ways that our judgments can go wrong. There have been many of these decision making models that have outlined our problems related to how our judgment system can create havoc in our lives, and have generally been described in three different categories outlined as traps, errors, and biases.

These models are subject to the same rules that govern our collective judgment systems and remind us about the importance of our decisions. The following parental judgment traps are presented so we can become more aware of the pitfalls associated with the choices we make as parents.

Parental Judgment Traps:

- *Impulsive traps* point out the danger associated with our tendency to 'shoot first and ask questions later.' It has been described as a form of "restraint bias" that "influences the available alternatives as quickly as possible," (Harreveld et al., 2009). It can also be called "rush to judgment blunders" (Nutt, 2009), when outcomes are compromised by hasty judgments. This type of judgment error is sometimes driven by our own ambiguity and the "subjective experience of missing information," (Baron, & Frisch, 1988), that can lead us into making ineffective snap decisions.

    Retraining our abilities in making quick judgments in the 'blink of an eye' can help us minimize the "power struggles" (Gordan, 2000) we can have with our children. This form of parenting sensationalism (Grabe et al., 2000) can create knee-jerk reactions based on the tabloids of our mind. When these judgments are skewed, or when we rely solely on these reactions, we are often destined to repeat the mistakes of the past. If we become more adept at looking beyond our immediate reactions, become more mindful, and use our judgments as information, we can began to model effective decision making for our children.

- *"Learning traps"* (Nutt, 2009) reflect our tendency to ignore our mistakes and/or minimize our successes. John Wooden, one of the most successful coaches in sports history, once said, "Success is never final, failure is never fatal. It's courage that counts." In other words, our "bad judgment is a by-product of bad learning, the failure to learn, or the cessation of learning," (Hannush, 2002). This research seems to reflect that learning to make better decisions can be reinforced through both our successes and failures.

How we deal with both our successes and failures is what allows real learning to take place. By becoming better students of how we use judgments, we, as parents, can use the tools found in both our successes and failures to break free from these learning traps. We can find the ability within to focus on the process of learning rather than accruing more information. As students, we can began to shift our mental schemas about learning so we can grow through both our successes and mistakes.

- *Self-fulfilling traps* are when we use and seek out information that will support our existing mental schemas. This is similar to "inference and confirmation biases" that state when we are faced with unfamiliar or complicated decision, we have a tendency to "interpret information in a way that confirms our own preconceptions," (Darley & Gross, 2000). It has been described as a "selective search for evidence" (Plous,1993), and is a type of bias in which we gather information that supports our current views but disregards other facts that support different conclusions.

  A parental "self-fulfilling prophecy" (Merton, 1973) inflates, deemphasizes, and misuses information to support our current frames of reference. As an example of this trap, I once had a father who brought me a copy of an obscure, highly opinionated article on the benefits of spanking, as a way to justify his own 'spare the rod, spoil the child' style of discipline. His judgments were strongly tied to his religious beliefs and it was only by bringing his pastor into the counseling sessions that we were able to reframe his misperceptions about discipline.

- *The ego trap* is based on our overconfidence in, and being overly optimistic about, our judgments. This overconfidence and assurance can result in all kinds of flawed and risky decisions. These 'mind traps' are the devious ways in which the ego works as a "merciless judge for the human psyche," (Borysenko, 1987). This is a type of "self-serving bias" that is a judgment trap that motivates people to "accept more responsibility for good deeds than for bad," (Myers, 2009).

    To avoid these traps, we must be willing to leave our egos at the doorstep of parenthood, so we can let go of the self-serving snares of pride, prejudice, and conceit. Deepak Chopra said, "If you want to reach a state of bliss, then go beyond your ego and the internal dialogue. Make a decision to relinquish the need to control, the need to be approved, and the need to judge." The self-serving needs contained within our psyche can lead to egos trips that divert us from our journey and create distance between us and our children.

- *Social traps*, or "groupthink," (Janis, 1972), are decisions made within cohesive groups whose members try to minimize conflict and reach consensus without critically testing, analyzing, and evaluating ideas. This trap is directed by our tendency to socially "go along and get along," (Strentz, 2006). Although there appear to be "several reasons why group decisions are superior," (Zastrow, 2009), we must try and avoid the subjective influences of the group decision making process. A good example of this type of judgment error is related to the NASA decision making processes that led to the "Space Shuttle Challenger Disaster" (Schwartz & Wald, 2003).

Parents have a tendency to seek homogenous groups or organizations that already support our current ways of thinking. This can create group conformity and lead to a "herd mentality" (Geist, 2003). This reinforces our current parenting status quo and limits our ability to see other options in the parenting continuum. To split away from the herd and set ourselves free from this trap, we can learn how to welcome diversity with open arms and facilitate the acceptance of individual differences. This will allow us, as parents, to evaluate our judgments more effectively and see the different sides of all choices within groups.

- *The complexity trap* is our tendency to get lost within the details of a problem. This means that "more is not always better," (Gladwell, 2005), and that being absorbed by complexity creates problems in judgment. Einstein said that we need to "make everything as simple as possible, but not simpler." This seems to suggest that we tend to make things more complicated while, at the same time, we are 'dumbing down' the problem.

    We, as parents, can either overcomplicate or oversimplify the problems we face in making decisions. It seems that finding a balance can give us the ability to use our judgment systems more effectively to establish healthy boundaries that guide the rules we use with children. We can develop an awareness that 'what is simple is often not easy,' and 'what is easy is often not simple.' Confucius once said, "Life is really simple, but we insist on making it complicated."

- *Maintenance traps*, or "status quo traps" (Hammond et al., 2000), stifle change and are focused on maintaining the current situation as it is. Fear of change, failure, rejection, or loss of control, often compounds this problem, shuts down the creative decision making process, and limits our choices to those that will keep things the way they have always been. Our unwillingness to embrace change so we 'don't rock the boat' is why "creative people and effective leaders often clash," (Catt, 2010).

    This process is described as a fear of change that creates a sense of "anxiety about things falling apart and becoming chaotic," (Chazan, 2003). She goes on to say that this "pathology" comes from a "lack of coherence and capacity to remain organized during transitions" and can lead parents "to extreme conclusions." Gordon (2000) also states that parents need to overcome this problem by accepting "the idea of making changes within themselves."

- *Perceptual traps* are also known as "anchoring traps or framing traps," (Hammond et al., 1998). These traps occur when we are unable to recognize, perceive, or misjudge situations or people. Inaccurate judgments can be based on limiting search parameters based on our current mindsets when "a decision maker becomes trapped into making poor, ineffective, unreasonable, and costly decisions," (Sawyer, 1998).

These ingrained and habitual mindsets trap us, as parents, into a process of developing tunnel vision—where we become blind to other opportunities, solutions, and alternatives. Parental blinders are not all bad, as they can provide us with focus and help set priorities. We have to be careful that we are not limiting our options in either seeing difficulties or finding solutions.

These "conceptual metaphors" (Lakoff & Johnson, 1980), shape the way we think and act as parents. An example of this can be seen during parent-child conflicts when we get into competitive frames of mind that direct the ways in which we view arguments within a "win-lose" context (Gordon, 2000). He states that these "power struggles" are formed by the way we perceive conflict. He suggests that by moving to "win-win" perceptions of conflict, we can resolve differences more effectively.

As we have outlined above, there are effective strategies to minimize the impact of these parental errors in judgment. The best protection we have is to become aware that they exist, that they are real, and that we can change them. We can then choose internal perceptual processes that uncover our errors in judgment before they become disastrous decision. This process should allow for the open use of information to accurately assess the situation, apply sound reason and logic, and use social feedback to determine if what we did fits the results.

It seems that we are again faced with a parenting paradox when it comes to using our judgment, as these can become double-edged swords. The expectations we focus on when judging others are often the same expectations we use to critically judge ourselves. Avoiding these traps requires a parental humility that is all about "acknowledging our weaknesses, but not dwelling on them," giving us the power to "avoid one of the easiest traps of parenthood—guilt." (Chapman, 2008).

The power of believing

"You can have anything you want if you will give up the belief that you can't have it."
-Dr. Robert Anthony

WARNING: The following information may challenge your beliefs and CAUTION should be taken because your reality depends on it. What we believe is real and is often beyond question, even if it's not reality.

Our impressions are developed by what we believe and what we believe is real. These beliefs tend to reinforce the phenomenon of what is real in our lives. Damasio (2000) sees our beliefs being used "to qualify a perception or recollection as true, false, or somewhere in between."

Although this is a highly volatile, controversial, and contested subject of study, it is, nonetheless, responsible for some of the most horrific and also the most beautiful aspects of what we, as humans, are capable of creating.

Mankind's tragedies, including war, terrorism, slavery, and genocide, as well as our accomplishments such as landing on moon, building civilizations, creating great works of art, and performing acts of compassion, are all subject to our belief systems.

I find it not only significant, but fascinating, that the power of our beliefs is responsible for so much pain and suffering, as well as so much joy and enlightenment. Our beliefs provide us a sense of purpose, meaning, and direction, and when skewed or out of balance, present us with a number of challenges. The question seems to be: How can something so intangible and elusive be such a powerful influence in our lives?

We must keep in mind that our beliefs are highly dynamic mindset that are contained within the social context of our attitudes, judgments, values, and motivations, as well as our thoughts, feelings, and behaviors. Our beliefs are, in essence, our preconceived expectation of what we know is real. They originate from direct, modeling, and learning experiences that all become integrated into the very fabric of our existence.

The structure of someone's beliefs makes it challenging to see beyond the horizons created in their own mind. "After all, the constrained domain in which we hold and express beliefs is closely related to the notion of self," (Damasio, 2000). This is why they are so difficult to change. For example, if I believe that the earth is flat, then I can't imagine the possibility of a new world. Beliefs put up barriers to change by saying, "This is real and there are no other alternatives." Wilson (2006) said, "Don't believe anything. Regard things on a scale of probabilities."

The history of mankind has been unavoidably altered by our collective belief systems, whether oriented by religion, science, reason, or even skepticism and disbelief. It is our willingness to accept and adapt to these preconceived notions as a way to resolve the issues of uncertainty in our lives that dictates our belief systems.

Our search for answers on both ends of the spectrum of our beliefs contains an element of hope in trying to find the solution to our most frightening dilemma—that is "the manner, time, and place of our own demise," (Shermer, 1997), which becomes the price we pay for the knowledge of our own mortality. Developing certainty out of chaos and reality out of the unknown is how we use our beliefs to make sense of a world of unknowns.

Our parental belief systems, according to Lightfoot and Valsiner (1992), "are assembled by coordinating our inductive and deductive logics." Their social perspective states that our parental beliefs "encompass a multitude of social suggestions communicated by the collective culture." They also point out that the individual variations of our beliefs suggest a "dialect co-construction" process for how our beliefs are formed.

Awareness as to how our beliefs are manifested and maintained can provide us the opportunity to direct positive change within the parent-child system. Research suggests three ways in which our core parental beliefs can be changed: 1) education and information; 2) reinforcing positive life experiences; and 3) supporting affirming "roles, characteristics and skills," (Divecha & Okagaki, 1993). Our parental beliefs make a difference. The direction we take in exercising these beliefs is what matters most in them becoming either "devastating or empowering," (Robbins, 1986).

Barber et al. (2005) have identified three dimensions of parenting that appear to characterize parental beliefs across multiple cultures, in both industrialized and non-industrialized countries. These differing parental beliefs are associated with differing parenting styles related to discipline, interactions, support, child development, social standards, and cultural expectations. The following is a list of these parent dimensional belief systems:

1. *Parental support*, which refers to a number of varied behaviors related to the 'affective, nurturing or companionate' views of the parent and is especially relevant to the perceptual mindset of the child's degree of independence and social initiative.
2. *Psychological control* refers to parents' actions that attempt to change the child's thoughts or feelings, ignores or dismisses the child's views and withdraws love or affection; such parental behavior has been associated with the development of depressive symptoms later in a child's life.
3. *Behavioral control* refers to parents' monitoring and knowledge of children's activities and is relevant to the extent of the child's anti-social behavior.

Fortunately there are no standardized parenting beliefs that make up a universal church of parenting. We are not required to adopt all-encompassing parental belief system and this leaves us free to find those that can be associated with more positive outcomes. Understanding our parental beliefs regarding the following four areas can facilitate a more positive parenting experience (Pecnic, 2007).

1. *Nurturing behavior* refers to activities that respond to the child's needs for emotional security, such as the provision of warmth and sensitivity within the relationship.
2. *Structure* refers to setting boundaries and guiding the child's behavior through modeling of positive behaviors, without physical or psychological coercion.
3. *Recognition* refers to the child's need to be respected and acknowledged by parents and to foster the potential for mutual understanding and influence to develop.
4. *Empowerment* refers to combining a sense of personal control with the ability to affect the behavior of others; this is conceptualized as a process that necessitates ongoing parental adjustment to the changing developmental tasks of children as they grow older.

True value

"Until you value yourself, you won't value your time. Until you value your time, you will not do anything with it."
                                                                              -M. Scott Peck

Our value system establishes our priorities and determines which aspects of life we regard as important and beneficial. These "constructs of importance" (Lewis, 2000), shape and form our tastes, styles, and preferences, and serve both prescriptive and descriptive functions. He states that our values are the positive adjectives our minds use to "give meaning and depth to our thoughts, feelings, and behaviors."

Of all the personal processing systems, our values are more susceptible to internal and external influences that come with the different experiences in our lives. It seems that our "value-driven decision system" (Pugh, 1976) also has a dual function with our "primary" core, or predictive values, staying with us throughout our lives, and our "secondary" prescriptive or descriptive values being transitional based on our situations.

Our personal value system is a set of organizing principles that focus our attention on developing goals and provide structure and purpose by helping determine what is "good, just, and beautiful," (Lewis, 2000).

Our primary core value systems, like our beliefs, represent an internalized moral code that defines 'what we want in life.' They are comprised of those positive personal traits that are influenced by our thoughts, feelings, and behaviors, as well as our spheres of influence, and are at the heart of our character.

They define our identity through our strengths, preferences, goals, and ambitions. Covey (2000) described these "core values" as our "character ethic" and the "true north" of our "core ideology" that form the "true principles" that we live by. These personal core values are the *positive* guiding principles that are describe within each sphere of influence in our lives and are explained in more detail below:

- *Physical values* are those core physical traits that we see as worthy of aspiring to, and define our positive physical characteristics. They are the values related to our identity, physical appearance, and body image. These include values such as attractiveness, beauty, strength, endurance, vigor, heroism, cleanliness, vibrancy, charm, magnetism, poise, and youthfulness.

- *Spiritual values* represent our positive connectedness us to all things and are the concepts associated with a sense of purpose and direction. Different from religious values, these provide us an understanding of the interrelated nature of things. These values include peace, harmony, oneness, contentment, truth, justice, decency, morality, awareness, tranquility, honesty, serenity, insight, hope, goodwill, and well-being.

- *Social values* are concerned with our connections with others and can include the cultural aspects of our family, friends, acquaintances, coworkers, church, organizations, communities, and the society that we are a part of. These values include things such as equality, diversity, freedom, cooperation, collaboration, diplomacy, extroversion, kindness, caring, respect, openness, loyalty, and fairness.

- *Psychological values* are represented by the best use and expression of our mental talents and abilities. These are often used to describe the positive attributes of the psychological, mental, and personality aspects of the working mind. These psychological traits include intelligence, creativity, curiosity, achievement, attentiveness, dependability, consideration, mindfulness, concentration, discernment, rationale, reason, and logic.

- *Emotional values* are the positive expressions and abilities that are associated with the regulation of our feelings and affect. They are our abilities, talents, and skills in using our emotions in dealing with life. These include empathy, sensitivity, understanding, responsiveness, sincerity, authenticity, genuineness, discretion, warmth, affection, tenderness, passion, and love.

Our secondary, descriptive, or character values, on the other hand, are positive descriptors for the different roles and situations of our lives. These transitory values are based on our situational circumstances and are the positive adjectives we use to describe ourselves in these differing roles. For example, at school we might describe ourselves as 'studious,' and at work describe this same trait as 'industrious.'

These are linked with our core physical values and have similar content but differ in context related to our environment. The key to value is adaptability and to make sure that all our values are in line with one another. If these values are in conflict, then we are forced to change or they can limit our ability to adapt.

These "lifestyle values," as outlined by Kamler (1984), "secure a person's sense of social identity; they are held precisely because of what others think" about their values. He goes on to say that if these value conflicts remain, they can create "an eruption of either a social or personal identity crisis."

Conflicts within our value system can provide us a process for positive change as it gives us a reason to question the value of these mindsets. "Values clarification" is a process that aligns our values and reinforces our ability to change what might not fit, as Covey (2000) suggests, and enables us "to adapt and respond to the forces of change."

The goal in evaluating our values is to become fully aware of their influence, and to explore how these are working in our lives. We can become more self-directed and effective as parents when we are more in touch with our values and use them as guiding principles in our everyday lives. Raths et al. (1978) state that our "most appropriate values come from using our intelligence freely and reflectively to prize, choose and act" so we can develop the character we aspire to become.

Let's get motivated

"People who are unable to motivate themselves must be content with mediocrity, no matter how impressive their other talents."

-Andrew Carnegie

Motivation is "why we do what we do" (Deci & Flaste, (1996), and relies heavily on humanistic perspectives for understanding what drives human behavior. Our motivations are directed by our wants and desires that are both psychologically and socially motivated. They reflect our intentions of self that interact with the outside world. Interest and research into these motivational processes is diverse and expanding.

The focus on this psychological phenomenon has shifted its attention and is now considered an important conceptual framework for human understating. There have been many motivational theories that focus on both internal and external motivators. Our motivation seems to be influenced by both intrinsic and extrinsic forces that link our unconscious individual needs and "implicit motives" to our social needs and "explicit motives," (Brunstein & Schultheiss, 2010).

Maslow's (1970) "hierarchy of needs" is arguably considered one of the most influential motivational theories and is still used extensively to describe how we are motivated. His humanistic approach deals with higher forms of consciousness in what might be considered "existential or spiritual motives."

The idea behind his motivation theory is based on a "hierarchy of needs." He divides these into two general categories; one category being our "deficiency needs" that include our basic "physiological and safety needs;" and the other category being our "growth needs," that include our higher "social, esteem, and self-actualization needs."

Maslow proposed that we must satisfy our basic needs first before we can focus on trying to meet our personal or social growth needs. If we are hungry, our focus is going to be on getting something to eat and not on learning—a prime reason that we have school-based free breakfast and lunch programs.

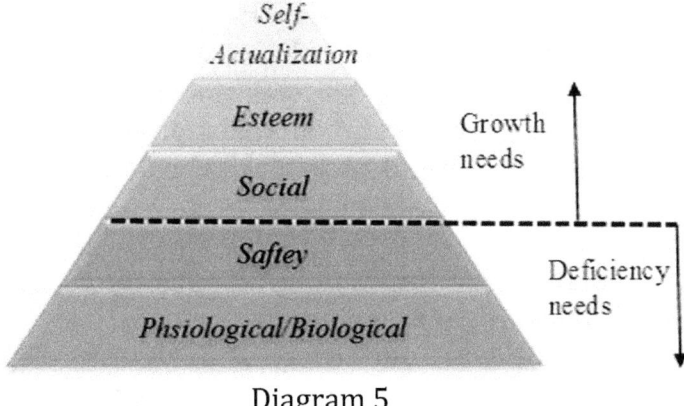

Diagram 5

Maslow's model above is excellent for conceptualizing how our intrinsic needs as parents formulate and drive our motivations. We can use this "hierarchy of needs" to better understand what motivates us and helps us to address our parenting needs that have not been met. By using this model, we can look at how to structure interventions that are based on what our needs are so we can take the steps necessary toward *becoming a better parent.*

It is important for us to we realize that we cannot take these steps towards parental self-actualization, as outlined in this book, while we have lower unmet needs. We cannot tap into the potential of our personal growth until we have met our deficiency needs first. In other words, if we are homeless and looking at the harsh reality of where our next meal is coming from, we are probably not going to be worried about teaching our children the importance of responsibility. These parental needs drive our motivations and are outlined as follows:

Deficiency Needs:

- *Biological needs* are related to the basic physiological aspects of what we need to sustain our existence. They form the base our existence from our most basic 'survival needs' such as air, water, food, health, and sleep, to our 'maintenance needs' that include the basic physical, and biological aspects in our lives that can include rest, exercise, nutrition, and play. These needs form the foundation for achieving a basic sense of physiological balance for our own health and wellness.

- *Safety needs* tap into our abilities to create the structure and boundaries in our lives that assure both our safety and security. These needs are based on our internal self-protective mechanisms and generate our emotional responses to threatening situations. These boundary-based needs are the representations of our emotional expressions. When this space is invaded, whether real or perceived, we feel threatened and must act to restore a sense of balance and safety.

Growth Needs

- *Belonging needs* are the social aspects of recognizing that we are social beings and need these connections in our lives in order to grow. These 'social needs' are a part of every relationship and form the basis for our connections with our spouses, children, families, friends, and acquaintances. These social needs are reinforced by our actives in our homes, at work, and in our communities that include family gatherings and outings, playing team sports, being involved in clubs, or organizations, and participating in civic events.

- *Esteem needs* are based on our accomplishments, achievements, and successes, as well as how we overcome and deal with our disappointments, setbacks, and frustrations. These needs are fostered by our ability to grow personally and drive our desires to learn. This growth helps us develop insight, make better decisions, and recognize our personal and psychological growth.

- *Self-Actualization needs* are related to the potential that exists within each one of us and drives our own continuous self-improvement project. It is a need that constantly takes into consideration what we are capable of becoming and is the granddaddy of all motivation. This need comes from our search for wisdom that can be only be sought, not acquired. It is an evolving masterpiece that is continually shaped throughout our lives and emanates from our willingness to grow. It is our experiences, struggles, and successes that form this pinnacle of balance within all spheres of influence in our life.

In order for us to make the most out of our motivational system within the parent-child relationship, we must recognize what our needs are and separate those from the needs of our children. This aspect of our "self-determination" (Deci & Ryan, 2003) focuses on the "perceived locus of causality" and the interplay of both the intrinsic and extrinsic motivators in people's lives. Their research has built upon the ideas of our "locus of control" (Rotter, 1954), and suggests that the quality of our experiences can be very different, based upon our own perceptions.

The interplay of our internal and external influences and our perceptions is critical for understanding what motivates people. "Parental motivation" (Buss, 2008) is "a core feature of human nature" and are the mental schemas that form our perceptions about parental love. These are the driving forces behind our actions as parents. Our growth as parental students is dependent on asking ourselves the simple question, "What motivates us to do what we do as parents?"

Motivation plays a significant role in the change process. Miller & Rollnick's (2002) work with "motivational interviewing" links states of readiness to an individual's inter- and intra- motivations for change. They state that "motivation is fundamental to change" and is based on our being "ready, willing and able."

If we are to become better parents, then our motivation holds the key for changing the problems that exist within our own personal processing systems. Our awareness of being 'sick and tired of being sick and tired' can support our willingness to change. Questioning the intentions of our motivations can determine our states of readiness and provide insight for the direction of change.

Self-confidence generates motivation and, if we are able to trust and accept change, we can grow beyond our current limitations and find the courage to change. Readiness for change is based on the motivators that include our levels of discomfort, security, commitment, capacity, confidence, and vision. These form the meaning and relevance for wanting to *become a better parent* and set the course future change.

Your perception is everything

"We're obsessed with how we appear to the rest of the world, yet desperate to win acceptance strictly by being ourselves."

-Amy Lago

I came across a comic strip called *It's All About You,* that points out the irony of our struggles to make sense of our fast-paced, espresso-driven, and sometimes neurotic views about our place in the world. Our concepts of self in the world are rapidly changing as we desperately try to keep pace. It is often our own rigid mental schemas as parents that get in the way of us being able to find the flexibility that we need to deal with, accept, and cope with an ever-changing world.

This "psychological flexibility is the ability to contact the present moment more fully as a conscious human being, and to either change or persist when doing so serves valued ends," (Hayes and Strosahl, 2004). They suggest that "acceptance" is the key to becoming more effective in how we deal with problems, by being "non-judgmental and actively embracing the experience of thoughts, feelings, and bodily sensations as they occur."

The structures of our mental schemas are instrumental in determining how flexible and accepting we can be in dealing with our everyday lives. We all possess sets of rules and scripts that are used to determine, interpret, and predict what goes on in the world. Piaget & Inhelder (2001) were the first to describe these "mental schemata" from a developmental standpoint, to explain the inner workings of the mind.

Schema theorists expanded on this concept and proposed that these mental constructs are "guided by the principle that every input is mapped against some existing schema," and that "all the aspects of that schema must be compatible with the input information," (Anderson, 1977). The individual and social characteristics of how these schemas are formed and maintained are the personal processing systems that are responsible for how we respond to the world.

These personal processing systems provide us an instantaneous and intentional way to filter, synthesize, and access information so we can effectively deal with our demanding lifestyles. The mental schemas that make up our attitudes, judgments, beliefs, values, and motivations, are intimately linked to one another and interact with our core *self* and the world around us. By expanding our understanding of these personal processing systems, we can increase our capabilities of handling whatever life throws our way.

These constructs process our worlds from an automatic and deliberate vantage point. Without this highly interactive, dualistic processing system, we become overwhelmed and shut down. "When we combine the effects of information overload and decision stress, we produce several common forms of individual maladaptation," (Toffler, 1970).

Our ability to respond effectively to incoming information is based on mental states of readiness that are pre-formed sets of expectations of how things should work. Oatley (1992) describes this as "action readiness" that is "normally based on an evaluation of something happening that effects important concerns." Our attitudes, judgments, beliefs, values, and motivations are often highly debated and contested psychological aspects of self.

The appeal of theses aspects of the inner *self* continues to drive our search for meaning and outlines the phenomenon of choice and free will that make us the most human. Without these self-defining constructs, we limit the possibilities that can exist and we subsequently stifle the process of change and personal growth for both ourselves and for our children.

The complexity of the human system has many variables and variations that can contribute to how these personal processing systems are structured. These dynamics make it impossible even for identical twins to be identical. Although there may be many similarities between all individuals, no one is exactly alike and, therefore, no two people think, feel, or act in identically the same way every time or in every situation.

When we develop mental constructs that are only based on similarities and don't include individual differences, we are setting our relationships up for problems. While it can be convenient, it is not necessary for parents and children to always agree, see things the same way, or be alike.

What seems to be more important is that we learn how to think together. By developing strategies that are focused on individual strengths, no matter how different, we can move to a position of 'agreeing to disagree' that does not resolve conflicts and allows us, as parents, to "pick our battles more carefully," (Maslin, 2004).

VI. It's All About the Relationship

"In the end, these things matter most: How well did you love? How fully did you love? How deeply did you learn to let go?"
                                                                -Buddha

'Letting go' does not mean giving up or giving in; it is all about having enough faith to trust in the ebb and flow of your relationships with your children. It's not about caring less, but about loving more. By letting go of the control of our children, we can free ourselves from the traps of parenting. Viorst (1998) states that "letting our children go, and letting our dreams for our children go, must be counted among our necessary losses."

As a result of our avoidance of loss, we can end up losing grasp of what matters most by clenching onto things out of love. This unhealthy interactional pattern is the primary driving force behind a number of serious problems from domestic violence to abuse, as suggested by Dutton (2006). His research states that these negative emotional experiences are a "by-product that produces the controlling behaviors that are the hallmark of abusiveness." Letting go is another parenting paradox and the more we try to hang on to this control, the more out of control our relationships get.

Our efforts to find a way out of this parenting dilemma can open the door for us to break free from the control that binds us to our old parenting values, attitudes, and beliefs.

Walking through these doorways means letting go of the illusion of control that will allow us to see the possibilities of what can be. We need to continuously redefine who we are as parents and this requires a good sense of *self*.

This new sense of *self* is forged in the furnaces of our minds where our thoughts are cast from the remnants of our pasts—where our emotional values are tempered, sharpened, and honed through a loving heart, and our actions are wielded through the internalized compassion of being a parent.

In the movie "*Star Wars Episode I: The Phantom Menace*," Yoda makes an interesting point about how these negative emotional experiences based on control can dictate our fate. He says, "Fear is the path to the dark side. Fear leads to anger. Anger leads to hate. Hate leads to suffering."

When our relationships with our children are centered on control, the control can take on a life of its own damaging the very thing we are trying to accomplish. If we want our children to know success, then we need to let go of the control and "focus on building stronger relationships with them," (Aldort, 2005).

The development of our brain in the context of a "social organ," can allow us to see the significance of our relationships with our children, where "our minds emerge and our emotions become organized through engagement with other minds," (Gerhardt, 2004). The social connectedness of our relationships influence changes and mold the emotional experiences that truly make a difference.

These interactional patterns must take on the key features of an effective relationship with our children that include "observing and listening, responsiveness, effective communication, relationship maintenance, emotional openness, functionally understanding and managing feelings, empowerment, coping with life successfully, support and protection, promote learning, acceptance and tolerance, and building a coherent family story," (Moore, 2006). It is only by honoring our relationships with our children that we can connect with them.

Becoming A Better Parent

It's worth the effort

"I'm a great believer in luck, and I find the harder I work, the more I have of it."

-Thomas Jefferson

The psychological, emotional, physical, social, and spiritual development of our children is the most important undertaking we face as parents. We cannot afford to overlook the wholeness of the developmental process with our children if we are to provide a positive direction in supporting their personal growth. Our relationships with our children provide the framework for these opportunities.

Its importance is so pervasive that many of our theories in the field of psychology are strongly rooted in area of human development. Historically, these early-stage theories have seen parenting as a centerpiece of human developmental, reflecting the firm belief that childrearing makes the child. Erickson's (1950) "psychosocial stage theory" is still commonly used today in describing the aspects of human development.

Erickson's understanding of human development was more inclusive and expansive than earlier models, and became instrumental in our developing views about the parents' roles in this process. He suggested that it is the influence of parents that matters most in the developmental process for our children. Carnegie's "How to Win Friends and Influence People," although not directed at parents, points out the importance of these influences and the problems that are associated with trying to control others in our relationships.

It is our children's own internalized processes of motivation, not our ability as parents to control them, which are the key to making a difference in our children's development. These parental efforts, directed at our own personal growth and development, are full of rewards and can support our children in moving toward their own procsses of "self-actualization," (Maslow, 1970).

Recent research has focused more intently on the role parents play in the developmental process and are showing strong links between parent-child relationships and our children's development. This research has "confirmed that what young children learn, how they react to the events and people around them, and what they expect from themselves and others are deeply affected by their relationships with parents, the behavior of parents, and the environment of the homes in which they live," (Shonkoff & Phillips, 2000).

Building relationships across the developmental continuum with our children can support their ongoing development and provide them every opportunity to become responsible, mature, competent members of society. Maccoby & Martin (1983) suggest that the effects of a parent on a child's development "cannot be viewed in isolation" and that a "parental behavior or parental personality trait is part of a complex system that, in some respects, is unique to each parent-child relationship."

The ways in which our relationships affect the entire parent-child system cannot be overlooked. The importance of these intra-inter-relational dynamics provides a substantial interconnectedness for the child's entire developmental continuum. Parental influence is more about choice and has increased our awareness of the "complex ways in which parenting intersects with the child's inherited strengths and vulnerabilities to affect the pathways that are followed en route to adulthood," (Shonkoff & Phillips, 2000).

This trend in understanding our roles as parents suggests that even more difficult developmental hurdles can be averted by building effective parent-child relationships. Delinquency, a serious social problem, seems to be attributed more to parenting difficulties such as "erratic, threatening, and harsh discipline, inadequate supervision of young children, and impaired parent-child attachment," (Sampson, & Laub, 1995).

Being in it for the long haul

"An ounce of prevention is worth a pound of cure."
-Benjamin Franklin

Efforts directed at building strong relationships with our children pay off in the long run and set the stage for the healthy development of our children. These developmental trends can follow our children into adulthood and make lasting impressions that span their entire lives. By becoming balanced in our own lives, we can move away from our control, set healthy limits, and build more supportive relationships with our children.

"Developmental systems theory" is a theoretical orientation to human development that is focused on "the complex nature of this parent-child relationship," (Lerner, 1986). He points out that the effective characteristics of this parent-child interaction reflect parents who are authoritative, accepting, firm, and democratic, as well as capable of building relationships that are warm, non-hostile, and supportive.

Establishing these fundamental foundations is often not fully recognized or valued until our children have crossed over into the dreaded stage of adolescence. It is then that we realize the haunting, unsettled echoes from the days when our parents once told us, "Wait 'til you have children of your own." Although our relationships with our children constantly change, adolescence is a brand new ballgame with different rules.

It is during this time that all our hard work in building our relationships with our children can have the greatest rewards. Armsden & Greenberg's (1987) study suggests that individuals who perceived a high quality of secure attachments in their relationships had "greater satisfaction with themselves, a higher likelihood of seeking social support, and less symptomatic response to stressful life events.'

Adolescence is a period of dramatic parental change that can put a great deal of strain on the parent-child relationship and that requires a great deal of flexibility. Understandably, both parent and child experience a number of reoccurring shifts from excitement to anxiety, happiness to fear, identity to confusion, and exploration to isolation. Adolscence is a confusing phase of life that can put an inordinate amount of pressure on even the most secure parent-child relationships.

Healthy relationships during this time are distinguished by "supportive interactions and positive connections between parent and child and are associated with our children's psychosocial developmental," (Steinberg, 1990). Change is the creativity of life and it's never too early or too late to refocus our attention on those aspects of *self* that can assist us in developing more significance in our relationships with our children.

Who said it was going to be easy

"It is easy to hate and it is difficult to love. This is how the whole scheme of things works. All good things are difficult to achieve; and bad things are very easy to get."
-Confucius

All relationships are two-way streets that require a great deal of dedication, hard work, time, energy, and effort, and we all know intuitively that this is not easy to achieve. Unrealistic expectations about our relationships with our children set us up for disappointments. What we believe about ourselves, our relationships, and our children, affects our thoughts, feelings, and behaviors toward the world and vice versa.

Many parents approach relationships with their children expecting that their love will make all things better. The reality is that love is only a starting point and we must continue to build loving relationships with our children in order for these relationships to work. There is nothing easy about it; however, if we choose to see this work as play, it can be fun and is definitely one of the most rewarding tasks we can undertake.

Taking responsibility in *becoming a better parent* means that we can embrace this task with an open heart, inquisitive mind, and an everlasting devotion to the ongoing development of our relationships with our children. Working on our relationships with our children often means that we need to adopt a philosophy of persistence that says, 'when things get tough, the tough get going,' and we can begin to see that it requires effort to obtain anything in life that is worth obtaining.

This personal ethic is a dynamic that can even be seen in our children's play. For example, as we watch our children playing, we often find ourselves wondering where they get all of that energy. We soon realize, from their joyful smiles, that it's all worth the effort. We can transform our efforts from trying to control our children's lives into efforts of building our relationships with them by practicing patience, tolerance, and forgiveness. Intimacy and love grow from this continual commitment, and the working parts you put into the relationship produce invaluable results that are gifts unto themselves.

"Parenting endurance" is a "daily marathon" (Donahue, 2007) that requires us to test the limits of our own resolve in the day-to-day job of being a parent. This is another primary reason why we need to have a good healthy sense of *self*. Yes, parenting is the hardest work we do, and if we take a somber, uptight, and too serious approach to this job, we only make matters worse. When we take ourselves and our jobs as parents too serious, it makes it difficult to 'whistle while we work,' and we can miss out on the most joyful aspects of our relationships with our children.

Training for a marathon is more about attitude than about the race, and more about giving the best effort as opposed to being the first to reach the finish line. It is our continued efforts in building our relationships with our children that provide an understanding of ourselves, our children, and our connections. If we only focus on the race, we lose sight of the personal joy and sense of accomplishment that our training provides us.

Cohen (2001)says, "The joy of our work as parents comes from the warm heartfelt experiences we get to share as gifts with our children,"—from the first time we experience the unconditional love of an infant's smile, or the warm clutching of our leg as our toddler's eyes say, "Take me for a ride, Daddy," to the intimate butterfly kisses on the cheek as our child giggles, and the contagious laughter that comes from our child's first attempt at telling a joke.

All these precious moments are the gifts of parenthood that we get share with our children throughout their lives and are the rewards we reap when we sow the seeds of our relationships. These are the gifts that keep on giving and make all the hard work of parenting worth the effort. By becoming consciousness parents, we can see the opportunities and pitfalls of parenting and avoid "the pull to return to the old way of doing things," (Segal, 2005).

It takes two to tango

"Opportunity dances with those already on the dance floor."

-Les Brown

At this point you are probably asking the question, "This is all good and well, but what happens when things go wrong?" This question makes up the 'what if' scenarios that are likely running through your mind as you read along. They are the most insidious aspects of the parent trap and represent our imperfect human efforts to deal with our own frail mortality. We struggle to make sense of the impermanence of our lives and are faced with the painful ill-fated reality that 'bad things happen to good people.'

Our parenting search reveals four more truths: 1)life is short; 2 there are no guarantees; 3) life is full of surprises; and 4) life is difficult. Nothing truer can be said when it comes to parenting. From our child crying when they fall and get hurt, to the pain suffered by our teenager laboring with the loss of their first love, we feel for our children at the deepest level.

Our feelings, no matter how deep they run, are ours alone and are separate from the emotions of our children. We must take ownership of our own feelings or we run the risk of projecting them onto our children. This emotional projection is a process that can impair healthy attachment and increase our children's vulnerability to a number of problems. It can create "a heightened need for attention and approval," (Bowen, 1994) and makes it difficult for our children "to deal with expectations or tolerate painful emotions."

This type of 'family projection' models poor emotional boundaries that make it difficult for our children to distinguish between their own feelings and the feelings of others. These emotional boundaries must be maintained so we can respond effectively within our relationships; thus remembering that we cannot dictate our children's happiness, destiny, or fate.

We are social beings and it is easy to confuse our feelings with those we are close to, especially our children. For example, if a child scrapes their knee while playing, and runs into the house with tears of pain rolling down their face, we are going to feel hurt. Our hurt is not their pain and vice versa; these are separate but shared association.

I have often seen young children stumble and fall and then look back to their parent's reactions for how they should emotionally respond to the situation. We must take every precaution to assure we are not projecting our emotions onto our children by realizing that we cannot deal with our own hurt by making our child's pain go away. Our greatest hope is that we can be there for our children to help them in their times of need.

Helping is a complex social process and, as such, is similar to change and the process of letting go. It represents another parental paradox that, if based on control, confounds and challenges our own intentions as a parent to manipulate the fates of choice. Our experiences in life as a parent are multidimensional and are based on personal choices.

Choice and control within the parent-child relationship are pivotal aspects of helping. These central themes reoccur throughout "*The Matrix*" trilogy and are ultimately revealed in "*The Matrix Reloaded*," when Neo tells the Architect, "Choice. The problem is choice." This somber reality also hits home in the movie "*A River Runs Through It*," when it is stated, "For it is true we can seldom help those that are closest to us."

Parents know the problem of choice all too well when it comes to their children's lives. We can often find ourselves struggling with this process as we try to prevent the unavoidable problems that are associated with the poor choices our children sometimes make. We can find good reason to let go in knowing that by building our relationships, we find the opportunities to teach our children how they can learn from their mistakes.

This process describes the difficulties we face in life and "that our finest moments are most likely to occur when we are feeling deeply uncomfortable, unhappy, or unfulfilled. For it is only in such moments, propelled by our discomfort, that we are likely to step out of our ruts and start searching for different ways or truer answers," (Peck, 1998).

Effective parental roles, unlike our traditionally held views, involve our ability to juggle a number of intersecting variables within and surrounding the choices in our parent-child relationships. Healthy parenting transcends the control trap and is centered on healthy boundaries, personal responsibility, supportive assistance, and empathy as opposed to control, blame, enabling, and sympathy.

It is essential for us to develop a parental leadership parallel so we can walk side-by-side and not in front, behind, on top of, or underneath our children. This model exhibits the flexible strength of our role as a parent in an ever-changing world.

Separate but connected, this dance of intimacy we share with our children cannot be forced. The dance of parenting is led by example where we can encourage our children to take the steps that flow from the rhythms of life. The dance of parenting is a place where we will come to know the uncomfortable stance of being alone in the middle of the dance floor with our arms wide open.

Our children's dance of choice, as they continue to develop, can have tragic consequences. We want to make sure that nothing bad happens and sometimes overstep our boundaries to prevent these mistakes for our children. Our attempts to control this process, no matter how well-intentioned, are often directed at avoiding the sometimes tragic endings of these choices.

Fey & Cline (2006) suggest that "parents need to hold children accountable for poor decisions" through the use of natural or logical consequences that are "locked in our empathy, love, and understanding." This 'love and logic' method promotes the parent-child relationship and allows our children to build self-confidence through their own struggles and achievements on the dance floor of life, with us by their side.

Hand in hand

"The first thing to know about parenting is: it's a dance."
-John Gall

Taking our child's hand in ours is a form of encouragement that provides the structure necessary to share the dance of intimacy with our children. It is the process of teaching our children so they can learn how to become interdependent and take chances on their own, without stepping on everyone else's toes.

It is a harmony that is felt within the rhythm and beat of the music contained within the patterns of life. By embracing the many variations within the dances of life, we, as parents, can take the necessary steps to understand and provide the flexibility for our children so they can have the confidence to find their own internal harmony.

Learning these dance steps allows us to break free from our "default modes," (Gall, 2002) and can give us the ability to effectively move along with life rather than fighting against it. Dancing allows us the ability to develop the joyful grooves that help us get out of the oppressive ruts we experience in life.

These can become newly-established parental dance patterns that can help us connect with our own internal rhythms. By dancing with the rhythms of life, our attempts to handle whatever life throws at us become effortlessly smooth glides across the dance floor.

Dancing with our children evolves developmentally and starts at birth as an internal connection we feel with the sway of an infant held tenderly in our arms. It is felt within our toddler's first steps as they stand on the tops of our feet as we stride across the floor. It is seen in our adolescent's individualistic discordant dance movements, as we try to keep up. It is the cascade of the formal ballroom steps shared with our children in their adult lives.

These changing dances lead us through a lifelong process with our children and developed by us becoming a student of dance. It is only by learning how to apply our own internal rhythms to the flow of the music that we can make the most of each opportunity. "Tuesdays with Morrie" (Mitch Albom, 1997, Doubleday, NY) hints at this internal vibration of life that is experienced by Morrie, who "would close his eyes and, with a blissful smile, begin to move to his own sense of rhythm."

Harmony and rhythm within the parent-child relationship allows us to become absorbed in the beauty of this dance. This can be seen as the synchronicity and sway between mother and infant rocking in unison, or in a father gently leading the way as the child follows closely in stride. It can be seen in an adolescent sharing their day's adventures in a flowing stream of conversation and the advice and guidance sought out by an adult child faced with making a difficult choice.

These rhythmic sways between parent and child can quickly change and become a dance of conflict when we shift to a position of control. This conflict can be seen when a mother frantically bounces a crying infant in her arms, trying to get them to stop crying, or a father dragging a crying child from the store in anger because the child wanted a toy.

It is also seen in the hostile yelling matches going when a parent says, "No, because I said so" to their teenager who wants to go to their first unsupervised party, and the silence and distance felt between an adult child and their parent due to some unresolved past resentment.

Dance patterns between parent and child can become ingrained automatic reactions to situations. Until we can find a harmonious path in learning how to dance with our children, we find ourselves stepping on the toes of our children. These negative patterns are destined to repeat themselves over and over again.

These dances of conflict can almost be choreographed and are the predicable habitual patterns that parents and children engage in every day. Thoman (1987) describes this "relationship dance" and argues that it is an important element in our child's development.

We can create an dance of intimacy with our children through sharing a warm, loving, reciprocal exchange—allowing our children the opportunity to learn about the nature of people and the world around them. This allows them the support and encouragement they need to grow cognitively, socially, and emotionally, so they can manage the dance with others on their own. It is then that we can get "on with the dance" of life and "let joy be unconfined," (Lord Byron).

VII. Love is Not Enough

"I had lots of love and good intentions, but without skill, they were not enough to change my children's behavior."
-Nancy Samalin

Contrary to the Beatles' song, "All You Need is Love," *becoming a better parent* requires an understanding of what constitutes *"parental love,"* (Unruh, 2010). He suggests that "the power of letting them know they are loved" is what shapes the relationships with our children. Love is a complex entity and represents another parental paradox that has many meanings and can create an imbalance in our relationships.

This is an *intra-relationship system dynamic* called a "dynamic systems framework," (Granic, Dishion & Hollenstein, 2006). This process moves us away from our narrow person-centered perspectives, and moves us toward what they see as "relationships, and the community within a cultural context in which these relationships are embedded." The dynamic system of *parental love* is described in the movie "*The Matrix Revolutions,*" when a computer program named Rama-Kandra explains his connection with his daughter, Sati, by saying, "Love is just a word. What matters is the meaning you attach to the word."

Love has many different meanings and we attribute a number of different concepts to this process. Since the time of ancient Greeks, it has been described as representing a triad of interpersonal factors and, more recently, has been described as a "complex set of emotions," (Rubin, 1973), (Lee, 1973), and (Sternberg, 1988). These descriptions range from intimacy to commitment, attachment to caring, and passion to compassion. These form the foundation for the different theoretical explanations of love that are combined and defined in more detail below:

- *Infatuation, Mania, or Puppy Love:* Obsessive feelings towards a love object that are largely based upon fantasy and idealization (instead of experience). Often occurring in the beginning stages of a relationship, and diminishing when partners get to know each other—a temporary crush on someone that you don't know well.

- *Eros, or Romantic Love:* An abiding love for a partner with whom you feel passion, attraction, caring, and respect. It can be a passionate love, usually involving a sexual attraction. This type of love covers everything from queasy stomachs and warm fuzzy feelings to strong sensual passion.

- *Companionate, Storge, Philia, or Brotherly Love:* Friendship and feelings of warmth towards a friend with whom you love to spend time. This connotes having a feeling of love for your neighbor, because all humanity is considered to be part of a larger family of human beings. This is the love of friendship, best friends, and the fellowship of being with those people you enjoy.

- *Agape, Spiritual, or Unconditional Love:* This represents a divine, unconditional, self-sacrificing, active, and thoughtful love. It is a type of affection and caring that is so strong that you feel it consistently, regardless of what that other person does. It recognizes the divine light in everyone and everything. It is a love that is given to everyone as an act of loving God.

- *Ludos, or Conditional Love:* This type of love requires a specific action or condition to be fulfilled in order to be maintained. It represents a game and is what people give to us when we do what they want, which makes ourselves and others feel good, temporarily. It is a performance-based requirement in a relationship and has been described as a 'game' of love.

- *Maternal Love:* This term has an instinctive biological component and usually describes a love and tenderness that is nurturing, accepting, and protective. In actuality, this love is not gender-specific and can be expressed by both parents.

- *Paternal Love:* This type of love has a social learning element and implies a love that involves guidance, instruction, and some authority. It is a love that is directed at preparing children for the outside world. Again, this type of love is not gender-specific.

- *Soulmate Love*: This recent description of love can be linked to a New Age view of love that has existed in past lives. However, it is better understood as an *enduring love* that is based on the laws of attraction that transcends both time and space.
- *Consummate Love:* This is a complete form of love, representing an ideal relationship toward which people strive. This ultimate form of love

represents closeness, connectedness, and a strong attachment in loving relationships.

- *Love for and Pride in Your Country, or Patriotism*: It is love and devotion to one's own country. This is a love for the place you live or the place that were born. It is a type of loyalty and a special feeling of belonging that you attribute to that that place you call 'home.'

- *Self-Love:* This is a positive feeling that you have about who you are. It is often expressed by treating yourself well, respecting yourself, wanting yourself to be happy, and expecting others to respect you, too. "Your relationship with yourself is the central template from which all others are formed. Loving yourself is a prerequisite to creating a successful and authentic union with another. The relationship you have with yourself is the central relationship," (Scott, 1998).

- *Tough Love:* This term is used to describe a love that is expressed by setting boundaries for the good of the other person. It is often used as an expression when someone treats another person harshly or sternly with the intent to help them in the long-run.

Intimacy between the love shared by a parent and child is formed through the emotional, physiological, psychological and social attachments that are built within our relationships with each other. *Parental love* involves different meanings that can be attributed to the fundamental aspects of the parent-child relationship. These forms of love include consummate, maternal, paternal, unconditional, and compassionate, as described above.

However, our love for our children also contains the aspects of love related to setting healthy boundaries, responsibility, accountability, self-respect, commitment, and bonding that contribute to our understanding of how love plays one of the most significant roles in our relationships with our children.

It is the interplay of commitment, caring, and attachment within all the aspects of *parental love*, that form these bonds that are created out of our shared relationships with our children. Commitment is formed from our expectations and established boundaries that allow for a mutual respect within the parent-child relationship. Being a good parent requires a tremendous investment and responsibility that continues to be an ongoing commitment throughout our children's entire lives.

Caring and compassion are expressed through the support and nurturing that builds the relationships with our children from an infant to a toddler, from elementary school through high school, to college and beyond. Finally, our "affectional bonding" (Bowlby, 1990), is the adhesive glue that holds this loving system together and is based on his "attachment theory," defining the glue of the relationship bonds between parent and child.

Parental love, then, is the basic ingredient that forms the basis of our relationships with our children, and contains a healthy multiple sense of meaning from which it can grow. It is an intricate set of emotional experiences which cannot be quantitatively measured or qualitatively analyzed, but is nevertheless a vital aspect of the evolving parent-child relationship.

The love shared between a parent and child forms the foundation for our relationships and determines our abilities as parents to make a difference in our children's lives. It is not merely confined to the elementary aspects of parenting, but encompasses the emotional, psychological, physical, and social elements of an individual's life. In other words, "There is no love. There are only proofs of love." (Pierre Reverdy)

Becoming A Better Parent

Balancing these complicated meanings of love within our relationships with our children is an important task so we can be consistent in creating an atmosphere of unconditional love while, at the same time, setting limits and teaching appropriate boundaries. We, as parents, can separate the behaviors from the child by letting our children know that we don't like what they did, and that we still love them, at the same time.

Parents can use a balance of consequences, encouragements, reflective listening, and self-statements to address behaviors while, at the same time, communicating unconditional love. Unconditional love for our children can free them from the fear that you will not love them if they fail to meet your expectations.

It will encourage them to give their best effort and achieve the highest level of which they are capable. At the same time, you can set consistent limits for their behaviors that will help them develop the attributes they will need to succeed in life and become self-actualized.

These conditional behaviors can be used to teach the essential qualities for success, such as hard work, discipline, patience, persistence, and perseverance, and give them the tools necessary to achieve their goals.

Similarly, the social values of compassion, caring, honesty, kindness, respect, and responsibility can be reinforced with our children through this balance of limits and unconditional love. In time, our children can learn to internalize this healthy separation between unconditional love and their behaviors as a guide for their own ethical and moral development.

Simply put, learning how to separate behaviors from the child is one of the key ingredients for *becoming a better parent*. Loving our children unconditionally while, at the same time, conditioning our acceptance of and responses to their behaviors, models healthy internal and external boundaries. This parental balancing act is the art of juggling the commitment, caring, and compassion that comprise the meaning of our love, as parents, for our children, and defines our relationship with them.

Lessons from a lifeguard

"Lifeguards consider swimming rescues a last resort due to the hazards presented by a panicked person in the water."
-United States Lifesaving Association (USLA)

According to the American Lifeguard Association, a rescue swimmer "should avoid personal hands-on contact with a victim" and the rescue method of "swim without an aid" should only be used as an absolute last resort. This is to prevent injury to both the rescue swimmer and the victim.

This holds true for parents as well, as we keep in mind that our love for our children can put us in dangerous positions. We can, however, find ways to help and empower them in their times of trouble so that they can rescue themselves. We can follow the same hierarchical guidelines that lifeguards use to rescue victims, as outlined below:

- Talk—The first rescue method is to talk with a victim so that, with instruction, they can help themselves. For parents, our first line of action in dealing with our children's behaviors is to provide instruction. This teaching process is a discussion that is directed at providing options and choices for our children.

- Reach—A lifeguard should try to reach the victim from a position of safety, such as the side of a pool or from the beach, using any aid that allows them to stay safe throughout the rescue, while keeping constant contact with the victim. For us to 'reach' our children, we must create safety and trust in our relationships so we can offer and teach them the rescue tools they need.

- Throw—The next method used, is to throw a rescue aid to the victim and encourage them to use it to swim to safety. As parents, when our children get beyond our reach, we can continue to talk with them and 'throw aids to them' so they can access the tools they need to rescue themselves from their own behaviors and find more effective ways to be safe.

- Wade—It is only when neither of these techniques is possible that a lifeguard should consider wading to a victim, and this will only work in shallow water. Parents who find themselves in precarious rescue waters still can talk, reach, and throw the tools that are necessary to assist our children in making the changes needed in order to help themselves.

- Row—This is using a personal watercraft to reach a victim. This is almost exclusively used in outdoor and open water environments. When we, as parents, venture out into the deeper waters to rescue our children, we can get close enough to talk, reach, and throw the necessary tools for our children to rescue themselves.

- Swim with an aid—When a lifeguard considers swimming with an aid to rescue a victim, it creates additional danger for both the lifeguard and victim. If we are going to risk swimming out to rescue our children from themselves, we better make sure that we are strong swimmers ourselves and are thoroughly trained in the use of these aids.

- Swim without an aid - Only as an absolute last resort should a lifeguard attempt a rescue with no equipment. We, as parents, know the futility of trying to control our children, and it is only when they become completely incapacitated that we can attempt such a risky hands-on rescue maneuver.

Too often I have seen the ill-advised approach of a parent jumping in headfirst to rescue their child from themselves—only to see the parent end up drowning alongside the child in the process. We, as parents, have a built-in "instinctual drive to protect our children," (Noriuchi, Kikuchi & Senoo, 2007). This drive often short-circuits our rational abilities to respond to these situations effectively.

Picture a drowning person flailing in the water, grasping at everything and everyone within reach. In their panic, they are only interested in getting their head above water to breathe and they have little or no visible concern for others. This puts both you and the victim at risk of being hurt, or worse. Any seasoned lifeguard will tell you, "You have to deal with your emotions if you want to save anyone in these situations."

Now, picture a child who is feeling out of control due to an unmet need, emotional upset, or environment disruption. If they are unable to find an effective way to resolve this internal conflict, they, too, will flail and fight against the very people that are trying to help. They often perceive this help as creating part of the problem. exposing their own weakness, and will often lash out against it.

Like a person who is drowning, this child is fighting just to get their heads above water. When we, as parents, instinctively jump in to rescue our children in these situations, we may be inadvertently damaging our children's self-esteem. These rescue attempts often end up "invalidating our children's abilities" (Leo, 2007), "enabling learned helplessness" (Seligman, 1975), and "pampering our children into weakness" (Grunwald & McAbee, 1999).

We can change this parent-child system dynamic by using the lifesaving techniques outlined above, and save ourselves and our children in the parenting process. By communicating effectively, talking, reaching, and throwing out these lifesaving devices, we can begin to understand and be more attuned to the underlying needs of our children.

Leo (2007) describes these behaviors as "a communication of need," and encourages us, as parents, to make a shift away from parenting approaches that facilitate the "dynamics of power and control." When we are able to do this, we help our children get to a place where they can better stand on their own two feet, deal more effectively with their fear, and listen more intently to their own inner voices so they can learn how to intuitively and effectively address their own needs.

Parenting can, at times, resemble working as a lifeguard, and our best tools are better directed at prevention, instruction, guidance, and supervision, so our children can learn how to stay out of trouble on their own. With reasoning and training, we can stop reacting to these emotionally charged situations and learn how to respond to our own fears of uncertainty. We can prepare ourselves and our children for the responses we need in life to assure our success.

These lifesaving tools can then be used to structure our interventions so we will know when it's OK to talk, reach, throw, step in, or swim out to our children. With these lifelines, we will provide our children the assurance they need to feel supported and loved as we stand on edge of life's pool while encouraging them on.

By helping our children build the self-confidence they need to venture out into deeper waters, they can develop the abilities necessary to rescue themselves and become self-reliant in an ocean of constant change.

Parents can be much more effective in saving their children by following these simple strategies. We must remember that we are no use to our children in these situations if we find ourselves flailing in the water next to them.

Robert Lang

Responsibility 'to' vs. responsibility 'for'

"Freedom is the will to be responsible to ourselves."
-Friedrich Nietzsche

Love does a funny thing to us when it comes to our responsibilities as parents, and often blinds us to the errors of our own ways of thinking. These misconceptions often stem from our misunderstandings and use of accountability and responsibility. Accountability and responsibility are two words that are often used synonymously with one another but, in actuality, they represent opposite ends of the same continuum.

Understanding the difference between accountability and responsibility is essential to our comprehension and development of healthy boundaries within the parent-child relationship. Basically, what this means for us, as parents, is that we cannot take responsibility for our children, we can only hold them accountable. Healthy *parental love* creates awareness that we, as parents, have a responsibility to our children and not for them.

According to the Oxford Dictionary, *accountability* stems from the old Latin word *accomptare* (to account), a prefixed form of *computare* (to calculate), which, in turn, is derived from *putare* (to reckon). The use of this word is related to the concept of accounting and has ancient roots that are associated with record keeping, governance and money-lending systems. Accountability, then, is our ability as parents to take into account our children's actions in holding them accountable.

It is a system of supervision within our relationship with our children that allows us to consider and surmise the behaviors and the ways of dealing with them more effectively. Many states have enacted "parental accountability" laws that hold parents 'legally responsible' for crimes committed by their children.

Although there is no empirical evidence to support that these laws either decrease youth crime or increase parental accountability, they continue to be a popular public policy.

These sweeping policy changes are less likely to make the kind of changes we want to see in our children for tomorrow, and only devalues the personal responsibility of the parent and the child.

On the other hand, the *American Heritage Dictionary* and the *Collins English Dictionary* define *responsibility* as "the state, quality, or fact of being responsible, something for which one is responsible; a duty, obligation, or burden." Being responsible means that one has the ability or authority to act or decide on one's own, without supervision.

Responsibility is a relatively new concept and only finds its way into the English language toward the end of the 18th century. It is related to governmental systems which are responsible to the people. Twentieth century philosophy began to emphasis responsibility in terms of its associations to the ideas of free will and determinism.

Responsibility, then, is a highly personal concept that separates the parent from the child and is an important marker for their individual success, achievement, motivation, happiness, and self-actualization.

The difference between responsibility and accountability is personal. Responsibility is a personal concept of free will and self-determination, while accountability is a social concept, based on fairness and equality. Every individual on this planet has a personal responsibility for their own thoughts, feelings, and behaviors, while simultaneously being held socially accountable for their actions.

Therefore, we have a personal responsibility to others and in making this world a better place to live while, at the same time, holding others and ourselves socially accountable. Accountability refers to making, keeping, and managing relationships and expectations, while responsibility is a personal sense of ownership. In other words, we take responsibility for ourselves and hold others accountable.

Starting in the 1960s, a public service announcement was created in an attempt to increase parental accountability and came over American television airways stating, "It's 10 o'clock, do you know where your children are?" Research done by Smetana (2008) has challenged the notion that vigilant parental monitoring is associated with less externalizing behavior among children.

Her research has shown that children who have close supportive relationships with their parents are able to "voluntarily disclose heir activities, associates, and whereabouts, and this is a more important factor in predicting their involvement in risky behavior."

This research seems to suggest that a positive parent-child relationship has more to do with 'how' and 'what' we do in our involvement with our children than it does with having 'our thumb on top of things.' It is this process that makes a significant difference for how we look at parental accountability and personal responsibility.

Responsibility and accountability are influential aspects that form the boundaries of our *parental love* and involve a shared give-and-take within the parent-child relationship. It is given through our responsibility to ourselves and for our children, and taken from our accountability for our children and to ourselves.

The parent-child relationship grows as we become responsible parents while, at the same time, holding our children accountable so they can, in turn, become responsible individuals. In understanding the differences in accountability and responsibility within the parent-child relationship, we can more effectively define the parameters of our relationships with our children so that our *parental love* can be expressed more freely and does not become another barrier in building the relationships with our children.

What's love got to do with it?

"We cannot do great things on this earth, only small things with great love."

-Mother Teresa

Becoming A Better Parent

It seems to be common knowledge that childrenneed loving, caring, and consistent parenting in order to survive and thrive, but there is also scientific evidence to support that these relationships with our children have long-lasting psychological, emotional, and physical health implications.

Studies done at both Harvard (Russek & Schwartz, 1997) and John Hopkins (Thomas, 1976), have concluded that "parental love seems to act as a buffer against later life illnesses." They speculate that the foundation of loving parental relationships helps to "lessen the negative impact of stress and pathogens in later life, protect the immune system, and strengthen the desire to live and heal."

These researchers, as well as many others, recently have suggested that there "is no other factor more significantly related to illness than the degree of parental closeness reported in the earlier years." Luecken's (1998) research has further indicated that "there are specific characteristics of a parent-child relationship that are key to good health in adulthood" which include "togetherness in the family, avoiding conflict, nurturing, closeness, and supportive behavior."

Loving and effective parent-child relationships are neither harsh or abusive, nor weak and ineffectual. It is a highly balanced elaborate social system that is characterized by the boundaries and nature of our relationships with our children. However, when our understanding of love goes wrong, it can create tragic outcomes.

When love is misperceived as a mechanism of control, it pollutes the parent-child interactions. This is often the case when parents don't have a healthy sense of self, lack consistent healthy boundaries, experience ongoing instability or imbalance, and when their hearts become twisted by this illusion of control.

These unresolved issues, as described by Voirst (1998), are instrumental in determining the very nature of the relationships we have with our children. She suggests that what is needed to *'save the children'* is the ability to be a "good enough parent" in the process of "dancing the dance of letting go."

When we are unwilling to embrace our past, come to terms with our insecurities, and accept our strengths and limitations as parents, we produce a perpetual wave pool that constantly disrupts our life's waters. The endless sufferings created by these parental insufficiencies lead to the many forms of child abuse and neglect that have long-lasting negative multi-generational effects.

These can range from children becoming abusive or neglectful parents themselves, to developing poor societal, social, and academic performance, and creating lifelong physical, emotional, psychological, and health problems. Control, as we have discussed, is the primary culprit that is at the heart of these parent traps and, when it is used as a defining element of *parental love*, the results can be disastrous.

Neglect and abuse can take many forms within the parent-child relationship and is currently defined by Federal and State laws. The Federal Child Abuse Prevention and Treatment Act (CAPTA) provides the definition of abuse and neglect as follows:

- "Any recent act or failure to act on the part of a parent or caretaker, which results in death, serious physical or emotional harm, sexual abuse, or exploitation, or an act or failure to act which presents an imminent risk of serious harm."

- "The employment, use, persuasion, inducement, enticement, or coercion of any child to engage in, or assist any other person to engage in, any sexually explicit conduct or simulation of such conduct for the purpose of producing a visual depiction of such conduct."

- "The rape, and in cases of caretaker or interfamilial relationships, statutory rape, molestation, prostitution, or other form of sexual exploitation of children, or incest with children."

Each state also provides civil definitions of child abuse and neglect and recognizes the different types of abuse, including physical abuse, neglect, sexual abuse, and emotional abuse. Some states also provide definitions in their statutes for parental substance abuse and/or for abandonment as child abuse. The U.S. Department of Health and Human Services has identified a number of characteristics that have been found to increase the parental risk for the maltreatment of children and are listed as follows:

- Parents' lack of understanding children's developmental needs.
- Parents' lack of understanding effective parenting skills.
- Parents' history of child abuse or neglect in their family of origin.
- Substance abuse and/or mental health issues, including depression in the family.
- Parents who are young, single, and have a large number of dependent children.
- Non-biological, transient caregivers in the home (e.g., mother's male partners).
- Parental thoughts and emotions that tend to support or justify maltreatment behaviors.
- Parents who are socially isolated, and have low education and low income.
- Family disorganization, dissolution, and violence, including intimate partner violence.
- Parenting stress, poor parent-child relationships, and negative interactions.

Strikingly, the risk factors that stand out the most are those that we, as parents, have the best chance of changing. Included in the factors that we have the best chance of changing, are our abilities in understanding our children's needs, taking the steps to heal from our own pasts, taking responsibility for our own problems, learning how to deal with the stresses of life, and getting the help and support we need. By becoming a student of parenting, we can break free from these cultural and family cyclical patterns of neglect and abuse.

There are also more subtle forms of child maltreatment that include emotional abuse and neglect that are often overlooked and fall outside of the above definitions. "Neglect is not only the most frequent type of maltreatment; it can be just as lethal as physical abuse" (Bagley, Wood & Young, 2005). Physical, emotional, educational, and medical neglect can all create serious long-term psychological, social, health, and developmental problems for our children.

Emotional and/or psychological abuse is probably the least understood of all forms of child abuse, yet it is the most prevalent, and can be the cruelest and most destructive for our children. Glaser (2002) finds that emotional abuse can be "more strongly predictive of subsequent impairments in the children's development than the severity of physical abuse." Besharov (1990) states that "emotional abuse is an assault on the child's psyche, just as physical abuse is an assault on the child's body." Children who are constantly ignored, shamed, terrorized, or humiliated, suffer at least as much, if not more, than if they were physically abused.

I have heard parents justify these misdirected actions toward their children through a number of irrational views and beliefs about *parental love* and often defend themselves by saying, "But, I did it out of love." You have probably heard the sayings, 'this is going to hurt me more than it will you,' 'might makes right,' or 'spare the rod and spoil the child,' all of which are misperceived notions about abusive forms of discipline.

Spanking is one of the most highly contentious and misunderstood forms of parental discipline and is often mistakenly attributed to our *parental love*. By emphasizing the importance of how any form of discipline can be misused, we can let go of these ineffective strategies and develop a more effective parenting plan. We can then take into consideration all the discipline strategies that are available to us so we can respond more effectively as a self-disciplined disciplinarian and use these learning opportunities to build our relationships with our children.

I have worked with parents who have told me that what they are doing, no matter how harmful, is 'out of love.' I have even had parents tell me that they 'love their child so much that they had to spank them to make sure they didn't make the same mistakes they did as a kid.' Climbing out of this ineffective shame-based control system of abuse and neglect can be difficult.

We must shed these problems from our past and seek a balance within all aspects of the parental continuum so we can stop these continued multigenerational family patterns. By finding a way out of these parental perils, we can turn to non-controlling ways to relate to ourselves and with our children. We will then be able to build the relationships with our children that are based on the true nature of *parental love* that give us the framework for change.

You're probably saying to yourself while you read along in this section that, "I would never abuse or neglect my child," and "What does this have to do with me?" You might even be hearing the resonating self-commitment you made as a child when you state, "When I have children, I will never do that to my kids." In spite of these resolutions to change, we often find ourselves unable to recognize that we are stuck in the same pattern.

If you are reading this book and actively taking the steps to become a better parent, then you are most likely not going to fall into one these destructive categories. You would also be well-represented by the same majority of parents who deny the existence of these problems, in spite of active dependency and neglect cases, toxic, and conflictual divorces, or their own untreated psychiatric or substance use disorders.

I work with many parents who are sometimes unable to see the devastation they are creating in their children's lives. Whether through domestic violence, hostile divorces, or neglect and abuse, this unsettling trauma leaves lasting imprints in our children's hearts. This form of parental "denial"

(Cramer & Brilliant, 2001) is a commonly used and difficult to overcome defense mechanism that ignores the unpleasant reality that parents have done something to harm their own child.

This identification process is not about blame or shame, but about change. We can make a difference for all our children's tomorrows through our resilience and acceptance of the problem and find the courage to change. The change that is necessary and is at the heart of every hurting child who has every suffered at the hand of a parent. These children often, even when separated from their parent, want nothing more than to have a chance at true *parental love*.

Listen to your heart

"Your vision will become clear only when you look into your heart."

-Carl Jung

Our heart has a truth of its own. Our social conditioning, on the other hand, teaches us that we need to be logical and use our heads. Using logic and reason can be sound advice, however. when we resort to only using our heads, our experience becomes limited. It is fascinating that the same neurological tissue found in the brain is also found in the heart.

Our heart is a metaphorical 'second brain' and represents our emotional nerve center, creating a body/brain connection that allows us to tap into our intuition. Paying attention to both your head and your heart is crucial to making good decisions that will improve our relationships with our children. Cloke & Goldsmith (2000) describe listening with the heart as an "empathic listener who genuinely cares about the speaker's message and who actively reaches out with authentic interest and gentle responses."

They affirm three active listening steps that outline our abilities to listen more effectively: 1) "Let go of your own ideas, roles, and agendas;" 2) "Search for the other person's meaning;" and 3) "Respond respectfully, acknowledging and addressing the other person's concerns." They propose that listening with your heart allows individuals to choose responses that support open communication by "encouraging, clarifying, acknowledging, empathizing, mirroring, reframing, and summarizing."

A healthy emotional system is the most important regulator in this process and if we are experiencing emotional imbalance, then our listing filters become skewed. Empathic, emotionally-based listening allows us to connect with our children at a deeper level and requires a genuine focus on our children's words, meanings, and feelings. So the next time your child is trying to communicate with you, make sure you are 'taking it to heart!'

"Actively listening," a phrase coined by Gordon (1977), requires that we listen with our hearts and our minds so we can empathize, interpret, and evaluate what is being said. He stated that "active listening is certainly not complex" and that "listeners need only restate, in their own language, their impression of the expression of the sender." He went on to say, however, that "learning to do *active listening* well is a rather difficult task." He also believed that the use of coercive power damages relationships and he developed an approach to help parents move to a position of influence rather than control.

The ability to listen actively can improve personal relationships, reduce conflicts, strengthen cooperation, and foster greater understanding. This idea is reflected in the Tao, where it states, "Love is of all passions, the strongest, for it attacks simultaneously the head, the heart, and the senses," (Lao Tzu).

The "Gordon Method" included a complete and integrated system for building and maintaining effective relationships at work, home, and school. "Parent Effectiveness Training" (Gordan, 1975) was one of the first skill-based training programs for parents that focused on teaching the skills of "active listening," "using I-messages," and "no-lose conflict resolution" to build the parent-child relationship.

His approach included more than just skills building and led the way for our further understanding of the *parent trap*. His revolutionary insights about parent system dynamics began to reveal those elements that interfere with our abilities to build close, caring, and supportive relationships with our children, and began to outline the true nature of *parental love*.

Take another little piece of my heart

"It is only because of problems that we grow mentally and spiritually."

-M. Scott Peck

It seems as though the entire parent-child relationship revolves around love and loss. At each stage of parenting we are confronted by both. We feel the loss-associated change and our love expressed in our connections with our children. Time and again, we have to deal with the transitions of life from the time our children are born to the time they move out and have children of their own.

We experience these as a world of 'parental firsts' and we hold on to these loving moments in time—our child's first smile, haircut, step, and day of school. These are the periods in time when our children sit, crawl, walk, and talk for the first time. These graduating steps of parenthood are experienced as both loss and love.

These "stages of parenting" (Galinsky, 1987) allow us to understand the developmental process we go through so we can grow and learn as parental students. Galinsky (1987) states that these *parental images* are the "visual expectations" of what we think should happen and what really happens with the struggles of each parental stage. He identified the following six stages of parental development that are not necessarily experienced in chronological order:

1. ***Image-Making Stage:*** This process occurs when we form our initial images about our

children and what we will be like as parents. It is a continual shaping of the *"parental image"* while we are growing up and is reinforced during pregnancy.

2. **Nurturing Stage:** This stage takes place from our child's birth until they are 18 to 24 months old. At this stage, parents compare their preconceived images of their child and themselves with their actual experiences.

3. **Authority Stage:** From our child's second birthday, until they are about 4 or 5 years old and enter into to school, is the stage when we, as parents, have to decide on the practical side of parenting; where we refine our images of style and approach.

4. **Interpretive Stage:** This stage is defined by our child's early school years and ends with the start of adolescence. In this stage, the concern shifts to our views and images as a parent in helping our children develop positive self-concepts.

5. **Independent Stage:** This stage covers our child's teenage years. We question and re-evaluate our images of parenting, and are focused on forming a different kind of relationship with our children.

6. **Departure Stage**: This is the time when our children leave home. This is a retrospective stage of evaluation and judgment about our parental images. Parents often look at how well they have done and how their image of their child fits the reality.

We are faced with the ongoing dilemma of wanting our children to grow up, yet, at the same time, struggle to keep their innocence. These are the "Necessary Losses" (Voirst, 1998) we experience in the normal process of letting go through each of the stages of parenthood.

Voirst believes that these processes are crucial in the development of healthy parent-child relationships and are repeatedly renegotiated throughout what she refers to as "the many stages of separation." These parental separations are associated with loss and are also outlined by the "five stages of grief" (Kubler-Ross, 2005) that include *denial, anger, bargaining, depression, and acceptance.*

Having an evolving model of parenting provides us the flexibility needed to address these ongoing losses and separations within the parent-child relationship and forms the supportive bonds with our children that help them prepare, navigate, and deal with the losses they will all have to face in their lives, as well.

VIII. Do What You Say and Say What You Do

"Today you are You, that is truer than true. There is no one alive who is You-er than You."

-Dr. Seuss

Too often, our words and behaviors send mixed messages and often don't match our true intentions. When our messages are inconsistent, they can limit our authenticity and deprive us of the understanding of our children's unmet needs. Communication, in its many forms and conduits, is the basis for how we relate to the outside world.

I have often used the phrase, "What you say might not be what others hear, and what you hear might not be what others say," in order to reflect the problems we have with communication. This statement points to the paradox of communication that outlines the two-way process of sending and receiving information.

Paying close attention to how we relay and receive messages through a filtered feedback system sets the stage for effective changes we communicate with our children. The game of *telephone* is often used as a good way to show how this communication process can often break down, where the more a message is passed on, the more the message changes.

There are many ways that messages get communicated and we need to remember that "actions speak louder than words, but not nearly as often," (Mark Twain). Mehrabian's

(1981) research suggests that more than 80 percent of communication is "nonverbal." He points out that it is the emotional context, paralanguage, and behavior, rather than our spoken communication, that creates meaning. In all forms of communication, success occurs when the receiver understands the message just as the sender intended it.

If we want to communicate effectively with our children, we must assure that all the elements of the communication system and processes are working. The following are the elements that make up the communication system and its processes:

- *Input.* This is the intent of the sender to communicate with another person. This intention makes up the content of the message.

- *Internal filters.* These are the mental schemas that provide us an internal frame of reference for analyzing and synthesizing information.

- *Sender.* In formulating output, we use an encoding system that funnels information down into the message sent. This is based on our internal system dynamics and experiences.

- *Channel.* This is how the message is delivered and is made up of both our verbal and nonverbal communications.

- *Social filters.* These are shared social reference points that are influenced by cultural factors that include family origin, socio-economic status, religion, customs, and gender roles.

- *Receiver.* The receiver decodes and translates the incoming message from a narrow perspective and drives meaning from their internal system dynamics.

- *Output.* This is the content of the message in the form of information that is communicated to the receiver.

- *Feedback loop.* Provides a regulatory function for the communication system and lets the sender know if the information was communicated effectively.

- *Fields of Experience.* These are the collective knowledge, values, and beliefs of an individual. It is comprised of our own thoughts, feelings, and behaviors, as well as our experiences.

Effective communication is a key factor in our ability to become better parents and is the structural foundation for building our relationships. "We are capable of understanding speech at rates up to 600 words per minute, however, the average person speaks between 100 and 140 words per minute," (Dreschler & Versfeld, 2002). These include the messages we actually send, the messages we interpret, our responses, our reactions, and how we interpret the information.

Communication can be a major stumbling block in creating significance in our relationships with our children. Increasing our awareness as to how this vital processing system works can provide additional insight for our own parental growth.

Research done by Maxwell (2008) indicates that "we hear half of what is said, listen to half of what we hear, understand half of what we listen to, believe half of what we understand, and remember half of what we believe," and, if you do the math, that means we only retain about 3 percent of what is said.

Robert Lang

Can you hear me now?

"To effectively communicate, we must realize that we are all different in the way we perceive the world and use this understanding as a guide to our communication with others."
-Anthony Robbins

Communication is a system-based network with continuous feedback loops that serve to regulate the exchange of information (see following illustration). This process and system is used to communicate a *message* from the *sender*, who formulates the *message* from their *field of experience* and then *encodes* and funnels the *message* through their *internal filter*. The *message* is *channeled* through various mediums and passes through a *social filter* to the *receiver*, who *decodes* the *message* through their own *internal filter*.

The *receiver then* formulates a *response* from their *field of experience*, in the *form of feedback* that is sent as a new *message* to the *sender*, and the process starts all over again. So, when we want to say something, it goes through a number of internal processes before it's sent, and then it goes through a number of communication processes before it's received, and it then goes through a number of receiving processes before it's returned as feedback.

This feedback process system is essential for effective communication and eliminates the need for parents to ask, "Can't you hear me?" Bowlby (1983) claims that these feedback processes are "goal directed partnerships" that are co-regulated by both the parent and the child. Our children have an intuitive curiosity that can be fostered by using these communication techniques to build a positive partnership in working with our children.

By taking a lead role in the communication process, we can set an example so we can use this process for instructing our children in how to communicate more effectively. Hopefully, by becoming better communicators, we can eliminate the statement that, ""My children never listen to me," and find more meaningful ways to communicate with our children.

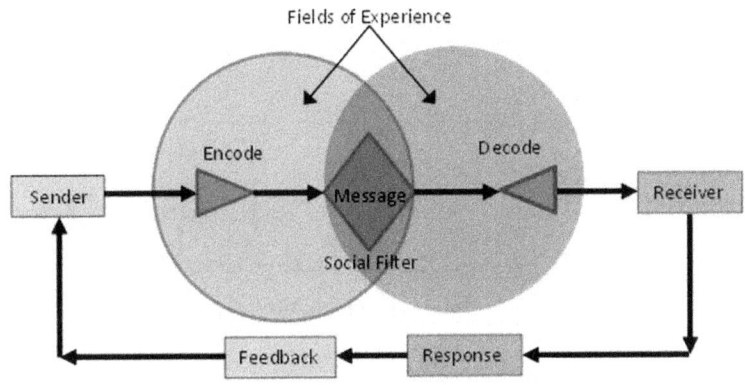

Systems Communication Feedback Loop
Diagram 6

The "Johari Window" (Luft & Ingham, 1955) is an effective tool for revealing the difficulties we have in communicating with our children, and can be helpful in understanding effective interpersonal communication. In using this tool, we can move to more open forms of communication so that our messages are known to both us and to our children (see Diagram 7). We can then escape the problems encountered in the communication process associated with "distancing, hidden agendas, and blindsides."

Johari Window

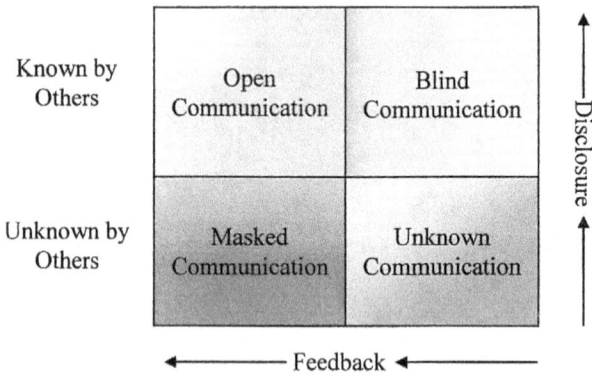

Diagram 7

Parents who are genuine, use appropriate disclosure-based knowledge, and are open to feedback, are more likely to have children who are willing to listen. When our expectations are clearly communicated, our children can feel secure, explore options freely, and cooperate more. There have been many studies on the effects of positive parent-child communication and, in summary, they state that warm, open, honest, direct, clear, consistent messages that build our relationships have long-lasting constructive outcomes.

As we examine the complex nature of parent-child communications, it is important that we take into account all the system "dynamics and variables that come into play," (Alexander, 1973). With this type of approach, we can look at "balancing cohesion and adaptability" (Olsen, 1997) and see how our views are "constituted and managed through relationships," (Adams & Marshall, 1996), suggesting that our parental self-concept is "inseparable from dynamic interaction in relationships."

Recent studies suggest that our identities are also strongly linked and co-created within an "embedded self, or self in relation" (Wilmot, 1995) within the communication process. So, if we want our children to listen, we need to first recognize that communication is a two-way street. If we, as parents, want to be heard, we must first learn how to listen.

Walk the talk

"Don't worry that children never listen to you; worry that they are always watching you."
-Robert Fulghum

Children's minds are hardwired to learn, but this does not happen automatically, and we need to take the necessary steps to teach them by 'walking the walk,' not just 'talking the talk.' We have to set an example and be consistent in letting our children know that we 'mean what we say and say what we mean..' Learning happens most easily by doing, insists Klontz (2009), who urges parents to get on top of their own issues so they can effectively "walk the talk with their children."

Although Klontz's orientations are directed at "financial psychology," his insights about the parent-child interactions in dealing with modern social pressures and in teaching financial responsibility are right on the money. When we can start to understand the importance of our roles in supporting these aspects of our children's development, we can becomes much better teachers of the parenting process.

Our children are experts at knowing when we are being inconsistent—when what we say and what we do are out of sync. We need to be asking ourselves as parents, "Are we practicing what we preach?" Preaching contains an element of elitist hypocrisy that limits our ability to educate our children by only telling them what's right.

When we practice good decision making, good communications, good emotional regulation, and good boundaries, however, we are modeling what works. To 'practice what we preach,' we need to be willing to follow the same advice we are giving. Our actions (what we do) need be consistent with our words (what we say), for the intent, purpose, and meaning of our message to be communicated effectively.

This gives our children the best opportunities to learn. For example, we would be hard-pressed to expect change when we are lecture our children about the ill-effects of smoking if we smoke ourselves. The more we can 'practice what we preach,' the more we can model the most enduring aspects of our own humanity that include "honesty, beauty, openness, love, and trust," (Ferrucci, 2001).

Parents often give their children mixed messages when they make statements like, "Do as I say and not as I do." If we, as parents, want our children to grow up into happy, healthy, responsible adults, then we must be willing to lead the way through example.

When we insist that our children do the right thing, even if we don't, we lose the respect and positive influence of our relationships. Parents that have these mindsets often find themselves saying, "You can't do that," and then turn around and do the same thing, saying, "I get to do it, because I'm an adult."

This sets the stage for "parental hypocrisy" that is "based on resentment, and amounts to an abuse of power," (Fisher, Sharp & Wichman, 2007). This abuse of power is about trying to control our children and, if we are unwilling to set a good example in leading the way for our children, we are destined to repeat the mistakes of the past.

These indirect messages imply that adults can get away with anything and reinfoce a system of diminished accountability and reduced personal responsibility. Our children can internalize these messages. This can, in turn, enhance defensiveness and foster the magical thinking in our children when they say, "I can't wait to grow up so I can do whatever I want." It is impossible to effectively communicate with our children by words alone.

We need to develop an internal parental constancy with our thoughts, feelings, and behaviors, so that what we say matches what we do. Our children are like sponges and we need to be consistent on all fronts with the messages that we deliver. We often don't seem to fully recognize that everything we do or don't do is reflected back by our children.

Our children are the mirrors that reflect the images we project. If we are unwilling to look into the 'mirror of our children,' we run the risk of becoming hypocritical and set the traps created by a double standard.

Lead by example

"If your actions inspire others to dream more, learn more, do more, and become more—you are a leader."
-John Quincy Adams

Study after study has revealed that children name their parents among their most influential role models. We all hope to be good enough, strong enough, and effective enough role models that possess the kind of qualities we want in our children.

Charles Barkley once claimed that sports figures should not be role models saying, "I am not a role model. Parents should be the role models." Samuel (2008) agrees, and reports that parents are "role models" and not "heroes." While I agree that parents need to be positive role models for our children, I also feel strongly that we all have a civic sense of responsibility to make this world a better place for our children, as well.

Our success in life is based on an internal consistency within our thoughts, feelings, and behaviors, and setting a positive example that flows from this source allows us to be true to our word and consistent with our values. These positive ways of thinking and acting for us, as parents, sets the tone for our own continued search toward *becoming a better parent*—remembering that our children are always watching and listening.

There are some variations in how every parent defines what it means to be a good role model, and Samuel (2008) has identified a "positive role model" as being a person "who carries out an exemplary role" that "values ways of thinking and acting that are generally considered positive." He goes on to say that parents, as positive role models, need to be "real, someone who lives by the highest code of conduct possible, cemented in integrity, impartiality, and honesty."

Being a positive role model may seem like an overwhelming task and we need to make sure it's not creating additional pressure. We must remember that there is no such thing as perfect parent and that our children are not expecting us to be superheroes. Hopefully, we are not projecting these unrealistic expectations onto our children as we begin to accept our strengths as well as our limitations.

This idea is stated by Rinpoche & Swanson, (2009) who say that, "within our perceived weaknesses and imperfections lies the key to realizing our true strength." Our children are looking to us for answers and guidance, and modeling our imperfections imperfectly allows our children to appreciate the flaws in themselves and others. It is with a sense of humility, acceptance, and forgiveness, that we can take a new look at our limitations and move to a place that fosters change, inspires hope, and instills the courage to not take ourselves too seriously.

We can only hope to do our best in becoming a "good enough parent" (Bettelheim, 1988) so that we can let go of our parental perfectionism. Modeling this sense of humility is one of the most fundamental values we need to be teaching our children in becoming positive role models. Making mistakes is part of being a parent and how we deal with those mistakes is what defines us a positive role model.

Our children are infinitely tolerant and provide us with limitlessness chances to change and grow. Motivating our children to belief in the power of our 'minds over matter,' we can recognize the potential of the underdog in all of us. By showing our children how to develop their own insights about how to cope and deal with our imperfections in an ever-changing world,
we can help them develop a stronger sense of self-confidence.

Becoming a role model gives us a way to make use of all the aspects we have outlined in *becoming a better parent,* so we can make a positive impact within the parent-child relationship. To make a difference in our children's lives, it is not enough to tell them what choices they need to make—we must be willing to make these choices ourselves, and put them into action. As teachers, mentors, and role models, we can more effectively prepare our children for the future if we involve them in these life-affirming processes.

We no longer have to live in the shadows of shame, fear, or failure, and can share our lives more deeply with our children. We can now start to take the steps we need to lead the way for our children toward developing the characteristics that will support their growth and future success. These changes are based on true *parental love,* healthy boundaries, realistic expectations, and nurturing relationships—not on the control, abuse, and rigidity of our past parental traps.

Live life as a role model

"Our lives are a sum total of the choices we have made."
-Wayne Dyer

Decisiveness in making choices and the ability to deal with the outcomes is an important aspect of being an effective role model. Misner & Morgan (2004) point out that our "successes" and how we deal with our "losses" have to do with our "choices." Allowing our children to take part in this process can help them develop strategies for success and give them the ability to see how decisions are evaluated, weighed, and measured.

This problem solving method is an effective life skill that will show children how to resolve issues on their own. Children also need to share in our bad choices so they can learn how to minimize and deal with mistakes, as well. Admitting to our mistakes, apologizing, and repairing the damage quickly, creates a "family culture of forgiveness," (King, 2006). We can then demonstrate an important, yet often overlooked part of being a role model—being humble.

Stick-to-itiveness is a form of self-determination that models honoring commitments and following through on promises. However, as parents, it is easy for us to get busy, distracted, and sometimes complacent with our own follow-through. Becoming self-determined "serves to define those contextual factors that tend to support versus undermine motivation, performance, and well-being," (Deci & Ryan, 2002).

As role models, we must be committed to being on time, finishing what we start, not giving up, keeping our word, and not backing off when things get challenging. When we follow through, it teaches our children that things can be accomplished if we develop a 'can do' attitude. Frankl (2006) said,"I am convinced that life is 10 percent what happens to me and 90 percent how I react to it. And so it is with you. We are in charge of our attitudes." Being in charge of our attitudes gives us energy and revives our spirit.

Respect and compassion speak volumes about the type of attitude it takes to successfully become a parental role model and mentor. Parents often tell children to 'treat others the way you want to be treated,' yet may not be willing to follow The Golden Rule themselves. This rule has ancient roots and is linked to our modern concepts of human rights, justice, and reciprocal responsibility.

Based on the aspects of personal and mutual respect, the Golden Rule is something that children will learn through a trusting relationship. Sears, Sears & Pantley (2002) suggest that there is reciprocity to this learning process and state, "Our children learn how to respect though our efforts to know their needs and respect them." If we model compassion, respect, and consideration, we can develop the bonds that facilitate our role as a parent in "tutoring and playing with our children" that will continue to build our relationships as they "grow and develop," (Shiota et al., 2004).

Being well-rounded and seeking balance in our lives shows our children how to seek harmony and interest in theirs. While we don't want to spread ourselves too thin, it's important to model diversity and good time management. By wearing many hats and juggling a variety of activities, we can encourage a curiosity about life in our children. Albert Einstein once said, "I have no special talents. I am only passionately curious."

As an effective role model, we can challenge ourselves to get beyond our comfort zones so our children can learn not to pigeon-hole themselves in order to be successful. Our children's natural curiosity has been linked to the development of "personality traits," as suggested by Saliva (2006), who indicates that this characteristic is formed within a "positive emotional-motivation system."

Confidence does not mean being boastful, arrogant, or conceited. It emanates a sense of pride in who we are and defines the direction of our lives. We can model being proud of the person we have become and of our dreams for the future. It may have been a long and bumpy journey, and we may have taken many divergent paths, but, it is our obligation to celebrate the lessons we have learned along the way.

The stories of our lives model personal strength, character, and integrity that define our sense of accomplishment. Goleman (1997) indicates that self-confidence is linked to our success and gives us "the strength to make tough decisions" and "exudes charisma." The concepts of parental bravery can help us model an apprehension for keeping our heads held high in times of adversity. It is the courage needed to make tough choices in riding out the stormy seas of life.

The characteristics of positive role models involve the same dynamics that can help us in *becoming better parents*. These driven character traits have been divided into six different "universal core virtues and strengths," (Seligman, 2002). He further states that it is our ability to use our own "signature strengths every day to produce authentic happiness and abundant gratification."

It seems that by flexing these mental muscles, we can produce the internal characteristics that will lead to our own success. "Good character is a core assumption" of what Seligman (2002) calls "positive psychology," and defines this as a combination of both our "adaptive characteristics and static personalities." These virtues and strengths are further expanded on below:

- *Wisdom and knowledge:* To be positive role models, we have to acquire knowledge and possess the wisdom to apply it. In becoming parental students, we need to have the desire to overcome our ignorance by learning the tools acquired through knowledge and seeking the wisdom that lies within. Kekes (1983) states, "Whereas intellectual *knowledge* is about the discovery of new truths, *wisdom* is about rediscovery of the significance and meaning of old truths."

- *Courage:* Being courageous is associated with a number of "character traits, states of mind, and social forces," (Hannah, Sweeney & Lester, 2007). There are many definitions of courage that emphasize a connection between "the notion of persistence in the presence of perceived threat," (Norton & Weiss, 2009). This concept of courage affirms what General Bradley once said, "Bravery is the capacity to perform properly even when scared half to death."

- *Love and humanity:* These characteristics are defined differently than the aspects of parental love discussed before, and include the personal traits such as "kindness, patience, forgiveness, courtesy, humility, generosity, and honesty," (Chapman, 2008). These are often spoken within a social context that is represented by what he calls "the personal languages of love" that include "words of affirmation, quality time, receiving gifts, acts of service, and physical touch."

- *Justice:* A character virtue that includes the melding of both traits and actions within their social context. This virtue represents a "moral maturity," as suggested by Russell (2009), that resembles a systems perspective of wholeness. It incorporates the mental processes of values and judgments, the social constructs of equality and fairness, and the regulation of our social character, including morality, altruism, benevolence, collaboration, and cooperation.

- *Temperance:* This virtue is defined by *Webster's* as "moderation in action, thought, or feeling; restraint." Historically considered a core value that can be seen consistently across time and cultures, it is the ability to control our own thoughts, feelings, and behaviors, and is generally defined by other traits that include chastity, modesty, humility, prudence, self-regulation, forgiveness, and mercy.

- *Spirituality and transcendence:* This spiritual dimension of our character is broken down into three aspects of our personality that include "self-forgetfulness, transpersonal identification, and spiritual acceptance," (Piedmont, 2005). He points out that this form of self-concept is derived from our "feelings of mystical participation, religious faith, and unconditional equanimity and patience." These aspects of our true connectedness with the universe are about altruism, meaning, and wholeness.

The Dalai Lama states that the pathways to peace and harmony lie within the qualities of the human spirit and include "patience, tolerance, and forgiveness," (Erricker & Erricker, 2001). In exercising free will and striving to practice these principals, we can become better parents and experience the gifts of serenity, tranquility, and harmony. However, if we allow control to dictate our thoughts, feelings, and behaviors, we can generate unrealistic expectations that will not only ruin just your parental peace of mind; it may also ruin your ability to act firmly and decisively with your kids," (Guarendi & Guarendi, 1985).

These models act as character references, which become part of our parental resumés, and provide us with the effective foundation for personal change. By adopting a process of progression rather than perfection we can lead our children by example. We are role models for our children. What we model is determined by how we exercise our choice and free will.

Give it another try

"Energy and persistence conquer all things."
-Benjamin Franklin

'Parenting persistence' is our ability to rise above the situations and circumstances we face as parents and to never say 'quit.' It requires the staying power, effort, and internal resolve to say that no matter how bad things get we can find a way to work it out. We can easily lose this internal battle as we start to look for an easy way out or just give up altogether. With all the stressors we face, it's amazing that parents can muster up the courage, capacity, and energy to grow our relationships with our children.

Thomas Palmer said, "If at first you don't succeed, try, try again," and this is an effective refrain that can be used by parents to support our efforts in creating positive change within the relationships with our children. Persistence and consistency are more than just behavioral reinforcement strategies and can be used to expand the level of influence we have in our children's lives. This influence, through our persistent efforts to connect with our children, is not about control, coercion, or manipulation; it's a way for us to model, teach, and display the value of never giving up.

Personal perseverance, determination, and dedication are characteristics which distinguish between those parents who are able to accomplish great things in their relationships with their children, and those who can only hope. Having a 'never give up' attitude means more than blindly trudging ahead; it means we are building our personal resiliency by becoming more open, willing, and agile in adapting to change.

"Good parents never give up, because to do so would be to give up responsibility and appear to abandon caring," (Pickhardt, 2004). Pickhardt says it is our "parental pursuit" that determines the outcomes in dealing with the day-in, day-out, struggles of parenting, and which makes a lasting impression on our children.

Never giving up is not about never giving in, and means we can become more imaginative and resourceful in finding ways to work harder and smarter in *becoming a better parent*. This 'get it done' attitude can be modeled for our children though our effort, innovation, and reason.

This evolved work ethic is based on our abilities as parents to recognize that our success is directly related to our determination and resourcefulness in using what we have in the best way we can. Parenting is hard work and, without our endless attempts in making a difference in our children's lives, we can fall short of our goals.

Parenting is also challenging and, without our intuitive perspectives to lead the way, we can end up becoming lost on the journey. Parents need to work harder and smarter to overcome parental traps and stay clear of the unhelpful myths we have created about parenting.

'Never' and 'always' are words that can become absolute ways of thinking that can become mindsets and easily lead us back into a parental trap. This type of 'all-or-none,' and 'black-and-white' thinking can be linked to more serious character flaws and they inevitably head us, as parents, into "win-lose or lose-lose power struggles" and coping strategies with our children, (Gordon, 2000). These types of extreme-thinking errors can lead to extreme behaviors and interfere with our ability to achieve a sense of balance. It is important that we separate these uncompromising attitudes of control from the industrious attitudes and actions of change. The paradox that exists within 'never' and 'always' is how we apply the meaning in our lives. Simply put, we never have to say 'never' and can always find a way.

IX. Parent, Heal Thyself

"It is the false shame of fools to try to conceal wounds that have not healed."

-Horace

In talking with families over the years, I have come to the realization that sometimes parents have a hard time taking care of themselves. From the simplest forms of self-care and problem solving, to the more profound psychological and emotional disorders, we, as parents, often seem to have a reluctance to take care of ourselves first.

Left unchecked, these deficits can be reflected onto our children. In other words, "A man reaps what he sows." (Galatians 6:7) If we are unable to sow the seeds of self-care and heal the emotional, psychological, and mental wounds from our past, we can become infected carriers of the parent disease and pass it on to our children. On the other hand, if we are able to take care of ourselves, we can reap the multigenerational grace of healing, and come to know that "he who sows virtue reaps honor," (Leonardo da Vinci).

The bitter fruits we bear from our pasts are deeply rooted in our dysfunctional family trees and placed on the table of life as a feast for our children. Taking care of ourselves creates a new menu that is no longer predestined to repeat the failed recipes of the past. Breaking free form theese negative familial patterns gives us a way to set a new course for our children so that they no longer have to bear these mutigenerational burdens

This is not to say that all bad parents have bad children or all good parents have good children, as there are always exceptions. There are children who grow up with horrific circumstances that are able to overcome and transform these experiences and become successful. Conversely, there are other children who grow up in loving, caring, and nurturing homes, that can have serious problems.

Choice and free will are the exceptions that give us the ability to rise above these oppressive confines in effectively finding ways to re-parent ourselves. Research shows that the greater our unresolved problems are, the "greater difficulties for parents in effectively meeting the needs of their children," (Velleman, 2004). The strongest social and psychological research can only account for correlations that are in the eightieth percentile; so if we can get through the school of parenting with a 'B' average, then we are on our way to becoming exceptional parents.

Whatever unresolved problems we may have, they are reflected as unhealthy patterns in our children's lives. We need to take the necessary steps to find a way to take better care of ourselves, or we might be setting the stage for our children's failure. Our greatest gift is the gift of ourselves. This cannot be given unless we can find a way to appreciate the gift itself. It is only by valuing, honoring, and cherishing this gift through the process of self-care, that we can hope it will be accepted.

We can't possibly expect to pass on the ideas of self-care if we don't know how to do it ourselves. Engle (2006) suggests that in order to take care of ourselves, we need to reunite with our inner self so we can raise "self-esteem" and overcome "self-blame, self-hatred, and self-destructiveness" that interfere with our ability to parent effectively. We need to remember that "practicing self-care is not the same as being selfish!" (Bluestein, 1997).

Finding effective ways to deal with our own emotional, psychological, and physical well-being is a difficult but necessary task for parents. We need effective coping mechanisms, problem solving skills, self-care strategies, and the ability to heal from within, if we want to build more healthy relationships with our children.

Parents often imply that they want to 'fix' their child when they bring them into therapy for the first time. The therapy process soon reveals that some of these parents had a number of unresolved issues, themselves, that were being negatively projected onto their children. The challenge in working with these families is that these parents are often not ready to help themselves, their children, or the relationship by accepting their own problems.

From serious dysfunctional parental patterns to over-indulgent parents, this level of "parental denial" is remarkable. Often used to deal with their own parental guilt, this form of denial, as defined by Miller (1994), is the parent's state of readiness in "dealing with a problem or its implications." This suggests that we must be ready and motivated to accept our own problems so that we can make changes toward *becoming a better parent.*

The oxygen mask rule

"The older I get, the more wisdom I find in the ancient rule of taking first things first—a process which often reduces the most complex human problems to manageable proportions."
-Dwight D. Eisenhower

Preflight routines have flight attendants reminding parents that if the airplane cabin loses pressure, you should apply your oxygen mask first, and then your child's. This 'oxygen mask rule' seems obvious because a parent without oxygen is likely to pass out before getting their child's mask in place. The same principle holds true for parenting; if we don't take care of ourselves first, we will make matters worse and will be unable to attend to our children's needs.

Our natural response, as a parent, is to take care of our children first, sometimes denying ourselves the means to effectively address our children's needs. Our problems in life can create stressful states, such oxygen deprivation, and can undermine our capacity to help our children. So, in times of stress, we need to remember to get our oxygen mask on first-- by taking the time to stop, take a deep breath, and responding from the heart. Taking care of ourselves is the gift of self that cannot be given if we don't possess it first.

Most parental experts, if such things exist, would agree that parents need to take care of themselves first. Like the 'oxygen mask rule,' it is an important step in finding a way to heal from within. Parents often find themselves overwhelmed with parenting and end up feeling as if they have nothing left for their children.

If we are unable to rise to the challenge, we can experience dissatisfaction, burnout, and depression. Learning how to make the most of our lives and taking care of ourselves, allows us to better care for our children. Barkley (2000) points out that "failing to take time to renew yourself leaves you increasingly less to give your child." Coping with the demands of parenting is not easy as we look for ways to balance the challenges we face in everyday life.

There is an old cliché that states 'first things first,' and for us, as parents, that means that we have to take care of ourselves if we want to develop respect within our relationships with our children. It is commonly understood that respecting others is impossible until we learn to respect ourselves. Parents that lack self-respect are mistakenly too focused on helping their children develop self-respect and overlook taking care of their own needs.

Self-kindness, self-care, and self-respect are powerful, intricately interrelated ways of relearning to reconnect with ourselves, our children, and the world around us. They help to counter the negative shame-based messages associated with our views about life that have been adopted as ways to minimize the importance of our own needs. This idea of self-sacrifice is an empty vessel in a world of scarcity, as we cannot truly sacrifice what we do not honor or value.

Interpersonal effectiveness skills, known as "self-respect effectiveness" (Linehan, 1993), emphasizes that we must ask for what we want and need while respecting our values and beliefs. Valuing ourselves builds self-esteem and self-worth, and means we can honor who we are and how we think, feel, and act. Linehan states that "self-care and self-respect go hand-in-hand and support our well-being."

Respect is earned, not given, and if we don't trust, we become insecure and unbalanced. By valuing who we are and taking care of ourselves, we can learn personal respect and start to believe that we are good, worthwhile, and deserve the respect of others. We must remain mindful that if we respect and value ourselves, we will treat others with respect. Bluestein (1997) suggests that modeling self-care "reduces the chances for you to feel resentful or disempowered in your relationships and enhances the quality of love and care you can give to others."

Teaching our children to fish

"Give me a fish and I eat for a day. Teach me to fish and I eat for a lifetime."
-Chinese Proverb

Effective problem solving strategies have been around for a long time and support our efforts to manage the complexity of our lives. Solving problems is a process rather than an event, and usually involves a number of steps that are taken to assure positive outcomes. These can be seen as parts of a larger system that include the individual and group dynamics that define and shape how we perceive problems.

Problem solving is considered to be one of the most complex of all intellectual functions. It has been defined as a "higher-order cognitive process that requires the modulation and control of more routine or fundamental skills," (Goldstein & Levin, 1987). Although there have been many problem solving models, they all share a number of common elements that include, but are not limited to, the following:

- *Problem identification* is the process that focuses on gaining an understanding of the scope and causes of a problem.

- *Problem acceptance* means taking responsibility, experience, and owning the problem so we can do something about it.

- *Identifying desired outcomes* is about setting and establishing measurable goals and objectives for changing the problem.

- *Identifying barriers* involves looking at the specific gaps and obstacles between the problem and what we want.

- *Developing a plan* is the process that will take us from the problem to where we want to be, and outline how we get there.

- *Facilitating change* is acquiring the resources, support, and assistance we need to implement and sustain the changes we want.

- *Taking action* is about knowing what we want, doing something to make it happen, and taking the steps to get it done.

- *Using feedback* is a process in comparing where we came from and where wanted to be; always asking, "Are we there yet?

Myers (1992) identified three general problem solving strategies. One is an "algorithm" that follows a step-by-step procedure. Another is a "heuristic" method that follows a general rule-of-thumb strategy. The last is an "insight" orientation that is an underlying mental process that is often outside of our awareness. Problem solving processes resemble the communication process, as shown in the following flow chart.

The components of this system require continuous feedback loops that occur on many levels, to achieve the desired outcomes. In other words, we need a way to evaluate whether or not what we are doing is really working. Effective problem solving relies on the application of two simple axioms; 'if it ain't broke don't fix it,' and 'keep it simple.'

It's imperative that we, as parents, develop an internal problem solving method to effectively address the situations and circumstances we face so we can start to feel a sense of accomplishment in our attempts to make decisions and deal with problems. This problem solving process reminds us that although parenting isn't easy, it can be simplified by eliminating common pitfalls, as outlined by Ashcraft (1994), that include the following:

- *Functional fixedness:* (Inflexibility) is a tendency to solve problems in only usual and customary ways.
  When the ways we deal with things become familiar and routine, they become fixed habits that are applied to every situation.

- *Confirmation bias:* (Stubbornness) is a driving force that supports our own way of thinking. It is an inclination to seek and use data to strengthen our own preconceived notions, while ignoring additional information that might help in solving problems.

- *Negative set:* (Stereotyping) is an approach bias that is based on how we overgeneralize things. This can lead to us holding on to a one-size-fits-all approach and develops a state-dependent process that minimizes change.

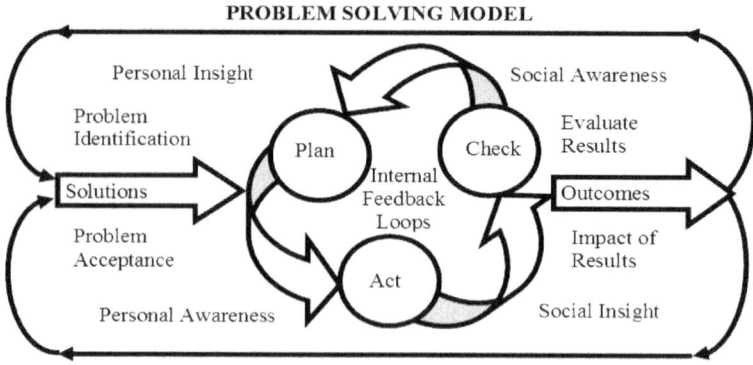

Diagram 8

The dynamics of problem solving listed in the PAC (Plan, Act, Check) model shown before, are determined by our ability to stay calm and centered within our own thoughts, feelings, and behaviors. Staying grounded in the here and now will allow us to recognize, accept, act, and check the problems and solutions as they arise.

Our ability to project beyond the current limitations can provide infinite opportunities that otherwise would remain hidden. If we become preoccupied with the drama of the problems we face, our full attention is diverted away from the tasks at hand. In addition to the problem solving strategies that have been developed over the years, there have been numerous coping dynamics that outline common practical steps we all can take to deal with the situations more effectively. These include the following:

- Stay objective, impartial, non-reactive to problems, and visualize alternatives.

- Resist power struggles, accept problems, and access resources.

- Don't be afraid to mix things up, take risks, and experiment.

- Be creative and playful, try novel approaches, and learn from your mistakes.

- Open up to all possibilities, acknowledge progress, and practice patience.

- Focus on how to make a difference, create dialogues, and stay flexible in the process.

- Know that all things serve a purpose and work together to create wonder.

The challenges we face in life are our greatest teachers and provide us the strength we need to grow and learn. Stay positive, be gentle with yourself, and focus on your strengths rather than the obstacles. Let go of the control and forgive yourself and others so you can feel the personal power to overcome difficulties.

Modeling effective problem solving strategies can help our children understand this process and prevents us from making problems worse. In addition to adopting effective problem solving strategies, we need to model and communicate these with our children. These problem-solving mechanisms do not exist in a vacuum, and our thoughts, feelings, and actions all contribute to this complex social system of change.

These are the "basic components of a resilient mind," (Brooks & Goldstein, 2001). They point out that "parents have countless opportunities to engage their children in problem solving and decision making opportunities that reinforce a sense of control and mastery."

Bags fly free

> *"The only real obstacle in your path to a fulfilling life is you, and that can be a considerable obstacle because you carry the baggage of insecurities and past experience."*
>
> -Les Brown

Some parents have become so lost on their journey of life that they have become momentarily unable to make good decisions, build healthy relationships, or find the personal power within themselves to create a successful balance in their lives. However, this does not have to be a permanent condition and parents can find a way out of the madness within their own minds.

These parents often need professional and supportive help to break free from the chains that bind them; often needing to overcome their own mental illness or substance use disorder. Parents can become lost within the pain from the emotional scars and residue carried by these problems and end up suffering needlessly because they are reluctant to seek help.

Someone once asked me to define 'mental illness' and I gave them my best *Diagnostic and Statistics Manual* criterion-based response. I felt as if this texbook answer lacked the wisdom needed to truly convey the horrific costs associated with these problems.

I eventually came to a more universal perspective of the problem, gathered from the shared stories of those who suffered from these problems: A hopeless sense that, no matter what the cause, what they did, or what they had to endure, they were unable to find a way out.

Hatfield & Lefley (1993) point out that "we ignore the fact that they are the insiders in the experience of mental illness and we are the outsiders." The one thing they all seemed to have in common, whether they had a psychiatric, substance, or personality disorder, was a sense of feeling totally lost.

Becoming A Better Parent

Parents who have lost their way are at times unable to recognize or admit that they need help and end up making the problems worse. They have pushed away, repressed, or protected the problems for so long that they become unaware of the devastation that is being created all around them.

Parents who are unable to maintain their recovery and are reluctant to find a way to heal from within, can create additional problems in parenting our children that include "inconsistency, unpredictability, arbitrariness, and chaos," (Whitefield, 1987). He indicates that these are often a result of "unfinished business" and can lead to "confusion, emptiness, and unhappiness." He suggests that parents need to "heal the child within" by a process of discovery, identification, experience, working through our "core issues," becoming our "real self," and getting our needs met in a safe and supportive way.

Our ability to cope with problems and our beliefs about our abilities to solve problems has been attributed to "self-appraisal and our psychological health," (Heppner & Lee, 2002). These strength-based resiliency factors of recovery are essential for helping individuals feel a sense of empowerment and make the changes needed to heal. I have always been fascinated by individual exceptions to our understanding of human nature.

How is it that some people can overcome insurmountable odds to achieve success while others, who are provided every opportunity, fail? These exceptions contain allusive variables and unaccounted for variations that are always changing within a system that cannot be controlled, only understood. These unique human conditions are comprised of our personal 'fields of dreams,' where all possibilities exist and true change can take place.

The personal narratives of these serious problems can be turned to success stories and are reflected by those individuals throughout human history that have made a positive impact by beating back their own inner demons. They contain the hope for those parents who continue to suffer from these serious problems.

These remarkable individuals are able to find their way out and share a common set of personal recovery steps that create stability and empower change. Although there are many different treatment approaches, the following are some of the basic standardized practices that can support parents in their recovery from serious psychiatric, personality, or substance disorders:

- *Accept the illness* and don't let it rule or run your life. You are much more than your illness, disorder, or disease, so take the opportunity to learn from it. By becoming a student of your diagnosis, symptoms, and treatment, you can take an active role in taking the steps needed in the recovery process. Linhorst (2006) states that by focusing on a "strengths and recovery perspective," individuals can overcome the stigmas and "self-perceptions of incompetence" and get the help they need.

- *Seek evidence-based treatments* that have been shown to work and are supported by outcome-oriented research. These are preferred treatment practices that provide significant evidence of effectiveness. Hayes (2008) points out that a "gap exists between research and practice," indicating that all treatment is not alike and some treatments are more effective than others. Evidence also suggests that "bonding with providers, provider competence/knowledge, and cultural/religious competence" (Bacon, et. all, 2004), is critical for your treatment outcomes so find someone that you like, connect with, and think will work.

- *Take an active role in your recovery* and be proactive in following your treatment recommendations. Ask questions, track your progress, participate in your treatment, and don't quit when it gets difficult. Sawyer (2005) reports that "although there is not a cure for severe mental illness, taking control of your recovery and living a healthier life is a reality." Being an active participant builds trust in treatment.

- *Work with your treatment providers* and develop a collaborative treatment plan that can help you set goals, stabilize symptoms, and build self-esteem. Don't be afraid to ask for help and stay with it. Davis (2008) and her colleagues suggest that it is important for both the treatment provider and patient to "have an active role in sharing information and developing an overall plan" as to empower consumers in their own treatment.

- *Advocate for yourself* you know yourself best and have the right to choose what course of treatment you are willing take. Consumer advocates and peer support specialists can assist you in this process. Dixon (1994) and others have indicated that "consumer advocates have made significant and valuable contributions" to the treatment process in working with, and advocating for, clients within clinical settings.

- *Develop effective coping strategies* and learn how to regulate your thoughts, feelings, and behaviors effectively. Finding effective ways to cope can reinforce new healthy habits, challenge negative thinking, and empower positive emotional experiences. Hatfield and Lefley (1993) suggest an "active-coping" strategy and support system to more effectively deal with both situational-based and emotional-based stressors.

- *Take it one step at a time* and learn to relax. Recovery can be a lifelong process, so be gentle on yourself and learn how to slow down the process. Acknowledge treatment progress and celebrate small successes. "Recovery does not refer to an end product or result. It does not mean that one is 'cured,' nor does it mean that one is simply stabilized or maintained in the community," (Deegan, 1996).

- *Find the support you need* and develop a positive support network. Use the resources that are available from family, friends, and peer support. Learn how to create power, control, and influence, by taking an active role in the recovery process so you can feel as if you are making a difference. Newton (1994) suggests "much of the support needed by people vulnerable to mental illness is best provided by 'natural' support networks, the community, and lay volunteers."

- *Find ways to deal with setbacks* and learn how to recognize your relapse triggers. Symptoms can reoccur, so set up a recovery plan to assist you in planning and preparing for these learning opportunities. Make sure to set up a "relapse prevention plan" so you can develop "procedures for identifying and interrupting the relapse process," (Spaulding et al., 2003). Recovery is a proces, not a cure, and you can regain the ability to manage the symptoms of your mental illness more effectively.

Becoming A Better Parent

Parents that suffer from these severe disorders are not incapable of becoming better parents and can find their way on this journey of recovery. Ackerson (2003) states that "these parents face great barriers in trying to demonstrate their parental fitness without the necessary supports and services they need to become competent parents."

What is often overlooked is the personal empowerment that parents with a mental illness are able to acquire through the process of their own recovery. This is a strength that can be used to build their relationships with their children and adds to the rich diversity that is parenting. However, Stanley et al., (2003) pointed out that "positive outcomes for parents with mental health problems, and their children, are rarely noted."

I have had the privilege of working with these parents and see the tremendous positive influence they are able to co-create with their children. Individuals with a mental illness can uncover their full potential as parents through their own road to recovery process. Parents need a more comprehensive "range of services essential to assist them with their mental illness in managing daily parental demands," (Blanch et al., 1994).

Parents who are unable to take the necessary steps to support their own recovery process can suffer tragic parenting outcomes. Sacket's research (1994) indicates that mental illness is the number one cause for having parental rights terminated. I have also worked with these parents, children, and families, and witnessed the sorrow of these heartbreaking losses. Shattered are their dreams that have faded away into the abyss of their own mind.

Unfortunately, these losses are felt in the deepest places in our hearts. They are the tears shed for those lost individuals that have been unable to find a way out. It is a grief shed for lost people whose lives have been torn apart by mental illness or substance abuse. Barton and her colleagues (2009) have shown that, if left untreated, "parental mental illness may affect children in a number of ways, including effects on all aspects of development, mental health, and increased vulnerability to abuse and neglect."

Parenting Yourself

"In every adult there lurks a child—an eternal child; something that is always becoming, is never completed, and calls for unceasing care, attention, and education."

-Carl Jung

"Reparenting" is a process of internal healing that is based on our ability to overcome the unmet needs from our past and find more effective self-care strategies for today. Schiff (1977) was one of the first to coin the term, and her treatment, through re-parenting clients considered "incurable," remains highly debated.

Her immersed experiential approach in taking the role of parent for these patients was considered radical and excessive. The notion of overcoming our own internalized pathological patterns from the past, however, remains a major component of most modern therapeutic approaches to healing. Ideas can be a powerful force of change; how we use these ideas determines the course and direction for our outcomes.

Our ideas about reparenting, like those of parenting, are more about the 'hows' than the 'whys' of their use. The whys of reparenting and healing from our past are still viable ways to empower healthy personal change from within.

Re-parenting is strongly tied to the theories of "transactional analysis," (Berne, 1996). Berne designed this approach as a "curative" therapeutic process that focused on re-orienting our internal "scripts," languages, and processes into healthier patterns. The most basic proponents of this theory are directed at resolving the conflicts within our personal narratives that are created within the "ego states of the Parent, Child, and Adult," and dictate the "Games People Play."

Becoming A Better Parent

These unhealthy transactional patterns within relationships are rooted in the unresolved issues from our past and can cause discomfort and suffering. This theory proposed that healing takes place within mastering "five conceptual clusters" in our lives that are related to social reinforcement, personal encouragement, individual narratives and habits, "ego states and transactions," and cognitive-behavioral change.

Modern reparenting approaches focused on coming to terms with our own unresolved issues from the past by parenting ourselves in the here and now. This empowering process is based on our own readiness to deal with the internalized perceptions we have created about ourselves, others, and the world around us.

By recognizing the challenges we all face in overcoming and coming to terms with our past, we can form new healthy mindsets and change our attitudes, judgments, values, beliefs, and motivations in *becoming a better parent* for ourselves and our children.

This healing process reframes our transfixed illusions from the past. It is not about making excuses for ourselves or blaming someone else, it's about developing new perceptual points of reference for learning to parent and take care of ourselves so we recognize the value of what have to offer. "In many ways, this is parenting yourself from the inside out," (Hartzell & Siegel, 2003).

Our mental constructs about parenting may have taken many forms and can be attributed to many different experiences in life. They may be based on past traumas created by abuse or neglect, or they may be attached to the normal challenges we all face in growing up. They can be related to situational difficulties or genetic predispositions and can be either self-induced or imposed by others.

The problem remains that if we continue to internalize and personalize these negative unhealthy patterns, they can become destructive remnants that can haunt us into our adult lives. These programmed self-defeating doctrines may interfere with our abilities to set healthy boundaries, make effective choices, and build significance in the relationships with our children.

By becoming an effective self-parent, we can let go of the shame and control, support and nurture the child within, and allow the adult we are to heal, grow, and learn.

Keep on keepin' on

"I do the very best I know how, the very best I can, and I mean to keep on doing so until the end."
-Abraham Lincoln

Once you stop growing, you start dying. Learning how to embrace this uncertainty and dealing with the knowledge of our own mortality can be the hardest lesson in life. It requires healing mindsets that are focused on process, discovery, and relationships in all their forms. Parents must recognize that there are no perfectly straight, clear, or certain paths that we all can take in living our lives.

The divergent paths we take are constantly changing and our very existence is dependent upon our continual growth in learning how to manage our lives. Being willing, open, and flexible to learning, change, and growth, is crucial to our physical, emotional, psychological, social, and spiritual selves.

Self-sustenance in life requires that we become autonomous in our efforts to feed, nurture, and support all areas of growth on our own. When we can break free from our efforts to control we can become more interdependent and "no longer need to rely others as a source of solace or support," (Cohler & Paul 2002).

We can start asking ourselves every day, "What are we going to do today in each area, to grow, learn, and change?" This question can be used to develop a balanced approach so we can set out with a plan, purpose, and meaning in the daily journeys of living our lives.

Becoming A Better Parent

None of us have all the answers and "your job is to hang in there and be the best parent you can be," (Parankimalil, 2009). He states that "raising children is not for the faint-hearted. It's a wild, exciting, and often chaotic adventure! So, hang in there, and keep on keeping on!" We can make the most of every opportunity we are given with our children if we 'just hang in there.'

We all make mistakes, so be forgiving, compassionate, and gentle with yourself, so you can make adjustments in managing your job as a parent. By focusing on all the areas in our lives, we can prioritize and focus our attention on where it's needed. Rather than trying to address everything at once, we can develop a sense of balance in our lives that will allow us the flexibility to stay somewhere in between becoming overwhelmed and being indifferent.

Bornstein (2003) states that "parenting is a job whose primary object of attention and action is the child." I would contest this point by saying that parenting is a job whose primary object of attention and action is the parent. The parent-child relationship is such that, without first *becoming a better parent*, we can hardly expect to do an effective job of parenting our children.

Without a better job description for being a parent, we are left with an incomplete view of parenting, where the work we do becomes a one-way, dead-end street. Managing our own job description can define our role as a parent more accurately so we can maintain healthy boundaries for the working relationships we have with our children.

Parenting is the best job you will ever have, so learn from it, have fun with it, love it with all your heart, and remember to make your job 'child's play.' "Defining your role as parent is your job" and is a "system of beliefs about what being a parent means to you and understanding your position in relation to your child," (Chidekel, 2002).

X. The Big Blue Marble

Together is a word that holds tomorrow in its hand, tomorrow's just another day to get together, and... Get closer, closer, closer..."

-Lyrics from "The Big Blue Marble"

Our life on this big blue marble, as shown by the photographs originally taken from Apollo 17, has allowed us "for the first time in history, to see ourselves as a single entity" and "a part of a global village," (Gaudelli, 2003).

Providing a new vision of this connected future can pave the way for us to see within while at the same time staying focused on the big picture. By letting go of our old parental patterns, we can make a difference in the relationships with our children so we can start to build a future for generations to come. We can then expand our parental horizons and start to make this world a better place for all of us, as we become closer.

Our advancements, over the last century, continue to make our world more connected, and we are starting to recognize that what affects one of us, affects us all. There is no longer any room for misperceptions that are based on prejudice, injustice, discrimination, or intolerance, as our beliefs, attitudes, judgments, values, and motivations affect how we think, feel, and act; and what we do today, will touch those that are yet to come

Becoming A Better Parent

To find a way for parents to keep pace with these changes can be challenging, but not impossible. The difficulty lies in trying to create new parenting prototypes for our ever-changing world. "Today, after more than a century of electric technology, we have extended our central nervous system, itself, in a global embrace, abolishing both space and time as far as our planet is concerned," (McLuhan, 1964).

We can ill-afford to hold onto outdated mindsets that limit our abilities to grow and connect with the world around us. This type of community consciousness can then become the cornerstone for our evolving parenting perceptions. Jung (1969) suggested that "there exists a second psychic system of a collective, universal, and impersonal nature, which is identical in all individuals." He called this the "collective unconscious" that can form our evolving views about parenting "archetypes" and can be used to symbolize the universal journey in *becoming a better parent.*

I had a mentor once tell me, "There are no mistakes, except for the ones we don't learn from." I now see that the mistakes that we don't learn from are often the ones we can't see, and the ones we can't see continue to haunt us throughout our lives. Finding the answers to these mistakes is never easy and our inner journey often only reveals more questions. The circular logic of the Tao, like Socratic questioning, provides us a way to see the world of parenting with 'soft eyes.'

Dyer's (2007) description of the Tao discusses how to surrender the ego's control that is "driven by power, judgment, fear, doubt, shame, guilt, and any other energy that clouds the light that is within the deepest heart of every human." He suggests that, through a process of "complete surrender," we can change our "old ways of thinking" by being compassionate, not explaining or defending our positions, considering all perspectives, and being open to new understandings. This process of living the "Great Way" is a "valuable resource for achieving a way of life that guarantees integrity, joy, peace, and balance," (Dyer, 2007).

Our big blue marble is getting smaller every day as technology simultaneously brings us closer together and expands our understanding of everything we know. This is not to say that the future is without challenges, as discussed by Sproat (2010), who states that we need "wisdom to ensure that the use of technologies does not endanger the future of human history."

We must be willing to embrace these changes as we move forward on our journey as parents. No longer needing to be driven by the archaic structures of scarcity, greed, control, and envy, we can break free from the shame that binds us as we began to open our eyes to the perceptual traps of parenting. The ever-expanding diversity within the realities of the parent-child system is based on the development of relationships, and can become inclusive and connected.

Parenting structures are rapidly being altered by our views of generational change. Our "success is based on our ability to overcome these new challenges, and our cultural competencies play a significant role in getting ahead of this generational curve," (Brinckerhoff, 2010).

It is only through our openness that we can move towards acceptance of our ever-changing expansive roles as parents and get beyond the stigmas of parenting that have been created in the past. As Pryor (2004) states, what matters is that "unconditional love and respect, monitoring and boundary setting, and fostering good development, apply across all settings."

Recognition and respect for diversity of settings in which they are applied is essential if we are to socialize our children as well-functioning adults in a rapidly changing world." Pryor seems to suggest that we need to move beyond our limiting notions of what make up a family, and focus on empowering the connectedness of the relationships that exist.

Human communities are becoming connected at every level and until we are able to put aside our prejudicial viewpoints, we are destined to repeat our parental history, as opposed to learning from our mistakes. By seeing a brighter future for tomorrow, we can share a vision with our children to create effective change.

Becoming A Better Parent

This is not accomplished through sweeping social change and public policy, but by the internal changes that start with us each 'thinking globally and acting locally.' Senge & Sterman (1990) state that our "problem lies, in part, with failing to recognize the importance of prevailing mental models.

New strategies are the outgrowth of new world views." It is being whole within the whole that we can make a significant difference in our roles as parents. By looking within, around, and ahead, we can facilitate change and build the relationships with our children, others, and the world around us. It is our relationship to all things that connects, binds, and holds the parent-child system together and generates the creative 'grassroots' power within, to change the world that we live in.

Lessons from the playground

"The true object of all human life is play. Earth is a task garden; heaven is a playground."
- G. K. Chesterton

Louis (2010) looks at the playground as a source of inspiration in the lessons we can learn from children in that "every new person you meet is a potential new friend; tools don't have to be used as everyone uses them; there are no boundaries, only obstacles; life is simple; and, failing is not failure."

Louis (2010) suggests that by tapping into our youthful spirit and showing genuine interest in meeting new people, developing an innovative attitude, embracing the possibilities of change, keeping things simply honest, and not being afraid to fail, allows us all the ability to make the most of every situation. This idea is reflected best by the last stanza from the poem "The Playground of Life," by Khalil Gibran:

This is life.

Robert Lang

Portrayed on the stage for ages;
Recorded earthly for centuries;
Lived in strangeness for years;
Sung as a hymn for days;
Exalted but for an hour, but the
Hour is treasured by Eternity as a jewel.

The playgrounds of parenting provide us a way to connect with our children on a level we never thought possible. Whatever form it takes, from reading a story to playing a video game, getting actively involved in the imaginary playgrounds of our children's minds reawakens our own inner child so we can find a common place in relating to our children. As distant as it might seem, the hopes and dreams of our childhood imaginations are only a thought away.

Reconnecting with the wonderment of our own youthful spirit through the playgrounds of parenting can reinforce the contagion effect within the relationships we have with our children. As parents, we can structure these experiences so we can "imagine how different the world would be if people were taught from the first days of life that the sharing they do on the playground would also serve them well in creating a peaceful world," (Mayer, 2002).

Fulghum (2004) discusses these *elementary* principles that are played out on the kindergarten playgrounds all over the world every day. It is a simple wisdom that breaks down social complexities into personal snippets of truth. He states that "it's hard to explain the cost and consequences of environmental pollution and destruction to a 6-year-old. But, we are paying a desperate price even now, because adults did not heed the instructions of kindergarten. Clean up your own mess; put things back where you found them; don't take what's not yours."

It seems we have not taken advantage of these learning opportunities from the playgrounds of our youth. If we can only find a way to reconnect, heal, and overcome these personal barriers, we can start to heal the scars and transform the world we live in. Chickering & Nuckols (1998) refer to the cliché "time heals all wounds" and indicate that "with these wounds come scars." They go on to state that "what's important is whether the scars create resentment and bitterness or lead to reflection and wisdom." It is our free will and choice that determines how these scars will be used to heal the suffering we all experience as parents.

The parent-child system

"How can children credit the assertions of parents, which their own eyes show them to be false? Few parents act in such a manner as much to enforce their maxims by the credit of their lives."

-Samuel Johnson

The new paradigm we are creating is that of the parent-child system. Developed out our evolving understanding of the dynamic, nonlinear, and self-organizing nature of complex social systems, we are now equipped with a means by which we can make sense out of the intricate road map of parenting. Laszlo (1972) and Sucharov (1994) discuss how any living system is part of a hierarchy. Each system contains subsystems, or elements, that constitute the whole. Two or more systems interacting cooperatively form a supra-system.

Our views of the parent, child, and their relationship are starting to take shape as we focus on conceptualizing the "emergent order and complexity; how structure and patterns arise from the cooperation of many individual parts." Based on the "dynamic systems theory" (Thelen & Smith, 1994), our new parenting paradigm can take into account all the "messy, fluid, context-sensitive" that is the parent child system.

Focus on the child's development under a system framework highlights the context-dependent nature of the child's self-regulatory processes (Thelen & Smith, 1994). They have drawn significance to the influences of these caregiving systems. This more encompassing view of the child-caregiver emphasizes the ongoing processes of "reciprocal mutual regulation" (Sander, 1985) within the dyad.

Both self-regulation and mutual regulation processes occur simultaneously within the parent-child system and are intimately interrelated (Beebe & Lachmann, 1994). Because of our concern with comprehending the process of change within the parent-child system, the relationship is based on the reciprocal interplays of a dyadic system.

The parent-child system is dyad comprised of a complex set of unique individualized internal elements that include our own thoughts, feelings, and behaviors, and are interconnected to other subsystems (i.e., attitudes, values, beliefs, motivations, and judgments) that interact with the world around us.

In this way, we can see this model unfolding to reveal the importance of all three major aspects of the parent-child system. These three major aspects consist of: the elements of a system, the internal dynamics of the system, and the interactions and boundaries that hold them together. Therefore, the parent-child system becomes more than just the parent, the child, or their relationship. An integrative system, this view provides us a way for us to see the true nature of parenting.

The parent-child system is a multi-system that is formed and maintained by strong binary bonds that exist between the parent and child. It is for this reason that our views and attitudes about parenting have been difficult to formulate, as our views of the role of parent as primary caregiver can include, but is not limited to, grandparents, foster parents, adoptive parents, and other non-traditional roles.

Each individual system, of both the parent and the child, has distinct internal elements that are connected by this bond that forms their relationship. The internal dynamics are the strong interconnected interactions that take place between the parent and child and provide the bond that holds them together. The external interactions being the exchange of information with our spheres of influence—physiological, emotional, physical, spiritual, and social energy.

The relationship between the parent and child is what provides a purpose for our interactional dynamics and allows us each to create the nurturing environment for our children's growth and prosperity. It is for this reason that we must be able to do more than just create a view of parenting based on the elements of system alone.

These internal and external interactional dynamics make up the bridges that span the gaps between and within the parent-child system and define the structures and boundaries that define who we are. The following is presented as a model for the parent-child system:

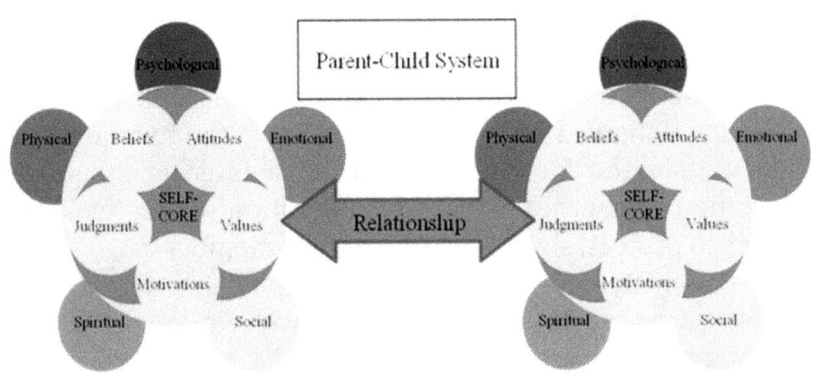

Diagram 9

The family system

"In every conceivable manner, the family is a link to our past, and bridge to our future."
-Alex Haley

Family systems are made up of interrelated elements, exhibit coherent behaviors and regular interactions, and are interdependent on one another and their interactions. The elements of a family system are the members of the family. These independent self-systems can include, but are not limited to, parent and child, and can also include biological, stepsiblings and half-siblings, grandparents, and extended family members.

The relationships between these elements function in an interdependent manner. All of these create a structure of its own that is more than the sum of the parts. The boundaries between these systems and its environment create repetitive interactional patterns that help maintain the family's cohesiveness. Family systems also contain subsystems, coalitions, or alliances. Each subsystem has its own rules, boundaries, and unique characteristics.

Bowen (1994) suggests that individuals cannot be understood in isolation, out of context from the family system. He views the family as an intact complex interactional system. He sees family members as living under the same "emotional skin," or boundary. A change in one person's functioning is predictably followed by reciprocal change in the functioning of others within the family. This emotional interdependence is determined by cohesiveness and cooperation within the family in order to protect, shelter, and feed their members.

Family systems theory is philosophy that searches for understanding as to why we are the way we are within the interactions and structures that exist between family members. The basic rationale is that all parts of the family are interrelated. Further, the family has properties of its own that can be known only by looking at the relationships and interactions among all members. The family system is based on several basic assumptions that include the following:

- Each family is unique, due to the infinite variations that are present within the personal characteristics of each member, the cultural influences of the family system itself, and the interactional patterns that are formed and maintained.

- The family is an interactional system whose component parts are in a constant of dynamic equilibrium, whose boundaries are in a constant state of shifting to accommodate the varying degrees of change that take place within and outside of the family.

- Family members have differing roles that fulfill a variety of functions for the family system. Each family and each of its members are both collectively and individually dependent on each other for its interdependent growth and development.

- Families are organized around interactions and within a hierarchy of interrelated subsystems. Boundaries, rules, and structures are all necessary components for the system to function, by defining who does what with whom.

- The family system is greater than the sum of the parts and each part of the system affects all others. Interrelations and interactional dynamics create system-wide ripples and reverberate down through all other family members.

- Families create reoccurring circular (mutual, reciprocal) causality that are recalibrated by self-regulating feedback loops that maintain the dynamic equilibrium.

Recently, the view of the family as a 'system' has become an increasingly accepted, popular, and important theoretical framework for understanding human behavior. By definition, a family system functions because it is a unit, and every family member plays a critical, if not unique, role in the system. As such, it is not possible that one member of the system can change without causing a ripple effect of change throughout the family system, as illustrated in the following:

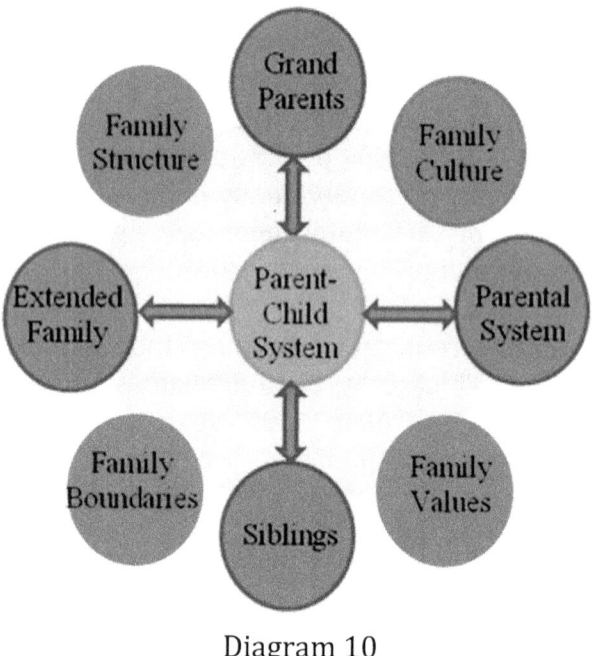

Diagram 10

Societal systems

"Every man is a creative cause of what happens, a premium mobile with an original movement."
—Friedrich Nietzsche

Our highly complex, evolving social world surrounds the parent-child system and is connected like the intricacies of a mobile molecule that, when in balance, resonates with the harmonic sounds of a wind chime. As we continue to unravel the mysteries of the individual and combined aspects of the parent-child system we can now turn our attention to the social context in which the parent-child system exists.

According to Parsons (1991), social systems consist of three major elements that include a number of other subsystems and elements. He proposed that complex social systems are independent systems unto themselves and include aspects of "social structures, social relations, and social actions." They can be considered "conglomerates" of similar oriented individuals or groups (subsystems) working together, and that often have separate identities and characteristics.

Connected by a common purpose, these systems act independently and add a layer of historical permanence. Change is more likely to occur from within these systems; they are more resistant to outside influences and remain relatively stable over time.

These extremely complex social systems are like the molecular structures of compound elements and follow the same rules of principle. Arnopoulos (2005) states that "social systems, like everything else, are basically physical, therefore, they obey space, time, and matter laws." He goes on to suggest that the stability of these social systems, like those of molecular structures, is dependent upon the energy bonds that form our relationships.

At the core of these structures are the nuclei that consist of the all the different subsystems that make up the variations that exist within the connections between individuals like those of protons and neutrons. The more individuals and groups the nuclei contain, the more complex the system. Surrounding these core systems are the shared elements and particles of other nuclei that make up a number of layers of a molecule and form the bond for each system.

Social systems, as defined by *Wikipedia*, are social structures that, in general, refer to "entities or groups in definite relation to each other; to relatively enduring patterns of behavior and relationships within social systems; or to social institutions and norms becoming embedded into social systems in such a way that they shape the behavior of actors within those social systems."

Our societies are based on these shared sets of experience that Luhmann (1995) describes as being driven by an "evolving sense of self-reference" that deal with the "enforced selectivity" and define our "functionally differentiated modern society." He states that these systems are defined by the development of both "interactive or societal systems," within what he calls either "simple societies," such as the parent-child system, or more "complex societies," such as communities.

Interactive systems are made up of smaller, more inclusive social systems like families, friendships, extended families, and situational-based relationships. These comprise what I call the 'hyphenated social systems' that include husband-wife, brother-sister, grandchild-grandparent, friend-friend, colleague-colleague, teacher-student, and parent-child.

These can make up the nuclei of more complex social systems and are functional-based systems. Vermeer (2006) states that these systems are "determined by the interconnectedness of their relationships and the use of a hyphen indicates the unity implicit in their function." He goes on to state that the translation of function within these systems "deals with the indeterminacy of meaning between social systems."

Meaning and purpose within these systems are defined by the relationships and feedback that are the driving forces that comprise the bonds and boundaries of the system. These systems, like that of the parent-child system, represent the self-systems of both individuals that are connected through their relationships.

Societal systems, on the other hand, can be considered institutions that contain a conglomerate of connected groups and/or individuals that operate together for a common purpose. These larger, more stable systems, like an organization, focus on the interconnectedness within a system in what Barabasi (2003) calls "a complex series of networks made up of interconnected hubs."

The "system dynamics paradigm," as proposed by Meadows & Robinson (1985), assumes that the world is composed of these types of systems that are "feedback-dominated, non-linear, time-delayed systems." In general, these set up distinctive dynamic patterns that are structured by time, space, and boundaries that characterize a world of uncertainty.

The concept of "turbulence," as described by Rosenau (1990), focuses on processes of disequilibrium within a system and how this sets the stage for change as "anomalies arise and irregularities set in as structures waiver, new processes evolve and outcomes become transitory." In other words, when a system no longer serves a purpose or has no meaning, it changes or becomes obsolete. This is what makes a dysfunctional system.

Our dysfunctional representations of the parenting system are currently in a state of 'turbulence.' We must begin to recognize the interconnectivity we have to these societal networks that make up the overall global community in which we live.

These represent molecular societal mobiles that are highly dynamic and flexible structures that contain both interactive and societal systems. These systems can change connecting points, individuals, and relationships, as they are continually redefining their purpose and identity.

Although these remain fairly stable, over time they are endlessly being challenged, as the influences of both internal and external factors shift and move through space and time. There are many different types of molecular structures, but one way this global system might appear through the parent-child looking glass, is illustrated in the model below:

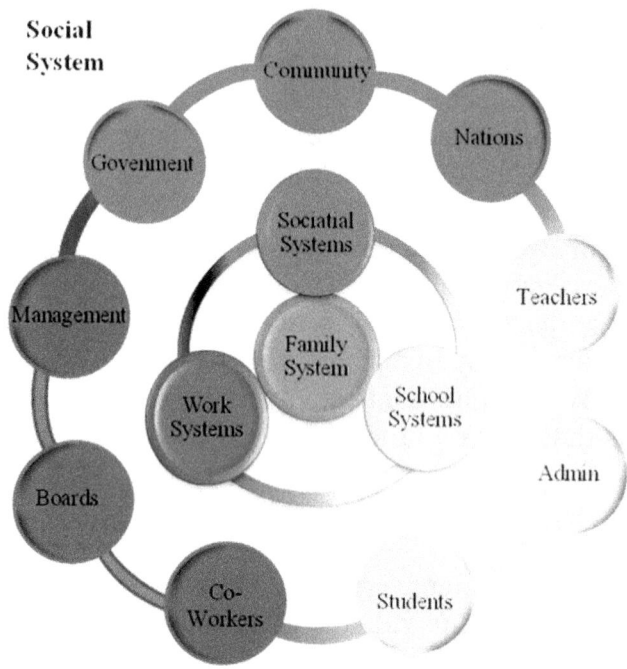

Diagram 11

These represent the layers of a complex social system that influence and impact the relationship between parent and child and provide the building blocks for other parent-child systems. They remind us that we exist on this big blue marble together, and what affects one of us, affects us all. Like many different wind chimes moving together in harmony, they resonate with the sounds of life.

It is only when we start to recognize our connection to all things that we can start to make a difference in our world. Lunden (2000) suggests that "making a difference in our world" comes from "our ability to answer a call to action." She states that "no one person can sincerely try to help another without helping themselves." It seems that "the business of changing the world" requires a "call to action," and "now is the time for all players in the private sector to identify the ways in which they can join in this movement," (Moore, 2007).

The sandbox is for everyone

"Most of us have lost track of these gifts somewhere between the sandbox and the workplace."
-Alan S. Gregerman

Our world is a giant sandbox and how we treat it is our choice—whether it's like kitty litter or sacred sand castles, is up to us. If we are to have a chance at peace, we all must be able to play in the sandbox together; not because of the concepts of social justice, but because it's the only sandbox we've got.

If we are to have a hope for our children's futures, we must learn to take care of what we have; not because of limited resources or scarcity, but because it's all we've got. If we want to promote basic human rights, we must value everyone and make room for all of us; not because of some higher social conscious, but because they're the only rights we've got. If we've only got one sandbox to play in, it would make sense that we do everything we can to make sure we take care of it together.

We are the stewards of our big blue marble and we need to take stock to make sure we are making it a better place to live for future generations to come. Becoming good custodians of the world means that "we should make every effort to understand the way the world is, to the best of our ability. Otherwise we cannot make informed decisions and can hardly be good or reliable stewards," (Alexander & White, 2006).

One of the major philosophical tenets of parenting throughout human history, if not often realized, has been making sure we are making this world a better place for our children. Modern parenting science has dedicated itself to the same ends, and Hirsh-Pasek, Golinkoff & Eyer (2003) stated that thousands of scientists "have devoted their lives to making the world a better place for your children to grow."

Emerson once said that we need to "laugh often and much; to win the respect of intelligent people and the affection of children...to leave the world a better place...to know even one life has breathed easier because you have lived. This is to have succeeded." If we want to make a difference, we need to look within and ask ourselves a simple question, "What have I done today to make this world a better place?"

Camping was one of our favorite family activities when I was growing up, and one of the rules we followed was to leave the campsite better than we found it. If we could only adopt this simple principle into our everyday lives, we would start to experience the success that can make a difference in our lives, the lives of our children, and the lives of those around us. These types of compassionate acts of kindness can create contagion effects like those in the movie "*Pay it Forward.*"

In this movie, these effects can be seen when a child touches a number of lives by thinking of something that will change the world and putting that thought into action. He sets out with a plan to do three good deeds for others that they cannot accomplish on their own, and the only obligation is that they agree to 'pay it forward' by doing good deeds for three other people, in return. In this way, these acts of kindness spread exponentially, with the goal of making the world a better place. By practicing random acts of kindness, we have "the secret to a happier world and the power to make it a nicer place!" (Wallace, 2004).

Our connectivity as humans on this big blue marble, is shrinking all the time, as is alluded to by Gladwell (2002), when he discusses the concepts of "six degrees of separation" and "connectors." He suggests that the social phenomenon of change is related to the world being more connected than we think, and is linked by small shifts within a few small factors that create "tipping points." This contagion model provides us insight into how these types of grassroots movements can become so instrumental in generating social momentum for change.

This is a process where "change feeds on itself" and cerates "snowball effects" that are self-sustaining as "positive feedback sets in motion reinforcing pressures that produce change in the same direction," (Kelman, 2005). Societal change is transformative, and small actions play a crucial role in facilitating a personal evolution and shared revolution for positive lasting change. This can be described as the initial kick- start we need to ignite and sustain the momentum for our parental change of the future.

While growing up, the sandbox was the cool place to be. It was a place of magic, where all things were possible. There was always enough room for everyone and everyone found their own place. It was an easy fit and everyone found their own niche. Watching children in the sandbox at play, I'm always amazed at the ease in which the welcoming spirit of acceptance transforms the nature of their play as being both together and separate.

This youthful spirit is the key to our psychological flexibility in being an individual and a part of something much bigger than ourselves. Gregerman (2000) points out that our success is linked to "rediscovering how to think and act more like small children...and mastering children's innate abilities to play, learn, lead, innovate, and create magical results." He suggests that by tapping into our childlike qualities that come straight out of the sandbox, we can use our "special gifts to create constant magic."

We create mental constructs of our world based on religious, political, and socio-economical frames of reference that are often a source of conflict. However, there is no room for such frivolous things within the sandbox, and a child has no time for politics, religion, or status. Their innocence often contains a sense of fairness, sharing, well-being, and contentment that flows naturally from a place deep within their unconsciousness.

This is not to say that there are no conflicts in the sandbox; it just seems as though children are sometimes better equipped to let go and move on without having to succumb to the trappings of the overvalued ideas of our ego's possessiveness. There are many forms of control that produce unhealthy preoccupations within our voracious appetite for self-significance.

It is both our uniqueness and our connectivity that provides us with meaning. Frankl (1946) suggests that it is precisely our "ability to choose our attitude in any given set of circumstances" that determines success. He believes that "when we are no longer able to change a situation—we are challenged to change ourselves."

Sands of time

"Lives of great men all remind us we can make our lives sublime, and departing, leave behind us, footprints on the sands of time."
-Henry Wadsworth Longfellow

The history of parenting has often been defined by the cultural aspects of the societies in which they existed. Our world has been moving "very rapidly towards wholeness since about 1870" (Robertson, 1992), and a new global culture of parenting is emerging. He states that the process of "globalization" has been transforming how we identify relationships in what he calls his "fourfold scheme" that includes "national societies, individual selves, international system of societies, and mankind."

If the developing culture of increased globalization defines the nature of relationships, then how we define ourselves as parents can be described by the interconnectedness of these relationships. Eliezer & Sternberg (2002) identify this process as "a global specialization of the social reality." They state that through the process of "transference, transformation, and transcendence," we can begin to see the world of our parent-child system through all its multi-faceted and connected parts.

Following the "law of unintended consequences," as purposed by Levitt & Dubner (2009), we can argue that the more our culture moves towards accessing the global community, the more empowered and autonomous we become. Not because of some overestimated sense of "altruism," or because of the development of some umbrella "global policy," but because it promotes our own "self-interest."

This future is dependent on our ability to build our relationships with our children, by working with what we have and not dwelling on what we lack. Sheffield (2006) would say that it is our own primitive instincts of "self-preservation, and propagation" through the love of our children, that propels mankind into the future. It is a strength-based approach to change that gives us a focused approach, as proposed by Wood (2008), where "we concentrate on making the most of what we have, not hankering for what we don't have."

Time with our children is time well spent, and is one of the greatest investments in our future and the future of the world to come. This proposition continues to drive our journey in *becoming a better parent* as we begin to realize the myth of quality vs. quantity time spent with our children. It is the recognition that every grain of sand we have is quality time that empowers us to truly treasure every moment we have with our children.

From the frantic get-ready-in-the-morning time, to the we-need-to-sit-down-and-have-a-talk time, the grains of sand within the hourglass slip slowly away, and it is what we do in those moments that creates the quality with our children. There seems to be a difference between the "big 'H' and the little 'h' of happiness," as proposed by Sandbek & Philbrick (2008), who state that it is when we are able set our priorities on the "big 'Hs' of life," such as "listening to music, going on walks with friends, or spending time with our children," that translates into our "psychological well-being."

Like Defoe's (1719) "Robinson Crusoe," we, as parents, have mistakenly thought we have existed alone on a deserted island, but can now see the footprints throughout the sands of time. Recognizing that we are not alone in our endeavors, we can now seek to find meaning in these connections that make up the social fabric of our lives.

Interconnected on many levels, we are able to appreciate the importance of the little things in life that determine both the quality and quantity of the time we have with our children. I would contest that it is when we can see the value of the time spent with our children as pleasurable, engaging, and meaningful, that we can experience the true rewards of parenting.

This slant towards "positive psychology," as coined by Seligman (2004), focuses on ways "to find and nurture genius and talent; to make normal life more fulfilling; and to build thriving individuals, families, and communities." He states that exploring our own interpersonal virtues and strengths, "like kindness, gratitude, and capacity for love," are what make life worth living and provide the guideposts for real world change. He suggests that our "lasting happiness is based on pleasure, engagement, and meaning."

Hope is the best of things

"Hope is a good thing, maybe the best of things, and no good thing ever dies."
-Frank Darabont (*"The ShawshankRedemption,"* 1994)

Ronald Reagan (1989) once said that we are bound to the dreams of our past and "we, too, dare to hope. We dare to hope for our children; that they, too, can share in the gift that guides us into a future of peace, freedom, and hope." Hope for our global future is based on those things we hold close to our hearts and starts within, for our hopes for our children.

Creating a "personally-generated culture" within an "industry-generated culture," as described by DeGaetano (2004), means that we must look beyond the limitations of our past parental perspectives, empower our human relationships, and generate our own culture of parenting.

It is this 'parental culture of the future' that can foster a new hope for our children. DeGaetano's efforts seem to be directed at minimizing the impact of modern influences of mechanization and depersonalization within our current cultural identity. She claims that our hope for our children's future comes from understanding "the conditions that are being imposed upon us, and transform them into conditions that work on our behalf."

In other words, it's not *what* happens to us, but *what we do with* what happens, that matters most. Making a difference in our lives and changing the future for ourselves and our children is an inside job. We can start by looking within to transform our perceptual mindsets that have locked us into our current traps.

Throughout the years, I have been asking a simple question, "What's the only thing in life you can change?" I must have asked this question of everyone—covering a wide range of age groups, cultural backgrounds, and socioeconomic statuses— and everyone, 100 percent of the time, comes up with the same answer: "Yourself." Yet, it seems that most of the difficulties we face in life are related to trying to change *everything else*.

This principle is a rare truism that states: You are the only thing in life you can change. The process of change comes from within, whether on an individual, relationship, or societal level. If we are to create a hopeful future for our children, we need to start from within. This seems to be the best place for us to focus our energy as "all change comes from within you, and, as you change, the world changes, because the planet can only be changed one person at a time," (King, 2009).

"True change is a process of systemic change," that impacts all aspects of the parent-child system, (Klein, 2004). Klein suggests that it is the "combined power of people, their internal approach, and systems support, that facilitates true change that becomes self-sustaining." Change is a complex process that is influenced, inspired, and supported by external factors, but is initiated from within.

Change, like a fire, generates from within as an intentional spark that ignites the external fuel and radiates heat outwards. This energy can light the passions and desires of others and create additional momentum that can set off chain reactions of change. This type of true change can be seen as a social chain reaction, as described by Phan (2004), who states that "the adoption of a single agent in a population may lead, by chain reaction, to a significant change in the whole population."

Our parental hope for a better future for our children lies within our ability to change. These are the creative flashes of inspiration that are orchestrated by our own thoughts, feelings and behaviors, and stir the imaginations of our transformation. These are internally-generated perspectives that set the stage for true change to take place from within. Our inclusive worldviews can fan the fires of social reform, from within, and illuminate the future for our children.

We can emerge from the darkness of control and begin to immerse ourselves in the rich tapestry of life. "What I'm suggesting to you is that this could be a renaissance. We may be on the cusp of a future which could provide a tremendous leap forward for humanity," (Jeremy Rifkin). Compassion within our connection to all things provides us the building blocks to develop healthy relationships and grow.

We can become participants in this new parental renaissance by developing a global dream for our children that can become the means by which we can "create a healthier, happier, more just world and thriving societies everywhere," (Wood, 2010). Taking these steps in *becoming a better parent* can open the door to a world of possibility that exists between parent and child, and plots the course for our relationships in the future.

ii. Prologue: Where Do We Go From Here?

"We may not be able to prepare the future for our children, but we can at least prepare our children for the future."

-Franklin D. Roosevelt

Many of today's time-pressured parents are hard-pressed to find more effective ways to deal with and prepare our children for the fast-paced changes of the world of tomorrow. The world is changing and, as the future advances towards us, our relationships with our children need to take center stage.

As we embark on this highly personal adventure, we can turn our attention to the future importance of how we research, analyze, and examine the parent-child system and the relationships that hold it in place. "It is increasingly obvious that the world into which our young children will enter as adults, will be nothing like the world their parents grew up in, or even the world we currently inhabit" (Bush & Codrington, 2009). They state that "we need a better understanding of the world of the future in order to prepare our children and to 'future-proof' them."

We have begun to break away from the modern myths of parenting; we are beginning to let go of the illusions of control; we have loosened the chains of our parental traps; we have started to lay the foundations for a better understanding of the parent-child system. Where we go from here can have endless possibilities as long as we can remember three basic steps: 10 "How we do things is more important that what we do;" 2) "Mistakes are opportunities in disguise;" and 3) "We need to practice patience, tolerance, and forgiveness," (Nelsen, 2009).

Unveiling these truths about parenting has given us the ability to see beyond our current perceptions and uncover the problems of the past. By looking at parenting data over the past 25 years, a recent study has found that "parents are more involved in their children's lives and spend more quality time together than they did in the past," (Nuffield Foundation, 2009).

In spite of the increasing rates of parental stress and youth behavioral problems, this study suggests that "parents are not to blame." This study points out that other factors may be contributing to these increased rates and draw attention to the "broader social environment." These trends may again be suggesting that something else is needed in how we see, study, and interpret the parent-child system.

It seems we need to turn our attention to parenting practices that work for the future of our children. Defining what works, however, has been somewhat challenging, and what often works for one parent, might not always work for another, or for the child, and vice-versa. To develop a better understanding of what works in the parent-child system, we must begin to look at the outcomes of parenting that support effective change across the entire system.

Outcomes, within the parent-child system, are based on the process rather than the results, continuously evolve within both time and space, and focus on building the relationships between parent and child.

"Parenting that works" is a process-oriented approach to parenting that focuses on how to build relationships with our children by "playing, teaching, and communicating effectively with them," (Christophersen & Mortweet, 2002). They suggest that building our relationships with our children through the process of "practice, patience, and support," will allow our children to develop the ability to "play independently, manage their moods, and respond appropriately to requests and expectations."

Psychologists have been interested in how parenting influences human development since the inception of the study of psychology. They have conducted rigorous research on the subject that goes back to its very beginnings. These studies have generally focused on parenting styles and have limited the scope of focus to the assumption that the primary role of all parents is to "influence, teach, and control their children," (Baumrind, 1989).

This research has captured two of the most important elements of the parenting continuum: "parental responsiveness and parental demandingness." This provides us with a "strong predictor for parenting function and child well-being," (Maccoby & Martin, 1983). They also point out that, despite this long standing tradition, a number of limitations remain that include the "definition, developmental changes, and the processes underlying what constitutes parenting."

If we can look beyond these parenting limitations, we can start to uncover what matters most and what makes a difference. By focusing on the entire system and our relationships, we can develop the insight and mental connections needed to make a more comprehensive model of parenting for the future.

Although scientific research has supported the role of parental influence and teaching in the parent-child system, it has also overemphasized the illusions of control over our children. Parenting styles, however, are an important element of parenting and can be better directed at creating more optimistic outcomes that provide us all with the resources necessary to help our children reach their full potential.

By becoming more inclusive in our approach to parenting, we can see beyond the individualistic aspects of the entire system so we can have "positive, pleasant experiences and interactions" (Latham, 1994) in the relationships with our children.

Positive parenting outcomes that reinforce our efforts to build relationships, recognize the futility of control, and empower the process of growth, are the best chances we have to believe in a future of tomorrows for our children. We, as parents, must come to recognize that our children are separate parts of the same system if we are to develop an understanding that will create positive change.

The promise of things to come

"Don't cry because it's over. Smile because it happened."
-Dr. Seuss

The more we understand about the intricacies of the parent-child system, the more we can appreciate the chaotic nature that makes up the science of parenting. Sunderland (2008) outlines "the science of parenting" as a scientific approach that provides research and demonstrates the importance of the interactions between parent and child. Although child-focused, her scientific overview of the parent-child interactional process is backed by solid social and neuroscience research.

Dewar (2006) also proposes a scientific approach to parenting with "no folk theories, no preachy advice, and no authoritarian pronouncements or pseudoscientific political dogma, but instead, an in-depth analysis with fully-referenced citations from the scientific and medical literature." What these scientific approaches emphasize, are the missing components that can further provide us a way to make sense out of all the variables that influence this highly complex parent-child system.

Never has the need been so great for us to develop a new scientific understanding of parenting that builds on our historical roots and includes a more "multidisciplinary approach to parenting," (Markie-Dadds & Sanders, 2002). They indicate that by drawing on "social learning theory, applied behavioral analysis, research on child development and developmental psychology, social information-processing models, and public health principles," we can create the flexibility needed to understand the links between "self-regulation and parenting skills."

These "behavioral family interventions" originate from earlier family systems models (Bowen, 1994, and Minuchin, 1974), and see the nature of parenting being related to a much "broader family, social, and cultural context." Family-systems-thinking shows a great deal of promise for the future as we continue to develop our understanding of a new science of parenting.

"Evidence-based" approaches to parenting are those that have been shown to be effective "based on the results of rigorous evaluations," (Cooney et al., 2007). They suggest that an effective approach to parenting is evidence-based if the "evaluation research shows that the program produces the expected positive results; the results can be attributed to the program itself; the evaluation is peer-reviewed by experts in the field; and the program is 'endorsed' by a federal agency or respected research organization."

The problem with this approach to parenting is that no two children and no two parents are alike, thus, no program works with all children, or all parents, all the time, or in every situation. Environmental, social, and family situations also vary and make the range of possible outcomes within the parent-child system almost endless. This variability seems to be suggesting "an integrated science of parenting," as proposed by Bradley & Corwyn (2006), who suggest the need for social science to develop our own parental theory of everything.

The use of "meta-analysis" in reviewing clinical trials, outcomes studies, and research in the science of parenting, can be a useful strategy in connecting a "statistical synthesis of results from a series of studies" for the purpose of integrating the findings, (Borenstein et al., 2009). They suggest that systematically combining outcomes across studies can strengthen the evidence to "estimate the magnitude of the effect more precisely than with any of the studies alone." This statistical method can be used in a new science of parenting not only to review parental research, but also to further understanding of the parent-child system.

This statistical method is not only used to integrate findings, but can also be used to take into account a number of variables that contribute to overall outcomes. The advancements in computer software that are specifically designed to conduct meta-analysis make entering and analyzing this statistical information a relatively simple task of data entry.

Unlike the statistical formulas used in "meta-analysis," we can also look to the use of abstract, heuristic, qualitative, and causal assumptions, as outlined within the formulas of a "structural equation model," (Judea, 2000). These equations can be used to assist us in developing a more thorough understanding of the complex interrelated nature of the parent-child system.

This technique can be used within our new science of parenting for testing and estimating the causal relations and the interconnected relationships between parent, child, and the world around us. These predictive equations can be used to take into account the latent variables that have an influence and create change for both parents and their children.

Using this information to develop abstract formulas based on our statistical inner connectedness within the entire system, can suggest new directions for the field of parenting. These formulas can expand "the horizons of knowledge by exploring those of its domains that have not happened to become objects for empirical investigation," (Diriwächter & Valsiner, 2008).

The use of the abstract theoretical formulas has been widespread throughout the social sciences and there have been many equations developed that outline the predictive aspects of complex social systems. Lewin (1943) was a modern pioneer in the field of social psychology, and was one of the first to develop one of these imaginative predictive formulas "in which behavior is conceptualized as a function of the field," and "encompasses the whole gestalt," (Shoda, 2004).

Lewin's theory and formula as follows:

$$B = fP \& E$$

states that an individual's (B) "Behavior" is a (f) "function" of the (P) "Person" and his or her (E) "Environment." This equation is one of the most well-known formulas in social psychology and contradicted most of the popular theories at that time. His work was one of the first to give importance to a person's momentary situation in understanding individual behavior, rather than relying entirely on the past or behavioral sequencing. A parenting formula might very well be a useful tool in taking into account the latent variables in predicting the outcomes for the parent-child system.

Chaos and butterfly kisses

"In all chaos there is a cosmos, in all disorder a secret order."
-Carl Jung

"Chaos theory," also shows promise for the future of a new parenting science, and is used to describe the "interdependence of all parts of a system and the continuous predictive values based on the variability of initial conditions," (Gleick, 1987). Simply put, it's the little things within a system that make a big difference.

Predicting these "what-if scenarios," associated with the term "butterfly effect" (Lorenz, 1963), deal with unpredictability in complex systems. The "butterfly effect" can be seen when something as trivial as the flapping of a butterfly's wings can effect a chain of events for the entire weather system and "you get rain instead of sunshine," ("*Jurassic Park*," 1993).

Predictability in highly complex social systems is a difficult challenge. However "chaotic and random behavior of solutions of deterministic systems is now understood to be an inherent feature of many nonlinear systems, and the geometric theory developed over the past few decades handles this situation quite nicely," (Devaney, 2003).

Parental chaos is an often seen but seldom understood phenomenon within the parent-child system. These nonlinear patterns and interactions between, within, and around the parent and child, represent the initial conditions and the flexible variables within both time and space. All these factors contribute to our overall understanding of how the parent-child system works and provide us a framework for the possible outcomes, based on our initial conditions.

Our ability to predict the outcomes within the parent-child system are, in effect, "dependent on the conditions of the system when change was initiated," (Luvmour, 2006). He goes on to say that "most important into our inquiry of transitions in human development, are the initial conditions as outlined by chaos theory."

Choice and free will are part of the highly complex nonlinear parent-child system and often resemble the variant paths of a decision tree called a "bifurcation decision making process," (Gutzwiller, 1990). The social phenomenon of change within a system is represented by "levels at which the momentum for change becomes unstoppable," (Gladwell, 2002).

These social "tipping points" within the parent-child system are sudden and significant transitions from one state of functioning to another and are created when systems reach "critical mass, a threshold, or the boiling point." These dynamics of social change have also been attributed to the concept of "incentives," as outlined by Levitt & Dubner (2009).

Whether driven by external social or internal motivational factors, the chaos theory can provide the means through which we are able to see the world of parenting in a new light; where the initial conditions, latent variables, and dynamics of a system can be taken into account in understanding the complex process that is parenting.

Understanding chaotic patterns in complex social systems has historically been problematic, but recent advancements in the area of social science through "synergetics" has turned its attention to and focuses on "the relationships rather than individuals," (Dumas, 2005).

Becoming A Better Parent

Social science is still struggling to find ways to make use of the models associated with the "chaos theory," and it seems that the complexity of the parent-child system is pushing the scientific envelope in this area. It is becoming ever more apparent that we need to embrace these evolving scientific values, so we can change, evolve, and grow.

The more integrated our models of parenting become, the more we can make a difference as parents. The closer our relationships are with our children, the closer we come to a new era in parental science. The better our questions are about parenting, the better we can understand what it takes to become a better parent. Places deep within our hearts—where we can appreciate the significance of something as small as a butterfly kiss on the cheek.

Parental harmony and universal strings

"Happiness is when what you think, what you say, and what you do, are in harmony."
-Mahatma Gandhi

"Superstring theory" is a theoretical model that is used to describe and define all the known fundamental forces, elements, and matter, in the entire universe. It has been described as a "theory of everything" and has evolved out of a series of "successive approximations," allowing us to make more accurate predictions of a wider range of phenomena (Ellis, 1986). Like the strings of a guitar, these universal vibrations can occur in multiple dimensions and make up the musical chords that echo throughout our lives.

These are the harmonious melodies that exist within the heart of every parent. Connecting all things, these superstrings are the binding forces within a "cyclic universe" that are bound by "the field," (Barrow, 1994). This "field" is what Einstein said "is the only reality" and is the key to understanding the concept of universal connectively. These superstrings are the vibrating energy loops within a "cosmic symphony" (Green, 2003) that play in the heart of every parent.

These resonating fields join all things and are the energetic charges that either attract or repel all time, space, and matter. It has been described as the "life force flowing through the universe," and is the "central engine of our being and our consciousness, the alpha and the omega of our existence," (McTaggart, 2002).

The field is "a place where the tides, and the seasons, the turning of the earth, all come together; where everything that is, becomes one," (*"The Legend of Bagger Vance,"* 2000). "Consciousness, not matter, is the ground of all existence," and "the universe has a self-aware consciousness that creates the physical world," (Goswami, 1993).

Somehow, it seems that the connectedness of our consciousness brings the actual world of our parenting into being. If we are the creators of our parental realities, then our relationships form the magical shared space between us and our children. Parental harmony plays a key role in our ability to sway with our children to the reverberations played on the strings of our multi-dimensional parenting universe.

Our parental harmony exists within this interconnectedness and is the sweet music that can be played within the parent-child system. Only by understanding the connective complexities between parent and child, can we unlock the harmonious vibrations that are created on the strings within the field.

"Harmonious parenting" moves away from the issues of control that can become parental oppressiveness and focuses, instead, on the "complex dance of parent-child interactions," (Greenspan, 2006). He states that it is "only when a caregiver can step back and not just forward can he/she hope to perform that dance skillfully."

A new direction for parenting

Becoming A Better Parent

"Human beings, viewed as behaving systems, are quite simple. The apparent complexity of our behavior over time, is largely a reflection of the complexity of the environment in which we find ourselves."

-Herbert Simon

"Systems theory" provides us with the best hope for the future of a parenting science, and is a model that creates a clearer picture of the chaos, harmony, and relationships that exist within the dynamics of parenting. Advancements in systems theory provide us with a "powerful conceptual framework for organizing the study of adaptive behavior and adaptive functioning applicable across the life span," (Cabrera et al., 2003).

These recent studies suggest that by using a systems theory, we can create a model of the parent-child system so we can understand the "ecological context" of its nature based on the "emergent, epigenetic, constructive, hierarchically integrated, potentially chaotic, and embedded interdependent components" of its ongoing relationship dynamics.

In other words, to understand the parent-child system, we need to take into consideration and understand all the aspects that influence the parent-child system so we can get the big picture of how we, as parents and children, work. This is an inclusive model that takes into account all the factors and variables influencing this complex social system.

Space, time, and matter, within the parent-child system, is connected to, influenced by, and generates outcomes that are based on the parts of the system simultaneously working together and separately. These dynamics are continuously shaping the system and its individual parts as it evolves.

This "synergy paradigm" proposed that systems in the real world work interdependently, both as a whole and individually. He goes on to state that it is precisely the very "nature of what and how we think, based on either the whole or part, that may limit our ability to understand complex systems."

Bailey (1994) also developed an ingenious integrative way to look at complex social systems by providing a detailed analysis of the types of systems and their interacting subsystems. He outlined the "multi-dimensional spatial aspects of complex living systems," and emphasized both "structure and process."

In combining the influences of all things within and around the parent-child system, we can establish the internal and external links that become the superstrings of our parental systems model that connect all things. Barabasi (2003) calls these dynamic processes "a complex series of networks made up of interconnected hubs."

Our ability to grow as parents is based on this interconnectedness and provides the foundation for adaptability, acceptance, and flexibility. The interactions of these "human system dynamics," (Eoyang, 2006) focus on "dynamical change" that "shift from rest to rhythmic oscillation to random thrashing," and determine the patterns of interconnectedness within the parent-child system. These provide the forces that bind or repel the elements of a system, define its boundaries, form its thoughts and feelings, transform its behaviors and create the families, groups, organizations, communities and societies for the world in which we live.

We have begun to reveal a glimpse at the road signs ahead and, as we look into the future of parenting, we have the tools necessary so we can pull over and ask for directions. Peeling back the complex layers of the parent-child system, we can begin to understand what it means to strive to become a better parent.

These new mental constructs can lead us through the maze of parenting, expand the horizons for future generations, and help us find our way out of the confusion that currently exists. These pathways are our ability to connect with all things and can open the doorways of our mind. Buddha said, "To walk safely through the maze of human life, one needs the light of wisdom and the guidance of virtue."

We can now light our way on this journey by bridging the gaps that exist within our studies of parenting. We can use this wisdom to guide us through the course of parenting so we can awaken to a brighter future for our children. We can use these strength-based virtues to repair the multigenerational damage and suffering caused by our unrealistic parenting traps. We can now focus on the ways in which we can continue to build more effective and healthy relationships to make the lasting differences needed for our children's future.

INDEX

Absolute; 34, 134-135, 167
Abstract; 89, 216
Abuse(s)(d); 31, 41, 52, 115, 142-145, 158-161, 183-185
Accept(s)(ed)(ance); 17, 20-21, 35, 40, 45, 51, 59, 64, 80-81, 85, 87, 97-102, 112-113, 116, 119, 130, 133, 142, 146, 150, 160, 165, 170-174, 176. 180, 190, 197, 205, 222
Accountability; 29, 31-32, 132, 138-140, 158
Achieve(ment); 82-86, 106, 110, 120, 125, 133, 139, 168, 175, 179
Active Listening; 53, 146-147
Active Involvement; 44, 47, 55, 60, 62, 113, 129, 180-182
Adapt; 102, 107
Adaptability; 12, 107
Adapting; 16, 39, 67
Adjust(ment)(s); 32, 37, 89, 93, 104, 187
Agenda(s); 146, 155
Attachment(s); 118-119, 123, 129, 131-132
Attitude(s); 31, 42, 47, 49-50, 56-57, 63, 87, 89-93, 102, 113-115, 121, 162, 167-168, 185, 88, 191, 194, 206

Beautiful (Beauty); 101, 105, 126, 158
Becoming a Better Parent; 9-18, 25, 27, 29-31, 39, 43-45, 50, 79, 81, 120, 128, 133, 159-160, 167, 171, 185, 187, 189, 207, 210
Belief(s); 9, 14, 20, 22, 24, 26-32, 34, 42, 49, 50, 56-57, 62, 80, 86-89, 97, 101-105, 113-117, 144, 153, 160, 173, 179, 185, 187-188, 194
Behavioral; 25-30, 49-51, 76, 89, 92, 103, 166, 185, 212, 214-217
Behaviors; 25-29, 64-65, 70-79, 83, 86, 89, 102-105, 115, 115, 120, 133-139, 143, 151, 153, 158-159, 165-168, 176, 181, 194-195, 201, 222
Belong(ing)(s); 55, 73, 110, 131
Best Parent We Can Be; 45, 49, 73-74, 186
Blind(ers)(s)(sides); 100, 138, 158, 167
Boundary; 70-74, 110, 190, 196
Boundaries; 23, 30-34, 69, 83, 98, 104, 110, 123-124, 131-133, 138, 140-141, 157, 161, 185, 187, 191, 194-197, 200-201, 222

Broke(n); 165, 175

Care Giving; 143, 193-194, 220
Care Taker; 14, 142
Caring; 46-48, 106, 115, 129, 132-133, 141, 148-149, 167, 170
Character; 106-107, 163-167
Characteristics: 26, 42, 44, 57, 103-105, 113, 119, 141-143, 161-163, 192, 199
Choice(s); 10, 25-26, 30, 36, 39, 65-66, 76, 79-80, 95, 98-99, 114, 118, 123-126, 134, 161-163, 170, 185, 193, 203, 218
Cognit(ive)(ions); 51, 89, 92, 127, 173, 185
Collaborative(ion): 58, 67, 106, 165, 181
Common(ly); 14, 25-26, 29, 32, 40, 42, 47, 53, 58, 66, 82, 94, 113, 117, 141, 146, 172, 174-178, 192, 199-200
Communicate(ion)(s); 13, 24, 54, 56, 60, 69, 75, 102, 116, 133, 137, 147, 151-158, 175, 177, 212
Compassion(ate); 8, 46, 58, 70, 101, 116, 129, 131-133, 162, 187, 189, 204, 210
Complex(ity)and Parenting; 9-21, 33-34, 40, 52, 54, 66, 71, 76, 87-88, 98, 114-123, 128, 147, 156, 171-173, 177, 209, 214-216
Complex Social Systems; 83, 193, 199, 200, 216-220
Cooperate(ive)(ion)(; 48, 54, 58, 60, 106, 147, 156,, 165, 193, 196
Conflict(s)(ual); 31, 41, 48, 77, 97, 100, 107, 114, 126-127, 136, 141, 145, 147, 184, 205
Consisten(t)(cy); 51, 54, 60, 92-93, 129, 133, 141, 151, 156-159, 165-166, 179
Control; 23-32, 40, 48, 52, 79-80, 103-104, 115-117, 121-125, 136, 145, 158, 165-166, 168, 173, 177, 181, 189, 205, 210, 213, 220
Culture; 14, 20, 37, 47, 102-103, 161, 165, 206-208
Curio(us)(usly)(ity): 47, 54, 106, 154, 163
Custod(y)(ians)(ial); 46, 203
Custodians; 175
Cycl(e)(s)(ical); 24, 30, 40-41, 81, 131

Dance(ing)(s); 58, 122-127, 141, 220
Defensive(ness)(ly); 74, 91, 158
Mechanisms; 146

224

Becoming A Better Parent

Depress(ed)(ion)(ive); 56, 103, 143, 150, 172
Development; 13, 26, 34, 43, 52, 59,, 61, 63, 70, 73, 77, 81, 88, 103-104, 113-121, 126-127, 133, 158, 143-148, 150, 157, 163, 183, 190, 193, 197, 200, 207, 213-214, 218
Disciplin(ed)(ary); 9, 11, 32, 38, 44, 51-54, 75, 82, 97, 103, 118, 133, 144-145
Discover(y), Self and Parental 15-16, 21, 28, 32, 39, 55, 61, 66, 164, 179, 186, 205
Distort(ions)(ed); 22, 28-29, 44
Dyad(ic) (Systems); 194
Dynamics (Systems); 49, 52, 69, 75-75, 78, 81, 83, 86-87, 93-94, 101, 112, 118, 121, 128, 136-137, 148, 152, 156, 163, 173, 176, 193-194, 200-201, 218, 221-222

Emotional; 24, 33, 49-50, 56, 61, 72-77, 81, 104, 106, 110, 115-116, 123. 132, 136, 142-147, 152, 157, 169, 178, 181, 196
Emotions; 24, 67, 77, 106, 116, 122-123, 129, 136, 143
Emotionally: 18, 83, 85, 123, 127, 137, 147
Empathy; 63, 106, 124-125
Environment(s) and Environmental factors in parenting; 43, 72, 107, 118, 135-136, 192, 195-196, 212, 215, 217, 221
Evolv(ed(s)(ing); 13, 15, 22, 25, 60, 83, 111, 126, 132, 150, 167, 189, 193, 198, 201, 205, 212, 219, 221
Expect(ing)(ations); 8, 13, 15, 27-32, 39, 42, 44, 48, 50-60, 67, 84, 100-103, 114, 118, 120-123, 131-133, 139, 148, 156, 158, 160-161, 166, 170, 2133, 215
Experience; 13, 21, 29, 49, 56, 63-67, 77, 82-83, 93, 104, 113, 119, 121, 125, 141-146, 148, 150, 154, 166, 172, 178, 193, 199, 204, 208
Experienced; 16, 22, 126, 148
Experiences; 15, 59, 65, 68, 79, 82, 97, 107, 127

Failure; 9, 28, 44, 80, 95-96, 99, 142, 161, 170, 191,
Families; 9, 12, 26, 40, 45, 47-49, 70, 110, 169, 171, 183, 197, 200, 208, 222

Family Systems; 70, 195-198,, 215
Famil(y)(ial) Patterns; 41, 49, 123, 145, 142, 169, 175
Fear; 23, 52, 59, 64, 80, 99, 116, 119, 133, 137, 161, 189
Feedback; 100, 15-156, 174-175, 197, 200, 205
Feelings; 24-28, 42, 44, 65, 70, 75, 78-89, 102-106, 113, 116, 120-123, 129, 139, 147, 153, 158-159, 165-166, 176-177, 181, 194, 210, 222
Free; 14, 26, 29-30, 41, 46, 50, 74, 96, 115, 125, 144, 178, 186, 190
Freedom; 41, 106, 138, 208
Free Will; 10, 30, 39, 114, 139, 165-166, 170, 193, 218
Flexibil(e)(ity); 12, 60, 63, 71, 74-75, 112-113, 119, 124-125, 150, 163, 177, 186,-187, 201, 214, 218, 222
Future; 8-10, 16-20, 27, 31-44, 50, 65, 74, 78-81, 84, 94, 112, 161, 163, 188, 190, 195, 203-217, 221-223

Gather(ings)(ed); 38, 94, 96, 110, 178
Generation(s); 9, 14, 18, 20, 31, 36-41, 50-51, 64, 74, 142, 145, 169-170, 189-190, 203, 222-223
Genetic(s); 42-43, 66, 185, 221
Gift(s)(ed): 44-45, 55, 65, 68, 79, 81, 121-122, 164, 166, 170, 172, 203, 205, 208
Goal(s); 48, 53, 67, 75, 82, 105, 107, 133, 154, 167, 174, 181
Good Parents; 14, 16, 20, 22, 29-33, 36, 38, 42, 45-46, 50, 75-76, 132, 167, 170
Gratitude; 87, 92, 163, 208
Group(s) Process; 50, 97-98, 173, 199-200, 209, 222
Growth; 8, 14, 16, 22, 30, 37-38, 50, 58, 62, 79, 81, 108-109, 111, 114, 117, 153, 161, 186, 191, 195, 197, 214
Guide for Parenting; 12, 15, 18, 34, 50-51, 57, 70, 86, 99, 104-107, 126, 130, 133-134, 137, 154, 160, 208, 222-223
Guilt; 100, 171,

Happiness; 65, 67, 82, 84-86, 119, 123, 139, 163, 179, 204, 207, 208, 210, 219
Happy; 49, 63, 124, 131, 158
Hidden; 43, 47, 74, 155, 176

225

Healthy Parenting; 24, 30, 38, 61, 63, 69-77, 80-83, 98, 119, 121-124, 132-133, 138, 141, 147, 150, 158, 161, 171, 178, 181-187, 210, 223

Heart of Parenting; 9, 13, 17, 21, 27, 33, 43, 46, 49, 59, 61, 63, 80-81, 85, 105, 116, 120-121. 141-142, 145-148, 172, 183, 186-187, 208, 219-220

Human Beings; 8. 17, 22, 74, 113, 129, 221

Humanistic; 11, 89, 108

Humanity; 129, 158, 164, 210

Human Nature; 11, 14-15, 21, 42, 61, 71, 88-89, 106, 111, 129, 179, 189, 221

Image(s) Parental; 32, 42, 44-47, 49, 64-65, 73, 93, 105, 148-149, 159

Imagination; 37, 44, 55-56, 63-66, 192, 210

Inconsistent: 151, 157

Insight; 16, 20, 28, 36, 38, 67-65, 71, 106, 111-112, 148, 153, 157, 160, 175, 204, 213

Intelligence; 46, 77, 81, 85, 106-107

Integrat(ed)(ion)(ive); 11, 21, 74, 76, 89, 102, 147, 194, 215-216, 219, 221-222

Interact(ive)(ion)(s); 10-11, 13, 34, 40-41, 56, 59-63, 66, 69-76, 83-89, 103, 108, 113-116, 119-120, 141, 147, 143, 157, 193-197, 210, 213-214, 218, 220, 222

Internal Processing; 10, 18, 22, 52, 67, 74, 77-78, 89, 100, 154, 158, 175

Internalization; 24, 44, 48, 58, 73, 77, 83, 87, 105, 116-117, 137, 158, 184-185,

Isolat(ed)(ion); 13, 17, 70, 118-119, 143, 196

Join(ing); 33, 46, 5, 59, 61, 202, 220

Journey Parental; 15-19, 21, 25, 34, 59, 97, 163, 167, 178, 182, 186, 189, 190, 207, 222

Joy(ful); 58-59, 61, 63, 66, 68, 90, 101, 121, 125, 127, 189

Judgment(s); 48, 57, 85, 88-89, 92-102, 113-114, 149, 165, 185, 188-189, 194

Justice; 32, 58, 106, 167, 165, 188, 203

Kaleidoscope; 90, 93

Key(s) to Parenting: 34, 39, 50, 61, 78, 107, 112-117, 133, 141, 153, 160, 205, 219-220

Kiss(es)(ed); 42, 122

Butterfly; 217, 219

Kindness; 106, 133, 164, 172, 204, 208

Know(n)(ing); 16, 34, 47, 51, 69, 79, 99, 124, 155, 157, 173-174, 196, 219

Knowledge; 8, 10. 14, 28, 50, 65, 102-104, 148, 153, 156, 164, 172, 180, 182, 186, 216

Language(s); 139, 147, 152, 164, 184

Learn(ing); 8, 17, 25, 29, 36-42, 45-58, 66-74, 80. 85, 92-98, 102, 108, 114-115, 124, 133, 137, 144-148, 157-164, 172-177, 180-191, 203

Letting Go; 49-50, 80, 115-116, 123, 141, 150, 188

Living; 52, 58, 66, 68, 80, 83, 86, 181, 186, 189, 193, 196, 208, 222

Limits; 51, 66, 70, 98-99, 118, 121, 133, 157

Link(s); 27, 31, 42-43, 49, 52, 78, 90-95, 107-108, 113, 118, 130, 156, 162-163, 167, 195, 203-205, 215, 222

Linear Thinking; 34, 50, 52

Logic; 34, 38, 100, 102, 106, 125, 146, 189

Longing; 61, 73, 110, 131

Loss; 12, 80, 99, 115, 122, 148, 150, 161, 183

Love; 24, 42, 62, 81, 102, 120-125, 128-134, 138, 140-148, 104, 173, 187, 190, 207

Meaning(s)(ful); 22, 25, 34, 50, 52, 56, 59, 66-68, 85, 88, 93, 101, 104, 112, 114, 128, 131-133, 147, 152, 155, 158, 164-165, 186, 200-201, 206-208

Mental Health; 62-63, 143, 183

Mind; 15, 21, 49, 60, 63-64, 79, 100-101, 122, 134

Mindset(s); 18, 53, 57-58, 62, 73, 87, 99-103, 107, 158, 167, 185-186, 189, 209

Mindful(ness); 66, 77-78, 95, 106, 173

Models of Parenting: 11-14, 21-24, 28, 34, 39, 53, 77, 166

Modeling: 51, 61, 102, 104, 157, 160, 173, 177

Moral(ity); 47, 105-106, 133, 165

Motivation(s); 43, 57, 86, 88, 89, 102, 108-114, 117, 139, 162-163, 185, 188, 194, 218

Narratives; 45, 179, 184-185

Narrow Views of Parenting; 13, 21, 23, 128, 152

Becoming A Better Parent

Nature of Parenting; 21, 24, 23, 32, 54, 63, 119, 141, 145, 148, 156, 194, 214-215
Natural Parents; 42-44, 54, 56, 125, 163, 171, 182, 205
Neuroscience; 62, 146, 214
Nonverbal; 152
Nurture; 42-43, 80, 185-186, 208
Nurturing; 47, 56, 75-76, 103-104, 130, 132, 141, 149, 161, 170, 195

Obsess(ed)(ive)(ion); 86, 112, 129
Obstacles; 12, 14, 19, 52, 66, 150, 153, 165
Open(ness)(ly); 17, 20, 27, 39, 55, 57, 59-63, 75, 80-81, 85, 87, 98, 100, 106, 115-116, 120, 124, 135, 147, 155-158, 167, 177, 186, 189-190, 210, 222
Opportunit(y)(ies); 36, 39, 50, 56, 58-61, 66, 73, 76, 79-80, 87, 100, 102, 117-118, 122, 124, 126-127, 145, 158, 176-182, 186, 192, 212
Organize(d); 54, 99, 116, 197
Organization(al)(s); 26, 58, 98, 106, 110, 200, 222

Parent-Child Relationship; 9, 42, 56, 59, 62, 70, 92, 111, 118-126, 131-132, 138, 140-148, 150, 161, 187
Parent-Child System; 9-14, 20, 26-27, 30-34, 39, 43, 52, 54, 71, 75-88, 103, 118, 136, 190-195, 198, 200, 202, 206, 209, 211-222
Parental Patterns; 22, 39, 41, 50, 57, 69, 77, 116, 125, 127, 144-145, 169-170, 184-185, 188, 193, 196, 199-200, 218, 222
Perception; 49, 55-58, 74, 78, 89-90, 97, 100-102, 111-112, 180, 185, 188-189, 221
Personality; 106, 118, 163, 165, 178, 180
Personal Processing System; 10, 87, 93, 105, 112-114
Perspectives; 8-9, 12, 14, 41, 49, 108, 128, 167, 189, 208, 210
Positive Parenting Components; 8-9, 25-28, 32, 39, 46, 50-59, 75, 85, 89-90, 102-107, 117, 120, 131, 140, 149, 154, 156-166, 173, 177, 179, 183, 204-208, 213-215
Preoccupied; 33, 47, 91, 176
Problem Solving; 62, 65, 161, 169, 171, 173-177
Purpose; 22, 25, 34, 66-68, 93-94, 101, 105, 142, 158, 177, 186, 195, 199-201, 206, 215

Quality; 79, 111, 119, 139, 164, 173, 207-208, 212
Qualities; 133, 159, 165, 205
Qualitative; 52, 71, 132, 216
Quantitative; 71, 132,
Question Parenting; 8, 18, 20, 22-26, 39, 62, 88, 92, 101, 107, 122, 149, 186, 209
Questioning; 9, 14, 38, 86, 112, 189
Questions; 36-38, 41, 49, 53, 73, 75, 88-89, 95, 180, 189, 219

Reality; 16, 26, 29, 37, 43, 58, 78, 83, 101-102, 109, 120-123, 146, 149, 181, 206, 219
Recovery Parental: 179-183
React(ion)(ive)(s); 16, 40, 49, 70, 94-95, 118, 123, 127, 137, 153, 162, 210
Reason; 9, 28, 88-89, 93-94, 105, 108, 127, 167-168
Receive(s)(r)(d); 50, 70, 151-154
Reflect(s)(ed)(ive)(ion); 11, 28-32, 38, 44, 52, 56, 83-85, 89, 93-96, 107-108, 117, 119, 133, 147, 151, 159, 169-170, 179, 191, 193, 221
Regulat(ed)(ion); 38-39, 70, 76-81, 83, 85, 93, 106, 147, 153-157, 165, 181, 193-194, 197, 215
Resolv(ed)(ing); 47, 54, 72, 77, 100, 102, 114, 121, 136, 161, 166, 184
Respect; 25, 32, 44, 70, 80, 104, 106, 118, 129, 131-133, 143, 137, 158, 162, 172-173, 190, 204, 215
Respond; 12, 73, 89, 104, 107, 113-114, 123, 136-137, 144, 172, 213
Response(ive)(s); 12, 16, 36, 49, 60, 70, 106, 110, 116, 119, 133, 137, 146-147, 153-154, 171, 178, 213
Reward(s)(ing); 17, 29, 45, 67, 117, 119, 120, 122, 208
Role model(s); 53, 159-166
Rule(s); 30-31, 48, 51, 53-54, 60, 66-68, 75, 98-99, 113, 119, 162, 172-175, 180, 196-199, 204

Satisfaction; 119. 172
Satisfy; 82, 108
Self-Aware; 77, 220
Self-Actualization; 108-109, 111, 117, 139
Self-Care; 169-173, 184
Self-Concept; 73, 149, 156, 165
Self-Confiden(t)(ce); 42, 112, 125, 137, 160, 163

Self-Determin(ation)(ed)(ism); 10, 111, 114, 139, 162
Self-Esteem; 42, 80-81, 136, 170, 173, 181
Self-Improvement; 8, 111
Self-System; 88, 195, 200
Situation(al)(s); 14, 47, 57, 64, 79-80, 94, 99, 100, 105-106, 110,, 114, 123, 127, 136-137, 166, 175-176, 181, 185, 191, 200, 206, 215, 217
Social Systems; 10, 83, 86, 141, 177, 193, 198-200, 207, 216-218, 221-223
Solution(s); 16, 36, 54, 92, 100, 102, 143, 145, 147, 176, 217
Special; 131, 163, 181, 206
Stages of Parenting; 129, 148, 150
Standard(s); 44, 48, 71, 103, 159, 180
Strateg(y)(ies): 13, 15, 30, 53-54, 59-60, 75-77, 100, 114, 137, 144, 161, 166-167, 171-177, 181, 184, 191, 215
Student(s); 14, 21, 34, 39, 41, 51, 53, 68, 80, 96, 111, 126, 144, 148, 164, 180, 200
Subjective; 13, 95, 98
Subsystem(s); 20, 193-194, 196-199, 222
Synergy; 11, 221
Systems models; 11, 21, 34, 215, 222
Synthesis(ize)(ing); 113, 152, 215

Tactics; 13, 25, 27, 47
Talent(s); 14, 33, 43, 106-107, 163, 208
Tendency; 40, 89, 94-98, 175
Tender(ness)(ly); 106, 126, 130
Think(s)(ing); 9, 25-29, 33, 38-39, 47, 52, 56, 58, 63-64, 73-74, 77, 99-100,, 104, 138, 148, 158-159, 167-168, 180-181, 189, 191, 204-205, 215
Thorough(ly); 9, 135, 216
Thought(s)(ful); 9-10, 15, 20, 24-28, 50, 57, 63-65, 70-71, 77-86,, 89, 102-105, 113, 116, 120, 129, 139, 143, 153, 158-159, 165-166, 176, 177, 181, 192, 194, 201, 207, 210, 222
Touch(ed)(s); 34, 61, 74, 77, 107, 164, 188, 204
Tradition(al); 14, 18, 41, 47, 66, 124, 194, 213
Transform(ation)(s); 18, 22, 27, 34, 48, 51-53, 57-68, 64, 67, 74, 121, 170, 192, 205-206, 209-201, 222
Transcend(s)(ence)(ing); 44-46, 124, 130, 165, 206

Understanding; 8-21, 28, 32-33, 38, 46, 52, 56-59, 76-82, 87-90, 104-122, 129, 133, 141-148, 152-156, 174, 179, 187, 193-197, 208-220
Unrealistic; 8-15, 27-28, 32, 39, 4, 37-48, 51, 121, 161, 167, 224
Unresolved; 36, 48, 73, 128, 142, 171-172, 185-186
Unwilling(ness); 100, 143, 159-160
Utilize(s)(ing)(tion); 27, 62, 65

Value(s)(ed); 10, 16, 20, 24, 26, 41, 47, 49-50, 57-58, 68, 80-90, 102-108, 114-117, 120, 134, 140, 154, 160-168, 173-174, 156, 189, 204, 206, 209, 218, 220
Vibrate(s)(tion); 73, 127, 220-221
Victim; 135-137
Views About Parenting; 8, 10-14, 20-27, 30-39, 44-50, 55, 66, 75, 82, 83, 90-91, 97, 104, 113, 118, 125, 145, 150, 157, 173, 190-197
Virtue(s); 66, 164-166, 170, 209, 223-224
Vision(s); 13-16, 34, 39, 42-44, 47, 61, 64, 82, 100, 105, 113, 119, 138-140, 147, 189, 19
Vulnerab(le)(ities); 75, 119, 124, 183-184

Want(ed)(ing); 9, 11, 15, 25-26, 29, 40, 47, 61-64, 75-82, 93, 98, 102, 106, 109, 112, 117, 125-132, 137, 140,, 147-160, 172, 175, 204-205
Watch(ing); 122, 158, 160, 206
Weak(en)(ed)(ness); 22, 40, 49, 72, 74, 101, 137, 147, 161
Wealth; 38, 83
Welcom(ed)(ing); 9, 65, 99, 206
Well(-)being; 56, 64, 86, 107, 163, 171, 174, 206, 208, 214
Wellness; 66. 111
Willing(ness): 9, 21, 31, 34, 48, 53, 61, 77, 88, 91, 100, 103, 12-113, 143, 157, 163, 168,, 182, 187, 191
Win(ning); 17, 66-67, 94, 113, 118, 156,, 199, 203, 205, 218
Wis(e)(dom); 8, 10, 13-17, 20, 35, 37, 47, 58, 64, 83, 112, 165, 172, 179, 193-194, 223
World Around Us; 8, 10, 15, 21, 31, 33, 59, 71, 87, 113-114, 128, 173, 186, 190, 192, 195, 217
World of Parenting; 60, 87, 190, 211, 219

Youth(ful); 56-62, 102, 139, 192-193, 206, 213

Becoming A Better Parent

References

A miracle on 34th street (1947). Twentieth Century Fox Film Corporation; NY. http://www.youtube.com/watch?v=tI_Rzl6KSYs

Ackerson, B. J. (2003). "Parents with serious and persistent mental illness: Issues in assessment and services." Social Work, Vol. 48.

Adams, B. "Straight from the heart." http://www.romantic-lyrics.com/ls13.shtml

Adams, G. R., & Marshall, S. K. (1996). "A developmental social psychology of identity: Understanding the person-in-context." *Journal of Adolescence,* Vol. 19, Num. 4.

Adams, J. Q. http://thinkexist.com/quotations/leadership/

Adams, J. T. (1931) http://en.wikipedia.org/wiki/American_Dream

Agazarian, Y. (2004). *Systems-centered therapy for groups.* Gilford Press; NY.

Agich, G. J. (2003). *Dependence and autonomy in old age: an ethical framework for long-term care.* Cambridge University Press; NY.

Albom, M. (2007). *Tuesdays with Morrie.* Random House; NY.

Aldort, N. (2005). *Raising Our Children, Raising Ourselves: Transforming Parent-child relationships from reaction and struggle to freedom, power and joy.* Book Publishers Network; WA.

Alexander, J, (1973). "Defensive and supportive communications in normal and deviant families." *Journal of Consulting and Clinical Psychology.* Vol. 40, No. 2, pp. 223-231.

American Lifeguard Association (ALA) http://www.americanlifeguard.com/lifeguarding.htm

American Proverb. "Don't judge a book by its cover." http://thinkexist.com/quotation/don-t_judge_a_book_by_its/171903.html

American Psychiatric Association, (2000). *Diagnostic and statistical manual of mental disorders: DSM-IV-TR.* American Psychiatric Association; VA

Received December 6, 1985; accepted March 19, 1987

Anderson, E. & Emmons, P. (1996). *Unlocking the mysteries of sensory integration.* Future Horizons; TX.

Anderson, R. C. (1977). "The notion of schemata and the educational enterprise: General discussion of the conference." In *Schooling and the Acquisition of Knowledge,* (eds.) Anderson, R. C., Spiro, R. J., & Montague. W. E. Hillsdale; NJ.

Anderson, D. L., & Moore, A. (2002). *Never act your age: Play the happy childlike role well at every age.* Bookhouse; GA.

Anderson, W. T. 1990. *Reality Isn't What it Used to Be.* Harper and Row; CA.

Anthony, R. (2004). *Beyond positive thinking: A no-nonsense formula for getting the results you want.* Morgan James Publishing; VA.

Anthony, R. http://thinkexist.com/quotations/belief/

Armsden, G. C., & Greenberg, M. T., (1987). "The inventory of parent and peer attachment: Individual differences and their relationship to psychological well-being in adolescence." *Journal of Youth and Adolescence,* Vol. 16, No. 5, pp. 427-453.

Arnopoulos, P. (2005). *Sociophysics: cosmos and chaos in nature and culture.* Nova Science Publishers Inc.; NY.

Ashcraft, M. H. (1994). *Human Memory and Cognition.* Harper Collines College Publishers; NY:

Bach, R. http://thinkexist.com/search/searchquotation.asp?search=controlling&page=3

Bacon, D., Fisher, S., Olmos-Gallo, A., Henley, A., Mason, K., & McQuilken, M. (2004). "Exploring the consumer's and provider's perspective on service quality in community mental health care." *Community Mental Health Journal,* Vol. 40, Num. 1, pp. 33-46.

Baer, J., Kaufman, J. C. & Baumeister, R. F. (2008). *Are we free?: Psychology and free will.* Oxford University Press; NY.

Bagley, C., Wood, M., & Young, L. (2005). "Victim to abuser: Mental health and behavioural sequels of child sexual abuse in a community survey of young adult males." *Child Abuse & Neglect,* Vol. 18, pp. 683-697.

Bailey K. D. (1994). *Sociology and the new systems theory: Toward a theoretical synthesis.* State University of New York Press; NY.

Bailey, K. D. (1990). *Social Entropy Theory.* State University of New York Press; NY.

Balber, L. G., & Barnes, D. L. (2007). *The Journey to Parenthood: Myths, Reality and What Really Matters.* Radcliff Publishing; UK.

Bandura, A. (1999). "Social cognitive theory: An agentic perspective." *Asian Journal of Social Psychology.* Vol. 2, pp. 21-41.

Barabasi, A. L. (2003). *Linked: How everything is connected to everything else and what it means.* Plume; Penguin Group; NY.

Barber, B., Stolz, H. and Olsen, J. (2005) 'Parental Support, Psychological Control and Behavioural Control: Assessing relevance across time, culture and method', *Monographs of the Society for Research in Child Development,* Vol. 70, No. 4.

Barber, N. (2000). *Why parents matter: parental investment and child outcomes.* Bergin and Garvey; CT.

Bardill, D. R. (1997). *The relational systems model for family therapy: living in the four realities.* The Haworth Press inc.; NY.

Barrow, J. D. (1994). *The origin of the Universe.* Basic Books; NY.

Baumrind, D. (1989). "Rearing competent children." In Damon, W. (Ed.), *Child development
today and tomorrow.* Jossey-Bass. CA.

Barkley, C. http://www.answers.com/topic/charles-barkley

Barkley, R. A. (2000). *Taking charge of ADHD: the complete, authoritative guide for parents.* Guilford Press; NY.

Baron, J., & Frisch, D. (1988). "Ambiguity and rationality." *Journal of Behavioral Decision Making,* Vol. 1, Iss. 3, pages 149–157.

Barton, J., Cox, J. & Henshaw, C. (2009). *Modern Management of Perinatal Psychiatric Disorder.* Royal College of Psychiatrists; London.

Basco, M. R. (1999) *Never Good Enough: How to use Perfectionism to your advantage without letting it ruining your life.* Simon and Schuster; NY.

Beatles (1967). *Magical Mystery Tour.* "All you need love." Lennon, J. Capital Records; CA.

Beebe, B., & Lachmann, F. (1994). Representation and internalization in infancy: Three principles of salience. *Psychoanalytic Psychology, 11,* 127-165.

Beck, M. S. (1988). *The road less traveled.* Touchstone: NY.

Ben-Rafael, E. & Sternberg, Y. (2002). *Identity, Culture and Globalization.* Brill; MA.

Berends, P. B. (1997). *Whole Child/ Whole Parent.* Harper Paperbacks; N.Y.

Berne, E. (1996). *The games people play.* Ballantine Books; NY.

Berner, G. P. (2007). *The ABC's of becoming super parents: Opening the door to the best children and a more civilized society.* Vintage Press Inc.; NY.

Besharov, D. J. (1990). *Recognizing child abuse: A guide for the concerned.* The Free Press; NY.
Betsch, C. & Betsch, T., & Plessner, H. (2008) *Intuition in judgment and decision making.* Taylor Francis Group; NY.
Bettelheim, B. (1988). *A good enough parent: a book on child-rearing.* Vintage Books; NY.
Big Blue Marble (1974). http://en.wikipedia.org/wiki/Big_Blue_Marble
Big Daddy (1999). http://www.youtube.com/watch?v=8HUvTp8ZcJs
Blanch, A. K., Nicholson, J. & Purcell, J. (1994). "Parents with severe mental illness and their children: The need for human services integration." The Journal of Behavioral Health Services and Research. Vol. 21, Num. 4 pp. 388-396.
Bluestein, J. (1997). *The parent's little book of lists: dos and don'ts of effective parenting.* Health Communications Inc.; FL.
Bly, R. (1992). *Iron John: A Book about Men.* Vintage; NY.
Bornstein, M. H. & Cheah, C. S. L. (2006). "The place of "culture in parenting" in the ecological contextual perspective on development science." in Rubin, K. H. & Chung, O. B. (Eds.) *Parenting beliefs, behaviors, and parent-child relations: a cross-cultural perspective.* Psychology Press, Taylor and Francis Group; NY.
Borenstein, M. H., Hedges, L. V., Higgins, J. P. T., & Rothstein, H. R. (2009). *Introduction to meta-analysis.* John Wiley and Sons; UK.
Bornstein, M. H. (2003). "Positive parenting and positive development in children." In Lerner, R. M., Jacobs, F. & Wertlieb, D. (Eds,.) *Handbook of applied developmental science; Volume 1.* Sage Publications; CA.
Borysenko. J. (1987). *Minding the body, mending the mind.* Addison-Wesley Publishing Co.; MA.
Bouchard, C., Malina, R. M. & Pérusse, L. (1997). *Genetics of fitness and physical performance.* Human Kinetics; IL.
Boulding, K. E. (1985). *The World as a Total System.* Sage Publications, CA
Bowen, M. (1994). *Family Therapy in Clinical Practice.* Jason Aronson; MD
Bowlby, J. (1983). *Attachment and loss.* Basic Books; NY.
Bowlby, J. (1990). *"The Making and Breaking of Affectional Bonds."* Routledge; NY.
Bradley, O. http://thinkexist.com/quotations/bravery/
Bradshaw, (1988). *Healing the shame that binds you.* HCI. Inc.: FL.
Bradely, R. H., & Corwyn, R. F. (2006). "The family environment." In Balter, L., & Tamis-LeMonda, C. S. (eds.) *Child psychology: a handbook of contemporary issues.* Taylor Francis Group; NY.
Brafman, O., & Brafman, R. (2008). *Sway: The irresistible pull of irrational behavior.*
Brazelton, T. B. (1983). "What Every Baby Knows" Lifetime Television, NY. http://www.brazelton-institute.com/berrybio.html
Brazelton, T. B. (1988). *What every baby knows.* Ballantine Books, NY.
Brinckerhoff, P. (2010). "Generation change." In CBHC *Total health: Moving towards the future.*
Bronfenbrenner, U. (1990). "Forward." in (Eds.)Cochran, M., Larner, M., & Riley, D. *Extending families: The social networks of parents and their children.* Oxford University Press: NY.
Brooks, R, & Goldstein, S. (2001). *Raising resilient children: fostering strength, hope, and optimism in your child.* McGraw-Hill Books; NY.
Brooks-Harris, J. E. (2008). *Integrative Multitheoretical Psychotherapy.* Houghton-Mifflin: MA.
Brown, H. J. (2000). *Life's Little Instruction Book: 511 Suggestions, Observations, and Reminders on How to Live a Happy and Rewarding Life.* Thomas Nelson; TN.

Becoming A Better Parent

Brown, L. http://en.thinkexist.com/search/searchquotation.asp?search=past+baggage

Brown, S. & Vaughan, C. (2009). *How play shapes the brain, opens the imagination and invigorates the soul.* Penguin Group; NY.

Brunstein, J. & Schultheiss, O. (2010). *Implicit Motives.* Oxford University Press: NY.

Buddha http://www.desiquotes.com/author/buddha/

Bush, N, & Codrington, G. (2009). *Future-proof your child: Parenting the wired generation.* Penguin Global; NY.

Buss, D. (2008). "Human nature and individual differences; Evolution of human personality." In (eds,) John, O. P., Robins, R. W., & Pervin, L.A. *Handbook of personality: theory and research.* Guilford Press; NY.

Cabrera, N., Fitzgerald, H. E., Mann, T., & Wong, M. M. (2003). "Diversity in caregiving context." In Lerner, R. M., Freedheim, D. K., Weiner, I. B., Easterbrooks, M. A., & Mistry, J. (Eds.) *Handbook of Psychology: Developmental psychology.* John Wiley and Sons; NJ.

Cambridge Dictionary. http://dictionary.cambridge.org/dictionary/british/judge_3

Carlson, E. (2009). "20th-Century U.S. Generations". Population Reference Bureau. http://www.prb.org/pdf09/64.1generations.pdf. Retrieved 22 May 2010.

Carlson, E. N., Furr, R. M., & Vazire, S. (2010). "Do we know the first impressions we make? Evidence for idiographic meta-accuracy and calibration of first impressions." *Social Psychological and Personality Science*, 1, 94-98.

Carnegie, D. (9181). *How to win friends and influence people.* Simon and Schuster; NY.

Carson, B. (2007) "There is no job more important than being parenting." In (Eds.) Allison, J., Gediman, D. & Gregory, J. *This I Believe: The Personal Philosophies of Remarkable Men and Women.* Henry Holt and Company; NY.

Carter-Scott, C. (1998). *If Life Is a Game, These Are the Rules.* Doubleday Dell Publishing; NY.

Castle, V. (2007). *The Trance of Scarcity: Stop Holding Your Breath and Start Living Your Life.* Berrett-Koehler Publishers; CA.

Catt, M. (2010). "ILR research finds leaders don't rock the boat." http://www.physorg.com/news/2010-12-ilr-leaders-dont-boat.html

Chapman, G. (2008). *Love as a Way of Life: Seven Keys to Transforming Every Aspect of Your Life.* Doubleday Publishing; NY.

Chapman, G. (2010). *The 5 love languages: The secret to love that lasts.* Northfield Publishing; IL.

Chazan, S. E. (2003). *Simultaneous treatment of parent and child.* Jessica Kingsley Publishers; NY.

Chesterton, G. K. http://thinkexist.com/quotes/with/keyword/playground/2.html

Chickering, B. & Nuckols, C. (1998). *Healing an angry heart: Finding solace in a hostile world.* Health Communications Inc.: FL.

Chidekel, D. (2002). *Parents in charge: Setting healthy, loving boundaries for you and your child.* Kingston Publishing Corp.; NY.

Csikszentmihalyi, M. (1997). *Finding flow: The psychology of engagement with everyday life.* Basic books; NY.

Chinese Proverb http://en.thinkexist.com/quotes/chinese_proverbs/

Chopra, D. http://thinkexist.com/quotes/with/keyword/ego/

Christophersen, E. R. (1998). *Beyond Discipline: Parenting that lasts a lifetime.* Overland Press Inc; KS.

Christophersen, E. R. & Mortweet, S. L. (2002). *Parenting that works: Building skills that last a lifetime.* Magination Press; DC.

Cinderella (1950). Disney Productions; CA.
Cline, F. & Fay, J. (2006). *Parenting with love and logic: Teaching children responsibility.* NavPress Publishing, MA.
Cloke, K., & Goldsmith, J. (2000). *Resolving Conflicts at Work.* San Francisco: Jossey-Bass.
Cohen, L. J. (2002). *Playful Parenting.* Ballantine Books; NY.
Cohler,B. J., & Paul, S. (2002). "Psychoanalysis and parenthood." In Bornstein, M. H. (Eds,.) *Handbook of parenting: Being and becoming a parent*, Volume 3. Lawrence Erlbaum Associates; NJ.
Collins English Dictionary – Complete and Unabridged (2003). HarperCollins Publishers: NY.
Cooney, S.M., Huser, M., Small, S., & O'Connor, C. (2007). "Evidence-based programs: An overview." What Works, Wisconsin Research to Practice Series, 6. Madison, WI: University of Wisconsin–Madison/Extension.
Confucius http://www.brainyquote.com/quotes/keywords/easy.html
Confucius http://www.brainyquote.com/quotes/keywords/simple_2.html
Corinthians 13:11. (2004). *Holy Bible: New living translation.* Tyndale House Publishers. IL.
Cosby, B. http://www.quotegarden.com/
Cowan, P. A. (2009). *The family context of parenting in children's adaptation to elementary school.* Lawrence Erlbaum Associates, Inc.; NJ.
Cramer, P. & Brilliant, M. A. (2001): "Defense Use and Defense Understanding in Children." *Journal of Personality* Vol. 69, no. 2 pp. 297–322.
Crano, W. D. & Prislin, R. (2008). *Attitudes and attitude change.* Psychology Press; NY.
Creed (1999). *Human Clay. "Never Die."* Wind up records; NY.
Cummings, M., Davies, P. T. & Campbell, S. B. (2000). *Developmental psychopathology and family process: Theory, research, and clinical implications.* Guilford Press; NY.
da Vinci, L. http://thinkexist.com/quotes/leonardo_da_vinci/
Damasio, A. (2002). "Thinking about belief: Concluding remarks. In eds. Scarry, E., & Schacter, D. L. *Memory, brain, and belief.* Harvard University Press; MA.
Darabont, F. (1994). *Shawshank Redemption.* http://sfy.ru/?script=shawshank
Darley, J. M., & Gross, P, H. (2000), "A hypothesis-confirming bias in labeling effects," in eds Stangor, C. *Stereotypes and prejudice: essential readings,* Psychology Press, NY.
Darling, N. & Steinberg, L. (1993). "Parenting style as context: An integrative model." Psychological Bulletin. Vol. 113: pp.487-496.
Darwin, C. (1998). *The origin of species.* (eds) Beer, G. Oxford University Press; NY.
Davis, D. D., Felgoise, S. H. & Freeman, A. (2008). Clinical Psychology: Integrating Science and Practice. John Wiley & Sons; NJ.
Deater-Deckard, K. D. (2004). *Parenting stress.* Penguin Group; USA.
Descartes, R. http://en.wikipedia.org/wiki/Cogito_ergo_sum
Deci, E. L. & Flaste, R. (1996). *Why we do what we do: Understanding self-motivation.* Penguin Group; NY.
Deci, E. L. & Ryan, R. M. (2002). *Handbook of self-determination.* University of Rochester Press; NY.
Deci, E. L. & Ryan, R. M., (2000). "Self-determination theory and the facilitation of intrinsic motivation, social development, and well-being." *American Psychologist*, Vol. 55, pp. 68-78.

Becoming A Better Parent

Defoe, D. (1719) *Robinson Crusoe*. W. Taylor: London. http://www.pierre-marteau.com/editions/1719-robinson-crusoe.html

DeGaetano, G. (2004). *Parenting well in a media age: Keeping our kids human.* Personhood Press; CA.

Deming, W. E. (1986). *Out of the Crisis*. MIT Press; MA

Devaney, R. L. (2003). *Introduction to chaotic dynamical systems.* Westview Press; MA.

Dewar, G. (2006). http://www.parentingscience.com/

Diriwächter, R. & Valsiner, J. (2008). *Striving for the whole: creating theoretical syntheses.* Transaction Publishers. NJ.

Divecha, D. J., & Okagaki, L. (1993). "Development of parental beliefs." In (eds.) Lucter, T., & Okagaki, L *Parenting: an ecological perspective*. Lawrence Erlbaum Associates Inc.; NJ.

Dixon, L., Krauss, N. & Lehman, A, (1994). "Consumers as service providers: The promise and challenge." *Community Mental Health Journal*. Vol. 30, Num. 6, pp. 615-625

Do you know where your children are? Public Service Announcement. http://en.wikipedia.org/wiki/Do_you_know_where_your_children_are%3F

Donahue, P. J. (2007). *Parenting without fear: Letting go of worry and focusing on what really matters.* Martin's Press; NY.

Donaldson, F. O. (1993). *Playing by heart: The vision and practice of belonging.* Health Communications; FL.

Douglas, A. (2004) "The Mother of All Parenting Books: The Ultimate Guide to Raising a Happy, Healthy Child from Preschool through the Preteens." John Wiley & Sons Inc; NJ.

Dr. Seuss (1959). *Happy Birthday to You!* Random House Books for Young Readers; NY.

Dr. Seuss http://thinkexist.com/quotes/like/anyone_can_give_up-it-s_the_easiest_thing_in_the/9586/

Dreschler, W. A., & Versfeld, N. J. (2002). "The relationship between the intelligibility

Dubner, S. J. & Levitt, S. D. (2009). *Super freakonomics: Global cooling, patriotic prostitutes, and why suicide bombers should buy life insurance.* HarperCollins; NY.

Dumas, J. E. (2005). "The dynamics of positive parenting: Psychological, social and cultural contexts." In Grietens, H. (Eds.). *In the best interests of children and youth: international perspectives.*

Dutton, D. G. (2007). *The abusive personality: violence and control in intimate relationship.* Gilford Press; NY.

Dyer, W. http://thinkexist.com/quotes/with/keyword/choices/

Dyer, W. W. (2007). *Change your thoughts - Change your life: Living the wisdom of the Tao.* Hay House Inc.; NY.

Eagly, A. & Chaiken, S. (1993). *The psychology of attitudes.* Fort Worth, TX: Harcourt, Brace.

Einstein, A. http://thinkexist.com

Einstein, A. http://thinkexist.com/quotes/with/keyword/moving/

Einstein, A. http://www.philosophersnotes.com/quotes/by_topic/Albert+Einstein

Einstein, A. http://www.janegoodwin.net/2010/03/13/quotation-saturday-curiosity/

Eisenhower, D. D. http://thinkexist.com/search/searchquotation.asp?search=%22first+things+first%22

Eisenstadt, T. H., Eyberg, S., McNeil, C. B., Newcomb, K. & Funderburk, B. (1993). "Parent-child interaction therapy with behavior problem children: Relative effectiveness of two stages and overall treatment outcome." *Journal of Clinical Child & Adolescent Psychology*, Vol. 22, 1. pp. 42 - 51

Elias, M. J., Tobias, S. E., & Friedlander, B. S. (1999). *Emotionally intelligent parenting: how to raise a self-disciplined, responsible, socially skilled child.* Three Rivers Press; NY.

Elliot, T. S. http://www.quotegarden.com/

Ellis, J. (1986). "The Superstring: Theory of Everything, or of Nothing?" *Nature.* Vol. 323, pp. 595–598.

Ellis, A. http://webspace.ship.edu/cgboer/ellis.html

Emerson, R. W. http://thinkexist.com/quotes/with/keyword/leave/

Emerson, R. W. http://thinkexist.com/quotes/with/keyword/journey/2.html

Engel, B. (2006). *Healing your emotional self: A powerful program to help you raise your self-esteem, quite your inner critic, and overcome your shame.* John Wiley and Sons; NJ.

Engell, A. D., Haxby, J. V., & Todorov, A. (2007). "Implicit trustworthiness decisions: Automatic coding of face properties in human amygdala." *Journal of Cognitive Neuroscience,* Vol. 19, pp. 1508-1519.

Eoyang, G. H. (2006). "Human systems dynamics: Complexity-based approach to a complex evaluation." In Imam, I & Williams, B. (Eds.). *Systems Concepts in evaluation: An expert anthology.* American Evaluation Association; EdgePress: CA.

Erikson, E. H. (1950). *Childhood and Society.* New York: Norton.

Erricker, C. & Erricker, J. (2001). *Contemporary spiritualities: social and religious contexts.* Continuum, UK.

Exodus (20:5). New International Version.

Eyer, D. E., Golinkoff, R. M., &Hirsh-Pasek, K. (2003). *Einstein never used flash cards: how our children really learn - and why they need to play more and memorize less.* Rodale, Inc.; NY.

Family Ties (1982). Paramount Television, NBC: CA

Father Knows Best (1954). Rodney-Young Productions, NBC; CA

Ferrucci, P. (2001). *What our children teach us: Lessons in joy, love, and awareness.* Warner Books; NY.

Fisher, E., Sharp, S. W., & Wichman, D. F. (2007). *The art of empowered parenting: The manual you wish your kids came with.* Ovation Books; TX.

Foehr, U. G., Rideout, V. A. & Roberts, D. F. (2010). "Generation M2: Media in the Lives of 8- to 18-Year-Olds." *A Kaiser Family Foundation Study.* http://www.kff.org/entmedia/upload/8010.pdf

Frankl, V. (2006). *Man's Search for Meaning.* Beacon Press; MA.

Franklin, B. http://thinkexist.com/quotes/with/keyword/early/2.html

Franklin, B. http://en.thinkexist.com/search/searchQuotation.asp?search=persistence

Franklin. B. http://www.ushistory.org/franklin/quotable/quote67.htm

Freud, S., (1905) *Three Essays on Sexuality,* in Stevens, R., (1983) *Freud and Psychoanalysis: An Exposition and Appraisal,* Milton Keynes: Open University Press.

Fromm, E. http://en.thinkexist.com/search/searchquotation.asp?search=journey

Fulghum, R. (1986). *All I Really Need to Know I Learned in Kindergarten.* Ivy Books; NY.

Becoming A Better Parent

Fuss, M. (1991). *Buddhavacana and Dei Verbum: A Phenomenological and Theological Comparison of Scriptural Inspiration in the Saddharmapundarika Sutra and in the Chri.* Brill Academic Publishers; MA.

Galatians 6:7 (1984). *The holy bible: New international version.* Biblica. CO.

Galdone, P. (1982). *Jack and the Beanstalk.* Sandpiper; NY.

Galinsky, E. (1987). *The Six Stages of Parenthood.* Perseus Books; NY.

Gall, J. (2002). *Dancing With Elves; Parenting as a Performing Art. The Parents' Handbook of Parenting Strategies.* General Systemantics Press; MN.

Gaudelli, G. (2003) *World class: teaching and learning in global times.* Lawrence Erlbaum Associates, Inc.; NJ.

Gerhardt, S. (2004). *Why Love Matters: How Affection Shapes a Baby's Brain.* Brunner-Routledge; London, UK:

Germer, C. K. (2005). *Mindfulness and psychotherapy.* Guilford Press, NY.

Ginsberg, K.R. (2007). "The Importance of Play in Promoting Healthy Child Development and Maintaining Strong Parent-Child Bonds." *American Academy of Pediatrics*, Vol. 21 http://www.aap.org/pressroom/playFINAL.pdf

Gladwell, M. (2002). *The tipping point: How little things can make a big difference.* Little Brown and Co.; NY.

Gladwell, M. (2005). *Blink: The Power of Thinking Without Thinking.* Little Brown and Co.; NY.

Glaser, D. (2002). "Emotional abuse and neglect (psychological maltreatment): A conceptual framework." *Child Abuse & Neglect*, Vol. 26, pp. 697-714.

Glasser, W. (1998), *Choice Theory: A New Psychology of Personal Freedom.* HaperCollins: NY.

Gleick, J. (1987). *Chaos: Making a new science.* Penguin Books: NY.

Goldman, A. I. (1993). "The Psychology of Folk Psychology". *Behavioral and Brain Sciences* Vol. 16, pp.15-28.

Goldstein F. C., & Levin H. S. (1987). "Disorders of reasoning and problem-solving ability." (Eds.) M. Meier, A. Benton, & L. Diller. *Neuropsychological rehabilitation.* London: Taylor & Francis Group.

Goleman, D. (1998). *Working with emotional intelligence.* Bantam Books; NY.

Goode. C.B. (2001). *Nurture Your Child's Gift: Inspired Parenting.* Atria Books/Beyond Words; NY.

Goodnow, J. J. (2006). "Cultural perspectives and parents' views of parenting and development: Research directions." In (Eds.) Rubin, K. H. & Chung, O. B. *Parenting beliefs, behaviors, and parent-child relations: a cross-cultural perspective.* Psychology Press; NY.

Gordon, T. (1977). *"Leader effectiveness training."* Wyden books; NY.

Gordon, T. (2000). *Parent Effectiveness Training (PET): The Proven Program for Raising Responsible Children.* David McCay Co.; NY.

Goswami, A. (1993). *The self-aware universe: How consciousness creates the material world.* Tarcher and Putnam; NY.

Grabe., M. E., Zhou, S., Lang, A., & Bolls, P. H., (2000) Packaging television news: The effects of tabloid on information processing and evaluative response. *Journal of Broadcasting and Electronic Media*, Vol. 44, pp. 581-598

Granic, I., Dishion, T. J. & Hollenstein, T. (2006). "The family ecology of adolescence: A dynamic systems perspective on normative development." In, Adams, G. R. & Berzonsky, M. D. (Eds) *Blackwell Handbook of Adolescence.* Blackwell Publishing Ltd

Greene, B. (2003). *The elegant universe: superstrings, hidden dimensions, and the quest for the ultimate theory.* W.W. Norton and Company; NY.

Greenfeld, J. M. (2009). *My Choice - My Life: Realizing Your Ability to Create Balance in Life.* Outskirts Press, CO.

Greenspan, S. (2006). "Rethinking 'harmonious parenting' using a three-factor discipline model." *Child Care in Practice*, Vol. 12, No. 1, pp. 5-12.

Gregerman, A. (2000). *Lessons from the sandbox: using the 13 gifts of childhood to rediscover the keys to business success.* McGraw Hill; NY.

Grunwald, B. B. & McAbee, H. V. (1999) *Guiding the family: practical counseling technique.* Taylor & Francis; PA.

Guarendi, R. & Guarendi, R. N. (1985). *You're a Better Parent Than You Think!: A Guide to Common-Sense Parenting.* Fireside; NY.

Gurian, M. (2002). *The soul of the child: Nurturing the divine identity of our children.* Atria Books: NY.

Gutzwiller, M. C. (1990). *Chaos in Classical and Quantum Mechanics.* New York: Springer-Verlag.

Haley. A. http://thinkexist.com/quotations/family/2.html

Hall, D. T. & Richter, J. (1989). "Balancing work life and home life: What can organizations do to help." *Academy of Management.* Vol. 2 No. 3 pp. 213-223

Hammond, J. S., Keeney, R. L. & Raiffa, H. (2002). *Smart choices: a practical guide to making better life decisions.*

Hannaha, S. T., Sweeney, P. J. & Lestera, P. B. (2007). "Toward a courageous mindset: The subjective act and experience of courage." *The Journal of Positive Psychology*, Volume 2, Issue 2, pp. 129 – 135.

Hannush, M. J. (2002). *Becoming good parents: an existential journey.* State University of New York Press; NY.

Harris, J. R. (1998). *The Nurture Assumption: Why Children Turn Out the Way They Do.* Free Press; NY.

Hartzell, M., & Siegel, D. J. (2003). *Parenting from the inside out: how a deeper self-understanding can help you raise children how thrive.* Penguin Putnam Inc.: NY.

Hastie, R., & Dawes, R. M. (2010). *Rational choice in an uncertain world: The psychology of judgment and decision making.* Sage publications; CA.

Hatfield, A. B & Lefley, H. P. (1993). *Surviving mental illness: stress, coping, and adaptation.* Guilford Press; NY.

Hayes, R. A. & Stout, C. E. (Eds.) (2005). *The evidence-based practice: methods, models, and tools for mental health professionals.* John Wiley & Sons; NY.

Hayes, S. C., & Strosahl, K. D. (2004). *A practical guide to acceptance and commitment therapy.* Springer Science+Buisness Media, Inc.; NY.

Headey, B. W. & Wearing, A. J. (1989). "Personality, life events and subjective well-being: Toward a dynamic equilibrium model." *Journal of Personality and Social Psychology,* Vol. 57, pp. 731-39.

Heppner, P. P. & Lee, D. (2002). "Problem-solving appraisal and psychological adjustment." (eds.) Snyder, C. R. & J. López, S. J. *Handbook of positive psychology.* Oxford University Press; NY.

Herrick, D. F. (2003). *Media management in the age of giants: business dynamics of journalism.* Iowa State Press; Iowa.

Hilden, A. (2007). "The family road trip: Discovering the self behind my eyes." (in eds.) McGowan, D. Parenting beyond belief: on raising ethical, caring kids without religion. AMACON; NY.

Hillyer, R. http://thinkexist.com/quotes/robert_hillyer/

Holden, G. W. (2010). *Parenting: A Dynamic Perspective.* Sage Publications Inc.; CA.

Horace http://thinkexist.com/search/searchquotation.asp?search=healing&page=3

Howe, N. & Strauss, W. (2000). *Millennials rising: the next great generation.* Vintage Press; NY

Jack and the bean stalk http://en.wikipedia.org/wiki/Jack_and_the_Beanstalk

Hannush, M, J. (2002). *Becoming good parents: an existential journey.* State University of New York Press; NY.

Janis, I. L., (1972). *Victims of Groupthink.* Houghton Mifflin Company; MA.

Jefferson, T. http://en.wikiquote.org/wiki/Thomas_Jefferson

Jefferson. T. http://www.brainyquote.com/quotes/quotes/t/thomasjeff104930.html

Jefferson, T. http://www.brainyquote.com/quotes/keywords/hope.html

Johnson, J. W. (1982). "Next, a Cure for Parents." *American Journal of Diseases of Children.* Vol. 136 num. 3, pp. 277.

Johnson, M., & George, L. (1980). *Metaphors We Live By.* University of Chicago Press; IL.

Jones, T. M., (1991). "Ethical decision making by individuals in organizations: An issue-contingent model." *The Academy of Management Review,* Vol. 16, No. 2, pp. 366-395.

Journal of the Acoustical Society of America, Vol. 111, pp. 401-408.

Judea, P. (2000). *Causality: Models, reasoning, and inference.* Cambridge University Press: MA.

Jurassic Park, (1993). Universal studios; CA. http://www.dailyscript.com/scripts/jurassicpark_script_final_12_92.html

Jung, C. C. (1969). *Four Archetypes.* Princeton Press; NJ.

Jung, C. G. (1969). *The Archetypes and the Collective Unconscious.* Princeton Press; NJ.

Jung, C. G. http://thinkexist.com/quotations/judgement/

Jung, C. G. http://www.quotegarden.com/

Jung, C. G. http://www.heartquotes.net/Heart-quotes.html

Jung, C. G. http://www.jungiananalysts.com/wp/?page_id=83

Juvenal (Decimus Junius Juvenalis), http://www.famous-quotes.com/topic.php?tid=866

Kahneman, D., & Lovallo, D., (2003). "Delusions of Success." *Harvard Business Review,* Vol.

Kamler, H. (1984). "Life philosophy and life style." *Social indicators research,* Vol. 14, Num. 1, pp. 69-81.

Katherine, A. (1994). *Boundaries: Where you end and I begin.* Simon and Schuster; NY.

Kaufman, J. & Kaufman, S. *The psychology of creative writing.* New York: Cambridge University Press.

Kofman, F. (2006). *Conscious business: How to build value through values.* True Sounds Inc.; CO.

Kekes, J. (1983). "Wisdom." *American Philosophical Quarterly,* Vol. 20, pp. 277–286.

Keller, H. http://thinkexist.com/search/searchquotation.asp?search=life's lessons&page=1

Kelman, S. (2005). *Unleashing change: a study of organizational renewal in government.* Bookings Institution; DC.

Kendler, K. S. (1996). "Parenting: a genetic-epidemiologic perspective." *American Journal of Psychiatry*; Vol. 153, pp. 11-20

Kennedy, J. F. http://thinkexist.com/search/searchquotation.asp?search=myths&page=3

Kerig P. K. (2006). *Implications of Parent-Child Boundary Dissolution for Developmental Psychopathology: Who Is the Parent and Who Is the Child*, Routledge, NJ.
King, J. (2006). *It's a Guy Thing: Helping Guys Become Men, Husbands, and Fathers*. Destiny Image Publishers Inc. PA.
King, J. D. (2009). *Transform your world through the powers of your mind: A guide to planetary transformation and spiritual enlightenment*. Author House; IN.
King, M. L. K. http://thinkexist.com/quotes/with/keyword/wheels/
Klein, A. (1989). *The Healing Power of Humour*. Tarcher; CA.
Klein, J. A. (2004). *True change: how outsiders on the inside get things done in organizations*. John Wiley and Sons; CA.
Klontz, B. (2009). *Mind Over Money: Overcoming the Money Disorders that Threaten our Financial Health*. Broadway Books, NY.
Kubler-Ross, E. (2005) *On Grief and Grieving: Finding the Meaning of Grief Through the Five Stages of Loss*. Simon & Schuster Ltd; NY.
Kurzweil, R. (2005). *The Singularity Is Near*. Viking Press; NY.
Lago, A. http://www.postwritersgroup.com/comics/itsallaboutyou.htm
Lamiell, J. T. (2003). *Beyond individual and group differences: human individuality, scientific psychology and William Stern's critical persoanlism*. Sage Publications Inc. CA.
Laszlo, E. (1972). *Introduction to systems philosophy*. Gordon and Breach: NY.
Latham, G. (1994). *The power of positive parenting : A wonderful way to raise children*. P & T ink; UT.
Leave It to Beaver (1957). Gomalco Productions, CBS; CA
Lee, J. A. (1973). *Colours of love: an exploration of the ways of loving*. New Press; NY.
Leo, P. (2007). *Connection Parenting: Parenting Through Connection Instead of Coercion, Through Love Instead of Fear*. Wyatt-MacKenzie Publishing; OR.
Lerner, R. M. (1986). *Concepts and theories of human development* (2nd ed.). New York: Random House.
Levitt, S., & Dubner, S. J., (2009). *SuperFreakonomics: Global Cooling, Patriotic Prostitutes, and Why Suicide Bombers Should Buy Life Insurance*. Harper-Collins Publishers; NY.
Lewis, H. (2000). *A question of values: Six ways we make the personal choices that shape our lives*. Axios Press; VA
Lightfoot, C. & Valsiner, J. (1992). "Parental belief systems under the influence: Social guidance of the construction of personal cultures." In (eds.) Goodnow, J. J., McGillicuddy-De Lisi, A. V., & Sigel, I. E. *Parental belief systems: the psychological consequences for children*. Lawrence Erlbaum Associates, Inc.; NJ.
Lewin, K. (1943). "Defining the 'field' at a given time." Psychological Review, Vol. 50, pp. 292-310.
Lincoln, A. http://www.alincoln-library.com/abraham-lincoln-quotes.shtml
Lincoln, A. http://thinkexist.com/quotes/with/keyword/keep_on/
Linden, A. (2008). *Boundaries in Human Relationships: How to Be Separate and Connected*. Crown House Publishing,
Linehan, M. M, (1993). *Cognitive behavioral treatment of borderline personality disorder*. Guilford Press; NY.
Linhorst, D. M. (2006). *Empowering people with severe mental illness: a practical guide*. Oxford University Press; NY.
Locke, J. http://thinkexist.com/search/searchquotation.asp?search=parenting&page=3

Long, N. *Handbook of parenting: theory and research for practice.* Sage publications Ltd.; CA.

Longfellow H. W. http://thinkexist.com/quotes/with/keyword/sands/

Lorenz, E. N. (1963). "Deterministic Nonperiodic Flow." *Journal of the Atmospheric Sciences* Vol. 20: pp. 130–141.

Lord Byron http://thinkexist.com/quotations/dancing/2.html

Louis, T. (2010). *Five entrepreneur lessons from the playground.* http://www.tnl.net/blog/2010/07/30/5-entrepreneur-lessons-from-the-playground/

Lucado, M. (2005). *Cure for the common life: Living in your sweet spot.* Thomas Nelson Inc.; TN.

Luft, J. (1969). *Of Human Interaction,* National Press; CA.

Luhmann, N. (1995). *Social systems.* Stanford University Press; CA.

Lundberg, G. & Lundberg, J.S. (2000). I Don't Have to Make Everything All Better. Penguin Books; N.Y.

Lunden, J. (2000). "Forward" in Dworkis, J. L. & Waldman, J. *The courage to give: inspiring stories of people who triumphed over tragedy to make a difference in the world.* Conari Press; MA.

Luvmour, B. (2006). *Optimal parenting: Using natural learning rhythms to nurture the whole child.* Sentient Publications; CO.

Maccoby E. E. & Martin, J. A. (1983). "Socialization in the context of the family: parent-child interaction." In, Heatherington E. M. (Eds.) *Handbook of Child Psychology* 4th ed. New York, NY: John Wiley; 1-101

Married With Children (1987) http://en.wikipedia.org/wiki/Married..._with_Children

Maslin, B. (2004). *Picking your battles: Winning strategies for raising well-behaved kids.* St. Martin's Press; NY.

Markie-Dadds, C. & Sanders, M. R. (2002). "Behavioral family interventions with children." In Patterson, T. (eds.). *Comprehensive handbook of psychotherapy: Cognitive-behavioral approaches.* John Wiley and Sons, Inc.; NY.

Maslow, A. H. (1970). *Motivation and Personality.* Harper and Row; NY.

Maté, G. (2003). *When the Body Says No: Understanding the Stress-Disease Connection.* John Wiley & Sons; NJ.

Matthew 19:14. (1984) *The Holy Bible; The new international version.* Biblica. MI

Maxwell M. http://thinkexist.com/quotes/maxwell_maltz/2.html

Maxwell, J. C. (2008). *Leadership gold: Lessons I've learned from a lifetime of leading.* Thomas Nelson, Inc., TN.

Mayer, V. J. (2002). *Global science literacy.* Kluwer Academic Publishers; MA.

Mayseless, O. (2006). *Parenting representations: theory, research, and clinical implications.* Cambridge University Press; NY.

McLuhan, M. (1964). *Understanding Media.* Gingko Press; NY.

McTaggart, L. (2002). *The Field: The Quest for the Secret Force of the Universe.* Harper Collins; NY.

Meadows, D.H., & Robinson, J. (1985). *The Electronic Oracle: Computer Models and Social Decisions.* John Wiley and Sons; England.

Magee, J. L. (1998). *Yield management: the leadership alternative for performance and net profit improvement.* CRC Press LLC; FL.

Mehrabian, A. (1981). *Silent messages: Implicit communication of emotions and attitudes.* Wadsworth; CA.

Menninger, K. http://www.quotegarden.com/

Merton, R. K. (1948). "The self-fulfilling prophecy." *Antioch Review*, Vol, 8: pp. 193–210.
Merton, R. K. (1973). *The sociology of science.* University of Chicago Press. IL.
Miller, M., Mangano, C., Park, Y., Goel, R., Plotnick, G.D. & Vogel, R. A.(2006). "Impact of cinematic viewing on endothelial function." *Heart*, Feb, 92(2): pp. 261-2.PMID
Miller, N. B. (1994). *Nobody's perfect: Living and growing with children who have special needs.* Paul H. Brookes; MA.
Miller, W. R., & Rollnick, S. (2002). *Motivational interviewing: preparing people for change.* Guilford Press; NY.
Milton Bradley (1943). "Chutes and ladders." Hasbro; RI.
Minuchin, S. (1974). *Families and Family Therapy.* Harvard University Press. MA.
Misner, I. R. & Morgan, D. (2004). *Masters of Success: Proven Techniques for Achieving Success in Business and Life.* Entrepreneur Media; CA.
Moore, C. H. (2007). "Forward." In Adler, C. & Benioff, M. *The business of changing the world: twenty great leaders on strategic cooperate philanthropy* .McGraw Hill; NY.
Moore, T. G. (2006). "Parallel processes: Common features of effective parenting, human services, management and government." In the *7th National Conference of Early Childhood Intervention Australia*, Adelaide, 5th- 7th March.
Mother Teresa http://thinkexist.com/quotations/love/4.html
Mother Teresa http://www.links2love.com/quotes.htm
Murphy, T. (2006). *It's all about you.* http://metrocartoon.blogspot.com/
Myers, D. G. (1992). *Psychology.* Worth Publishers; NY.
Myers, D. G. (2009). *Psychology in Everyday Life.* Worth Publishers; NY.
Nash, L. L. & Stevenson, H. (2004). *Just enough: tools for creating success in your work and life.* John Wiley & Sons; NJ.
National Center for Fathering (2009)
 http://www.fathers.com/documents/research/2009_Fathering_in_America_Summary.pdf
National Fatherhood Initiative (2007)
 http://www.uwex.edu/ces/flp/conference/files/ftp07_graham_fathers.pdf
Nelsen, J. (2006). *Positive Discipline.* Ballantine Books; NY.
Newton, J. (1994). Preventing Mental Illness in Practice. Routledge; NY.
Niebuhr, R.
 http://skdesigns.com/internet/articles/prose/niebuhr/serenity_prayer/
Nietzsche, F.
 http://thinkexist.com/quotes/like/play_is_the_beginning_of_knowledge/13476/
Nietzsche, F. http://thinkexist.com/quotations/responsibility/2.html
Nietzsche, F. http://www.brainyquote.com/quotes/keywords/mobile.html
Nordgren, L. F., Harreveld, F., & Pligt, J. (2009) "The Restraint Bias; How the illusion of self-restraint promotes impulsive behavior." *Psychological Science.* Vol. 1, Num. 1. pp.1-6.
Noriuchi M, Kikuchi Y, Senoo A. (2007). "The functional neuroanatomy of maternal love: mother's response to infant's attachment behaviors." *Biological Psychiatry.* Vol. 15; Number 63(4): pp. 415-23
Norton P.J., & Weiss, B. J. (2009). "The role of courage on behavioral approach in a fear-eliciting situation: a proof-of-concept pilot study." *Journal of Anxiety Disorders.* Vol. 23 pp. 212–217

Nuffield Foundation (2009). *"Time trends in parenting and outcomes for young people.*
Nuffield Foundation; London.
Nutt, P. (2009). *Why Decisions Fail: Avoiding the Blunders and Traps that Lead to Debacles*. Berrett-Koehler; CA.
O'Malley, A. http://www.brainyquote.com/quotes/authors/a/austin_omalley.html
Oatley, K. (1992). *Best laid schemes: the psychology of emotions*. University of Cambridge; NY.
of time-compressed speech and speech in noise in young and elderly listeners,"
Olsen, D. H. (1997). "Family stress and coping; A multi-system perspective." In Dreman (eds.), *The family on the threshold of the 21st century*. Mahwah, NJ.
Ossorio, P. G. (2005) *What Actually Happens: The Representation of Real World Phenomena (The Collected Works of Peter G. Ossorio, Vol. IV)*. Descriptive Psychology Press; SC. http://www.sdp.org/sdp/rap99/rap99.html
Oxford English Dictionary. http://oxforddictionaries.com/?attempted=true
Palmer, T. H. (1840). *Teacher's Manual*. Education press; MA.
Parankimalil, J. (2009). *Progressive parenting: The definitive resource book*. Unicorn Books Pvt Ltd; India.
Papalia, D. E.; Wendkos-Olds, S.; Duskin-Feldman, R. (2006), *A Child's World: Infancy Through Adolescence*. McGraw-Hill; NY.
Parenthood (1989). Imagine Entertainment. http://www.imdb.com/character/ch0015096/quotes
Parsons, T. (1991). *The social system*. Rutledge; London.
Patricia E. Deegan, P. E. (1996). Recovery and the Conspiracy of Hope. Presented at: The Sixth Annual Mental Health Services Conference of Australia and New Zealand. Brisbane, Australia. http://www.bu.edu/resilience/examples/deegan-recovery-hope.pdf
Pay it Forward (2000). http://www.imdb.com/title/tt0223897/
Peck, M. S. http://thinkexist.com/quotations/growing_up/
Peck, M. S. (1998). *The Road Less Traveled. A New Psychology of Love, Traditional Values and Spiritual Growth*. Touchstone; NY.
Pecnic, N. (2007) 'Towards a Vision of Parenting in the Best Interests of the Child'. In: M. Daly
(ed.), *Parenting in Contemporary Europe: A Positive Approach*. Strasbourg: Council of Europe.
Peter, L. J. (1982). *The Laughter Prescription*, Random House; NY.
Peterson, C., Park, N. & Seligman, M. E. P. (2005). "Orientations to happiness and life satisfaction: The full life versus the empty life," *Journal of Happiness Studies*, Vol. 6, No. 1,: pp. 25-41.
Petronio, S. S. (2002) *Boundaries of privacy: dialectics of disclosure*. State University New York Press, NY.
Phan, D. (2004). "From agent-based computational economics towards cognitive economics." (In eds.). Bourgine, P. & Nadal, J. *Cognitive economics: an interdisciplinary approach*. Springer; NY.
Philbrick, P. W. & Sandbek, T. J. (2008). *The worry free life: Take control of your thought life by weeding out the bad and nurturing the good*. Green Valley Publishing; CA.
Piaget, J., & Inhelder, B. (2001). *Mental imagery in the child*. Rutledge; NY.
Piedmont, R. L. (2005). "The role of personality in understanding religious and spiritual constructs." In, Paloutzian, R. F. & Park, C. L. (Eds.) *Handbook of the psychology of religion and spirituality*. Guilford Press; NY.

Pickhardt, C. E. (2004). *The everything parent's guide to positive discipline: professional advice for raising a well behaved child.* Adams Media, MA.
Plato. http://thinkexist.com/quotations/play/
Pleasantville (1998). New line Cinemas; CA.
Plesman, J. (1986). *Getting off the hook: treatment of drug addiction and social disorders through body and mind.* Shepson Printing; Australia.
Plous, S. (1993). *The psychology of judgment and decision making.* McGraw Hill; NY.
Preskill, H. & Torres, R.T. (1999). *Evaluative inquiry for learning in organizations.*
Prickett, S. & Carroll, R. P., eds (2008). *The Bible: Authorized King James Version.* Oxford University Press, USA.
Primason, R. (2004). *Choice parenting: A more connecting, less controlling way to manage any child behavioral problem.* IUniverse Inc.; NE.
Proverb http://thinkexist.com/quotes/proverb/
Pryor, J. (2004). "Parenting in reconstituted and surrogate families." In (eds.) Hoghughi, M. &
Pugh, G. E. (1976). "Human Values, Free Will, and the Conscious Mind," Zygon, vol. 11, pp. 2-24.
Ramey, S. L. (2009). "The science and art of parenting." In (Eds.) Borkowski, J. B., Ramey, S. L., & Bristol-Power, M. *Parenting and the child's world: Influences on academic, intellectual, and social-emotional development.* Lawrence Erlbaum Associates Inc.; NJ.
Raths, L., Harmin, M., & Simon, S. (1978). *Values and teaching: Working with values in the classroom.* (2nd ed.). Columbus, OH: Charles E. Merrill.
Reagan, R. (1989). *Speaking my mind: Selected speeches.* Simon and Schuster; NY.
Reamonn (2008). "Through the Eyes of a Child" Universal; Island label.
Reverdy, P. http://www.happiness-project.com/happiness_project/2007/08/keeping-a-diffe.html
Rifkin, J. http://www.brainyquote.com/quotes/authors/j/jeremy_rifkin_2.html
Rinpoche, J. Y. M. & Swanson, E. (2009). *Joyful Wisdom: Embracing Change and Finding Freedom.* Harmony; NY.
Robbins, A. http://thinkexist.com/quotations/communication/
Robbins, T. (2003). *Unlimited power: the new science of personal achievement.* Free Press; NY.
Robertson, R. (1992). *Globalization: Social theory and global culture.* Sage publications; CA.
Rogers, F. http://thinkexist.com/quotes/fred_rogers/
Roosevelt, T. http://thinkexist.com/quotes/with/keyword/discipline/2.html
Rosenau, J. N. (1990). *Turbulence in world politics: a theory of change and continuity.* Princeton University Press. NJ.
Rotter, J. B. (1954). *Social learning and clinical psychology.* Prentice-Hall: NY.
Rubin, Z. (1973). *Liking and Loving: an invitation to social psychology.* Holt, Rinehart & Winston: NY.
Russ, S. (2009). "Pretend play, emotional processes, and developing narratives." In (Eds.)
Russek, L. G. & Schwartz, G. E. (1997). "Feelings of parental caring predict health status in mid-life: A 35-year follow-up of the Harvard Mastery of Stress Study." *Journal of Behavioral Medicine,* Vol. 20(1): pp. 1-13.
Russell, D. C. (2009). *Practical intelligence and the virtues.* Oxford Press; NY.
Sackett, R. S. (1991). "Terminating Parental Rights of the Handicapped." Family Law Quarterly. Vol.25 pp. 253, 290.

Samalin, N. (1998). *Loving Your Child Is Not Enough: Positive Discipline That Works.* Penguin; NY.

Sampson, R. J. & Laub, J. H. (1995). "Urban Poverty and the Family Context of Delinquency: A New Look at Structure and Process in a Classic Study." *Annual Progress in Child Psychiatry and Child Development* (Chap. 13, pp. 366-393). Brunner/Mazel Publishers, New York.

Samuel, J. (2008). *Parenting for tomorrow: A results-oriented approach to preparing your child for tomorrow's world.* Vantage Press; NY.

Sander, L. (1985). Toward a logic of organization in psychobiological development. In H. Klar & L. Siever (Eds.), *Biologic response styles* (pp. 20-36). American Psychiatric Association: DC.

Sanna, L.J. & Chang, E.C. (2006). *Judgments over Time: The Interplay of Thoughts, Feelings, and Behaviors.* Oxford University Press; NY.

Sanna, L.J. & Chang, E.C. (2006). *Judgments over Time: The Interplay of Thoughts, Feelings, and Behaviors.* Oxford University Press; NY.

Satir, V. http://www.abundance-and-happiness.com/quotes-for-kids.html

Satir, V. http://www.brainyquote.com/

Santoro, M. V. & Santoro J. S. (2004). *Realizing the power of love: How a father and teenage daughter became best friends...And how you can too!* Publishamerica; MD.

Sawyer, D. C. (1998). *Getting It Right: Avoiding the High Cost of Wrong Decisions.* Lucie Press,

Sawyer, V. (2005). *Journey from Madness to Serenity.* iUniverse; NE.

Schaefer, C.E. (2002). *Play Therapy with Adults.* Wiley; NJ.

Schiff, J. L. (1977). *All My Children.* Jove Pubns; NY.

Schwartz, J. & Wald, M. L. (2003). "Smart people working collectively can be dumber than the sum of their brains: 'Groupthink' is 30 years old, and still going strong." *The New York Times.* March, 9. pp. 5

Schwartz, L. L. & Isser, N. (2007). *Child homicide: parents who kill.* Taylor Francis Group; FL.

Schwitzgebel, E. (2006), "Belief," in Zalta, E. *The Stanford Encyclopedia of Philosophy;* CA. http://plato.stanford.edu/entries/belief/

Sears, W., Sears, M. & Pantley, E. (2002). *The successful child: What parents can do to help kids turn out well.* Little, Brown and Company; NY.

Segal, B. (2005). *Why did you do that?: Solving the mysteries of parenting.* iUniverse, Inc.; NE.

Seligman, M. E. P. (2002). *Authentic happiness: Using the new positive psychology to realize your potential for lasting fulfillment.* Free Press; NY.

Seligman, M. E. P. (1975). *Helplessness: On Depression, Development, and Death.* W.H. Freeman; CA.

Senge, P. & Sterman, J. D. (1990). "Systems thinking and organizational learning: Acting locally and thinking globally in the organization of the future." *Conference on transforming organizations.* Sloan School of Management, MIT: MA.

Sheffield, S. L. (2006). *Women and science: social impact and interaction.* Rutgers University Press. NY.

Shermer, M. (1997). *Why people believe weird things: pseudoscience, superstition, and other confusions of our time.* Henry Holt and Company; NY.

Shinn, F. S. (2011). *Spiritual Secrets for Playing the Game of Life.* Ronin Publishing, CA.

Shiota, M. N., Campos, B., Keltner, D. & Hertenstein, M. J. (2004). "Positive emotion and the regulation of interpersonal relationships." In (eds.) Philippot, P. & Feldman, R. S. *The regulation of emotion*. Lawrence Erlbaum Associates, Inc.; NJ.

Shoda, Y. (2004). "Individual differences in social psychology: Understanding situations to understand people, understanding people to understand situations." In (eds.) Sansone, C., Morf, C. C., & Panter, A. T. *The Sage handbook of methods in social psychology*. Sage Publications; CA.

Shonkoff, J. P. & Phillips, D. (2000). "From Neurons to Neighborhoods: The Science of Early Child Development"

Silvia, P. J. (2006). *Exploring the psychology of interest*. Oxford University Press; NY.

Smetana, J. G. (2008). "It's 10 O'Clock: Do You Know Where Your Children Are?" Recent Advances in Understanding Parental Monitoring and Adolescents' Information Management. *Child Development Perspectives*. Vol 2, Issue 1, pp 19 – 25.

Socrates http://refspace.com/quotes/Socrates

Solomon, J. & George, C. (1996). "Defining the caregiving system. Toward a theory of caregiving." *Infant Mental Health Journal*, Vol. 17, pp. 183-197

Soloveychik, S. (2008). "Parenting for Everyone: Where Do Good Children Come From?" Wordclay; IN.

Spaulding, W. D., Sullivan, E. M., & Poland, J S. (2003). *Treatment and rehabilitation of severe mental illness*. Guilford Press; NY.

Sperry R. W. (1993). "The cognitive revolution: a new paradigm for causation." *Italian Journal of Psychiatry and Behavioral Sciences*, Vol. 3, Num. 1, pp. 3-9.

Sproat, R. (2010). *Language, Technology, and Society*. Oxford University Press, Inc.; NY.

Stagnitti, K., Cooper, R. & Whiteford, G. (2009). *Play as therapy: assessment and therapeutic intervention*. Jessica Kingsley Publishers; PA.

Stanley, N., Penhale, B., Riordan, D. & Barbour, R. S. (2003). Child protection and mental health services: interprofessional responses to the needs of mothers. The Policy Press; UK.

Star Wars (1977). 20th Century Fox; CA.

Star Wars Episode I: The Phantom Menace (1999)
  http://en.wikipedia.org/wiki/Yoda

Steinberg, L. (1990). "Autonomy, conflict, and harmony in the family relationship." In S. S. Feldman & G. R. Elliott (Eds.), *At the threshold: The developing adolescent* (pp. 255-276). Cambridge, MA: Harvard University Press.

Steinberg, L. (2004). *The Ten Basic Principles of Good Parenting*. Simon & Schuster; NY.

Sternberg, R. J. (1988). *The Triangle of Love: Intimacy, Passion, Commitment*. Basic Books; NY.

Stienberg, D. & Pianta, R. C. (2006). "Maternal representation of relationships: Assessing multiple parenting dimensions." In (Eds.) Mayseless, O. *Parenting representations: theory, research, and clinical implications*. Cambridge University Press; NY.

Stone, W. C. http://thinkexist.com/quotes/w._clement_stone/

Strentz, T. (2006). *Psychological aspects of crisis negotiation*. Taylor Francis Group. FL.

Sucharov, M. (1994). *Self psychology and intersubjectivity: A converging alliance*. Paper
presented at the 17th annual conference on the Psychology of the Self, Chicago.

Suedfeld, P. (2009). *Attitude Change: The Competing Views.* Transaction Publishers; NJ.

Sunderland, M. (2008). *The Science of Parenting: Practical Guidance on Sleep, Crying, Play, and Building Emotional Well-Being for Life.* Dorling Kindersley, NY.

Taffinder, P. (2006). *The leadership crash course: how to create personal leadership value.* Thanet Press; UK.

Temperance: http://www.merriam-webster.com/dictionary/temperance

Thelen, E., & Smith, L. (1994). *A dynamic systems approach to the development of cognition and action.* MIT Press: MA.

The American Heritage Dictionary of the English Language (2009). Houghton Mifflin Company: NY. Fourth Edition.

The Brady Bunch (1969). Paramount Television, ABC: CA

The Cosby Show (1984). Bill Cosby, NBC; CA.

The Federal Child Abuse Prevention and Treatment Act https://login.qualifacts.org/prod54/frameset.pl?system=coconsortium

The Incredibles (2004). Pixar Animation Studios, Walt Disney; CA.

The Legend of Bagger Vance, (2000). Twentieth Century Fox. http://www.script-o-rama.com/movie_scripts/l/legend-of-bagger-vance-script.html

The Roseanne Barr Show (1988). http://en.wikipedia.org/wiki/Roseanne_(TV_series)

The Simpsons (1989) http://en.wikipedia.org/wiki/The_Simpsons

The Twilight Zone. (1962). "Kick the can." Episode 86, Cayuga Productions, CBS; CA.

Thoman, E. (1987). *Born dancing: How intuitive parents understand their baby's unspoken language.* New York: Harper & Row.

Thomas, C. B. (1976). "Precursors of premature disease and death: the predictive potential of habits and family attitudes." *Annual Internal Medicine*; Vol. 85 pp. 653–658.

Thommen B., & Wettstein, A. (2009). "Dynamic models for research and education." In Chaudhary, N., Lyra, M. C. D., Molenaar, P. C. M., & Valsiner, J. (Eds.) *Dynamic process methodology in the social and developmental science.* Springer: NY.

Thousand Oaks, CA: Sage Publications.

Toffler, A. (1970). *Future shock.* Random House; NY.

Torrey, E. F. (1998). *Out of the shadows: confronting America's mental illness crisis.* John Wiley & Sons; NY.

Tracy, B. (2005). *Focal point: a proven system to simplify your life, double your productivity, and achieve all your goals.* AMACOM; NY.

Tracy, B. (2010). *No Excuses!: The Power of Self-Discipline.* Vanguard Press, NY.

Tuck, W. P. (2003). *Through the eyes of a child. Living while alive.* IUniverse; NE.

Tversky, A. & Kahneman, D. (1986). "Rational choice and the framing of decisions." *The Journal of Business,* Vol. 59, No. 4, Part 2. pp. S251-S278.

Tversky. A., & Shafir, E. (1991) Decision under conflict: An analysis of choice aversion.

Twain, M. http://thinkexist.com/quotes/mark_twain/

U.S. Census Bureau, American Families and Living Arrangements, 2003.

U.S. Department of Health and Human Services, Administration on Children, Youth and Families. *Child Maltreatment 2008* [Washington, DC: U.S. Government Printing Office, 2010] available at: http://www.acf.hhs.gov

United States Lifesaving Association (USLA) http://www.usla.org/

Unpublished manuscript, Stanford University. Vol.16, Issue 2, Pages 366-387

Unell, B. C. & Wyckoff, J. (2002). *Discipline without shouting or spanking: Practical solutions to the most common preschool problems.* Meadowbrook Press; NY.

Unruh, G. M. (2010). *Unleashing the Power of Parental Love: 4 Steps to Raising Joyful & Self-Confident Kids.* Lighthouse Love Productions LLC; CO.

Vasiloff, B. C. (2003). *Teaching Self-Discipline to Children: 15 Essential Skills.* Twenty-third Publications; CT.

Velleman, R. (2004). "Alcohol and drug problems in parents: An overview of the impact on children and implications for practice." (eds) Göpfert, M., Webster, J. & Seeman, M. V. in *Parental psychiatric disorder: distressed parents and their families.* Cambridge University Press, UK.

Vermeer, H. J. (2006). *Luhmann's "social systems" theory: preliminary fragments for a theory of translation.* Frank & Timme. Germany.

Viorst, J. (1998). *Necessary Losses: The Loves, Illusions, Dependencies, and Impossible Expectations That All of Us Have to Give Up in Order to Grow.* Free Press; NY.

Wachowski, A. & Wachowski, L. (2003) "The Matrix Reloaded." Warner Bothers Pictures, http://www.leesmovieinfo.net/special/MatrixReloadedSpeech1.php

Wachowski, A. & Wachowski, L. (2003). *Matrix Revolutions.* Warner Bothers Pictures, http://www.imdb.com/title/tt0242653/quotes

Wallace, D. (2004). *Random acts of kindness: 365 ways to make the world a nicer place.* Ebury Press; UK.

Waltzlawick, P., Weakland, J. & Fisch, R. (1974). *Change.* W. W. Norton; NY.

Watzlawick, P., Beavin, J., & Jackson, D. D. (1967). *Pragmatics of Human Communication. A study of interactional patterns, pathologies, and paradoxes.* Norton; NY.

Webster-Stratton, C. (1992). *Incredible Years: A Troubleshooting Guide for Parents of Children Aged 3 to 8.* Umbrella Press; Toronto. http://www.incredibleyears.com/

Weil, D. K. (2004) "Socratic questioning: Helping students figure out what they don't know." In (Eds.) Weil, D. K. & Kincheloe, J. L. *Critical thinking and learning: an encyclopedia for parents and teachers.* Greenwood Press; CT.

Weinstein, N. D. (1980). "Unrealistic optimism about future life events." *Journal of Personality and Social Psychology*, Vol. 39, No. 5, pp. 806-820.

Wharam, J. (2009). *Emotional intelligence: Journey to the centre of yourself*. John Hunt Publishing: UK.

Whitfield, C. L. (1987). *Healing the child within: discovery and recovery for adult children of dysfunctional families.* Health Communication; FL.

Whitfield, C. L. (1994). *Boundaries and relationships: knowing, protecting, and enjoying the self.* Health Communications Inc., FL.

Wikipedia. http://en.wikipedia.org/wiki/Category:Social_systems

Wilder, L. I. (1953). *Little House in the Big Woods.* "The Little House on the Prairie." HarperCollins Publishers; N. Y.

Wilmot, W. W. (1995). *Relational Communication.* McGraw-Hill; NY.

Wilson, R. A. (2006). *Quantum Psychology: How Brain Software Programs You and Your World.* New Falcon Publications; AZ.

Wood, G. (2008). *Don't wait for your ship to come in... Swim out to meet it: Tools and techniques for positive lasting change.* Capstone Publishing ltd.; UK.

Wood, R. L. (2010). *The Great Shift: Catalyzing the Second Renaissance.* Renaissance 2; France.

Wyss, J. (1812). *The Swiss Family Robinson*, (eds) Seelye, J. (2007) Penguin Classics; NY.

Zastrow, C. H. (2009). *Social Work with Groups: A Comprehensive Workbook.* Brooks/Cole; CA.

Ziglar, Z. & Ziglar-Norman, J. (2009). *Embrace the Struggle: Living Life on Life's Terms.* Simon & Schuster; NY.

Zisser, A., & Eyberg, S.M. (2010). Treating oppositional behavior in children using parent-child interaction therapy. In A.E. Kazdin & J.R. Weisz (Eds.) *Evidence-based psychotherapies for children and adolescents* (2nd ed., pp. 179-193). New York: Guilford.

Robert (Bob) Lyman Lang Jr,
LPC, LAC, MAC, SAP
Licensed Professional Counselor,
Licensed Addictions Counselor,
Masters Addictions Counselor,
Substance Abuse Professional

Bob received his Master's degree from Northern Arizona University in 1986, has 60 Post Master degree credit hours in Counseling Psychology, and over 5,000 hours of continuing educational credits in the counseling field. He has been in practice since 1983 and founded Family Treatment Centers in 1996. He is licensed as both a Mental Health and Substance Abuse professional and writes a family column for Living with Loss Magazine. He is a family systems expert and assists individuals and families in developing creative solutions to facilitate proactive change.

www.ingramcontent.com/pod-product-compliance
Lightning Source LLC
LaVergne TN
LVHW052100090426
835512LV00036B/2744